For Iain Charlerton

In gratitude — all good wishes.

2007

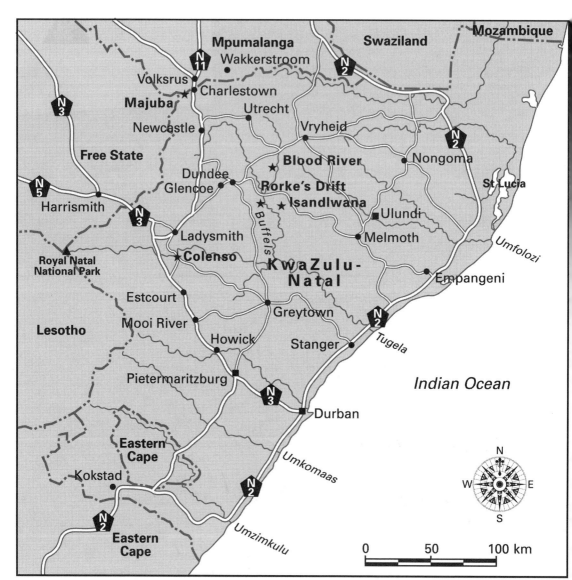

Road map to KwaZulu-Natal battlesites

GREG MILLS & DAVID WILLIAMS

Battles 7

THAT SHAPED SOUTH AFRICA

Tafelberg

Tafelberg Publishers
a division of NB Publishers
40 Heerengracht, Cape Town, 8000
www.tafelberg.com

Gratitute is expressed for the financial assistance of the Ernest Oppenheimer Memorial Trust.
It should be noted that any opinions expressed are the responsibility of the authors and
not that of the Ernest Oppenheimer Memorial Trust, or Tafelberg.

Cover design by Michiel Botha, ALINEA Studio, based on a painting by Sylvester Reisacher (1862–1916),
'The Battle of Colenso', National Cultural History Museum (NFI, Pretoria), HG54275.
Book design by Nazli Jacobs
Edited by Magdalena Mouton
Proofread by Fred Pheiffer
Index by Mary Lennox
Maps by Bennie Kruger
Printed and bound by Paarl Print, Oosterland Street, Paarl, South Africa
First edition, second printing 2006

ISBN 10: 0-624-04298-7
ISBN 13: 978-0-624-04298-3

The soldiers' graves are the greatest preachers of peace
ALBERT SCHWEITZER, Nobel Peace Laureate

Contents

Foreword

I t is a sad reflection but a truism that the history and fluctuating fortunes of nations can be tracked through military events. Nations and nation-states are formed and shaped through adversity, as are international relationships. This is particularly true for the intersection of British and South African history, from the eighteenth to the twentieth century – from the battlefields of Natal to those in far-flung places like the Somme and the Western Desert.

But battles are not only about empires, nations and states. At their core they involve people – citizens and soldiers – whose lives can change and turn on the decisions of others and according to the good or bad choices made on the battlefield. Instinct, training, fear, sweat, hardship and good, old-fashioned courage all play their part in shaping personal destiny in these trying circumstances, and even more so in today's high-intensity, technologically-driven and increasingly impersonal warfare.

Likewise battlefields are not just dots on a map in a textbook, nor are the participants merely markers on a featureless table. Rather they involve a complex interplay of elements such as weather, landscape, climate, culture, levels of technology and, of course, history and personality.

In this volume by Greg Mills and David Williams, a long-overdue and welcome addition to military history literature, we are told the story behind the known stories and are shown the main factors that affected each battle and its outcome. In identifying the key battles that shaped South African history from Blood River in 1838 to Cuito Cuanavale in Angola exactly 150 years later, the authors have traced the threads and described the circumstances that bound the destiny of nations and the fate of men and women.

LT.-GENERAL DAVID J RICHARDS CBE DSO
Commander Allied Rapid Reaction Corps
Kabul, 2005

Foreword

I am very pleased to offer a foreword to this volume on seven battles that shaped South Africa's history, from Blood River to Cuito Cuanavale, through Isandlwana, Rorke's Drift, Majuba, Colenso, Delville Wood and El Alamein.

There are always two sides to every story, and military history is no exception. For the one side, Blood River might have been a symbolic victory, for the other it was not only known by a different name – Ncome River to the Zulu nation – but also signalled the beginning of a long period of hostility and oppression. Indeed, the selection and analysis of these seven battles also encapsulate South Africa's political and ideological divisions and preoccupations over the past two centuries: Boer versus Zulu, Zulu versus Britain, Britain versus Boer, South Africa versus Germany, imperialist versus republican, the West versus the Soviet bloc and, critically, liberation against apartheid.

It is equally important to identify those links that bind rather than separate South Africans from one another and the world. These battles contained common political features that represented the ebb and flow of imperial ambition and conquest, and the extension of racial rule. These experiences not only bring South Africans together through mutual suffering, but also inextricably bind the fate and fortune of nations in the wider international arena.

In offering us an in-depth look at and various perspectives on our own past, Greg Mills and David Williams have not only filled the gaps and reminded us of how much there is to be proud of, but have also made a significant contribution to South African history, especially our military and political history.

PROF. KADER ASMAL, MP
Former Minister of Education
Chairperson: Portfolio Committee on Defence, South African National Assembly
Cape Town, 2005

Preface

The motivation for this book came as a result of a conversation between the authors in December 2002 at the site of the Italian prisoner-of-war memorial at Zonderwater near Cullinan, 45km east of Pretoria. Both of us were astounded to discover the impact of Italy's participation in the Second World War, not only in terms of the cost in lives and resources in East and North Africa, but also in terms of its effects on South African society.

Some 90,000 Italian POWs, captured in the African campaigns, were incarcerated in South Africa during the Second World War, and as many as 65,000 at Zonderwater alone, in the years 1941–47. Around 30,000 of those Italian POWs chose to stay in South Africa. The legacy they left goes beyond people and even culture to their effect on South Africa's rail and road networks (such as the building of the Du Toitskloof pass outside Cape Town by POWs) and general engineering standards.

That conversation at Zonderwater led to a discussion of South Africa's long and complex experience of military conflict, and provoked the challenge of identifying the most influential battles.

This book is thus more than a study of military events. It details the nature and impact of key battles and/or campaigns that shaped South African history, highlighting the nature of the events and the personalities behind them. The battles/campaigns selected are:

- Blood River, 1838
- Isandlwana/Rorke's Drift, 1879
- Colenso ('Black Week'), 1899
- Delville Wood, 1916
- El Alamein, 1942
- Cuito Cuanavale, 1987–88.

The selection might be controversial but it is not arbitrary. The following key criteria were used to select the battles:

- Their impact on South African history: were things the same after the battles?
- Their impact on particular South African communities and on political life.
- What is the relationship between the mythology flowing from these battles (given their wider impact) and the events themselves?
- Their impact on South African (and global) military practice and culture.

This book does not, however, pretend to be an exhaustive, encyclopaedic account of South African military history. But it does aim to focus on a number of other relevant and hitherto neglected aspects.

First, it will trace South African political developments through these battles. As Professor Kader Asmal has noted in his foreword to this volume, they encapsulate South Africa's military preoccupations over two centuries: Boer versus Zulu, Zulu versus Brit, Brit versus Boer, South Africa versus Germany, (white) South Africa versus Communism, white versus black, imperialist versus republican, and the West versus the Soviets.

Second, the book is also intended as a 'rough guide' to the battlesites, which occur in five main areas: three in the 'battlefield province' of (then) Natal; another close by in the (then) Transvaal; one in Namibia/Angola; and two in France and Egypt. The book is therefore not solely aimed at a specialist audience of military historians (and there are plenty of those about), but also at the general public and tourists/travellers interested in visiting South Africa's battlesites and keen to understand the link between battles and certain political events and history. It is hoped that in helping to make these battlefields more accessible to the reader, this book will stimulate renewed interest in crucial – and sometimes highly dramatic – battles and the often fascinating personalities and events behind them.

Acknowledgements and thanks

The travelling for the research behind this book was funded by a generous grant from the Ernest Oppenheimer Memorial Trust. Thanks go to the trustees for their faith – and patience – in seeing this study to fruition.

The staff at the SA Museum of Military History in Saxonwold in Johannesburg – a world-class institution – were generous with their time and in availing their research resources. Special mention should be made of the curator and his staff.

The process of research involved trips to each of the battlesites with the exception of Cuito Cuanavale, which proved difficult to access and for which the research process relied on interviews in South Africa and Cuba with former combatants and diplomats on both sides. Special thanks are expressed by Greg Mills to Martin Edmonds who proved, as always, insightful and good company on the Somme and elsewhere in France; and to Janet Wilson who was dragged without any complaint and, indeed, providing much encouragement, with two children over KwaZulu-Natal's battlefields. Michael and Franziska Lange were, as always, gracious and generous hosts in Egypt. The staff and Executive Committee of the South African Institute of International Affairs (SAIIA) also generously allowed Greg Mills, then National Director of the SAIIA, time to undertake the research trips to the Somme and Egypt. Thanks to Terry McNamee at the Royal United Services Institute on Whitehall who located photos and facts when no-one else could.

Special thanks are expressed by David Williams to Rob Caskie and David Rattray of Fugitives' Drift Lodge in KwaZulu-Natal, who were enormously helpful and enthusiastic about the project; to Alison Chisholm of the Wits School of Education library; to the historian John Laband for his time and insights; to General Jannie Geldenhuys for his recollections of the Cuito Cuanavale campaign; to David's son Robbie, who took the photographs at Blood River, Isandlwana and Rorke's Drift; and to Patricia and Morgan, who had to give up much family time.

Erika Oosthuysen and Maggie Mouton of the publishers displayed impressive diligence and patience, too, in the preparation of this volume.

Much of South Africa's history is entwined with that of Britain, and the various battles bear testament to this. We thus thought it most appropriate to invite the 'descendants' of those men and women caught up in these many conflicts to each write a foreword to this study: Lieutenant-General David Richards CBE DSO, the commander of NATO's Allied Rapid Reaction Corps (ARRC), and Professor Kader Asmal MP, the Chairman of the Portfolio Committee on Defence in the SA National Assembly, graciously agreed to do so.

Finally, a donation from the author royalties will be made to the Princess Alice Adoption Home in Westcliff, Johannesburg.

GREG MILLS & DAVID WILLIAMS
March 2006

Introduction

The great German philosopher of war, Clausewitz, pointed out that war is the continuation of policy by other means. That sounds so glib that it can easily obscure the fact that the essence of war is extreme violence. Therefore it is not entered into lightly, even by eagerly aggressive leaders. For war to take place, both sides must calculate that they have more to gain by fighting than by not fighting, that the considerable risks of battle are worth accepting.

South Africa has seen many wars, campaigns, expeditions, battles and skirmishes where the risks have indeed been accepted by both sides. One recalls a remark by the American travel writer Paul Theroux. When he visited Vietnam, he said, he found the country so beautiful that he could understand why it had been fought over so fiercely. And there is another remark, attributed to the great South African general and statesman, Jan Christiaan Smuts: 'The best and the worst never happens in South Africa.'

The selection for this book started as six battles, then it became ten, and the number finally settled on was seven. The final choice was of battles that were decisive in shaping the political geography as well as the political psychology of the modern South Africa. Three of these battles took place in what is now KwaZulu-Natal, formerly the province or colony of Natal, and before that a territory split into Natal and Zululand. It is the area that hosted a military 'triangular tournament' – Boer against Zulu, British against Zulu, British against Boer.

Our first selected battle was that between the early Boer trekkers and the Zulu nation. The Battle of Blood River (1838) ensured the survival of the trekkers in Natal, while establishing the themes of a conscious racial bitterness on each side that endures to this day. The second and third battles – British versus Zulu at Isandlwana (1879), British versus Boer at Majuba (1881) – represented the worst defeats suffered by British imperial forces in the 19th century. However, these battles, while humiliating for the British, failed to change the long-term strategic balance in southern Africa, and ironically set up later shattering defeats for the Zulus and the Boers, destroying them as independent nations.

The Battle of Majuba ensured that the Boer republics survived as political entities, which prepared the way for our fourth battle, Colenso (1900), and the many other encounters of the 1899–1902 Anglo-Boer War. Colenso was chosen because, as the third crushing British defeat in 'Black Week' in December 1899, it finally confirmed to the British that this war would be more than the usual imperial skirmish, and would require the commitment of massive resources for victory over a skilful and elusive enemy. Colenso rendered obsolete the popular songs that expressed the usual British arrogance about taking on far-off peoples:

Old Mr Kruger
What do you want us to do?
Do you want us to teach you the lesson
We taught the French at Waterloo?

The second Anglo-Boer War ended in victory for the British, but at such a cost that it necessitated a political accommodation between the two white races that was expressed in the Act of Union in 1910. However, this emphasis on reconciliation between the two language groups excluded black Africans, Indians and mixed-race coloureds. For the next 80 years, Afrikaners dominated political life, with varying degrees of loyalty to the British crown, and every prime minister or state president was an Afrikaner.

The next two battles that shaped South Africa, Delville Wood (1916) and El Alamein (1942), were not fought anywhere near the country. They reflected a commitment to British interests that is hard to understand in the 21st century. It was an allegiance that was both powerful (tens of thousands of South Africans volunteered to fight in Europe) and destructive

(in that it undermined reconciliation between Afrikaners and English-speaking South Africans). In each case the experiences of the men who fought (and those who refused to fight) shaped the political perceptions of a generation of whites.

Finally there is Cuito Cuanavale (1987–88), referred to as a single battle but, in fact, a year of fighting that brought nearly two decades of guerrilla and conventional war in Namibia and Angola to an end. In some ways it was a Cold War conflict in miniature. Ironically, less is publicly known in South Africa about Cuito Cuanavale than of any of the other six battles.

As is often the case with relatively recent history, the emotional dust has yet to settle on Cuito. Apologists for the old South African Defence Force argue that the battles achieved their objective – to stop the advancing Angolan, Cuban and Soviet forces – and created the space for an equitable diplomatic settlement for Namibia (and, later, South Africa). The military analyst (and former part-time SADF officer) Helmoed-Römer Heitman argued that Cuito was

British patrol, Second Anglo-Boer War: victory in the end, but at unexpected cost. (*NARSSA*)

Timeless slog of the guerilla and the infantryman: Unita's long campaign in Angola was also war by proxy for the South African Defence Force. (JS)

'an interesting demonstration of how carefully applied and directed force short of all-out war can be used to bring about a political result.'[1]

Strategy should identify the objectives for which a battle is fought; tactics are about how it is fought. Cuito can be seen as the culmination of one long holding operation, that (in Pretoria's strategic sensibility) depended on preventing a military defeat, while accepting that apartheid was discredited and would have to go. From the time of Prime Minister John Vorster's reluctant and cautious commitment to Operation Savannah in 1975, through to the anxious micro-management by senior generals of the Cuito battles, it was clear that Angola and Namibia were never going to be South Africa's Vietnam.

For the present ANC government and its allies, however, Cuito is symbolic of the smashing of the power of the SADF. It is also a victory that the ANC needs to claim. Of all the insurgent movements in southern Africa – Frelimo in Mozambique, the MPLA and Unita in Angola, Swapo in Namibia, Zanu and Zapu in Rhodesia – the ANC is the only one that did not fight a major guerrilla or conventional military campaign. This is not to denigrate its achievement in bringing an end to white rule. For the ANC, the traditional Clausewitz dictum can be inverted: political organisation, external sanctions and internal struggle were the continuation of war by other means to achieve the objective. Nevertheless, there was not the satisfaction of a military victory that would enable the winner to dictate terms to the loser – hence the importance of Cuito in ANC mythology.

Cuito was the only one of our seven battles in which the British played no part, which reflects their dominant role in South Africa's history since their first occupation of the Cape of Good Hope in 1795. The enduring and complex relationship with Britain also helped to make South Africa part of the global economy that imperialism created.

The simplistic view of imperial conquest attributes the success of the European powers in subjugating native peoples to superior firepower, and this was certainly a factor. However, the historian Douglas Porch points out that 'from its earliest period, imperial warfare was considered a hazardous and difficult enterprise.'[2] The conquering soldiers from Europe were generally outnumbered and they had to overcome the threat to men and animals from disease, as well as huge logistical difficulties – two vital factors that many historians, enamoured as they are with the actual fighting, tend to ignore. An element of superior European firepower was of course artillery – but guns were heavy and awkward to transport, and difficult to deploy quickly because they often had to be re-assembled. In southern Africa, the absence of navigable rivers exacerbated any British commander's logistic problems.

The imperatives of logistics made imperial forces extremely vulnerable. Lord Chelmsford, for example, in his advance to Isandlwana, had to deploy no less than half his fighting force to protect the wagon trains bringing in his supplies. It was not inferior firepower (on the part of the Zulus) that prevented them from attacking Chelmsford's supply lines, but rather the lack of a broader military strategy and a cultural inclination towards the set-piece battle where most personal glory might be won. Where the local opponent understood the value of indirect guerrilla operations, as the Boers did, the British were forced to muster enormous resources (over half a million men by the end of the Anglo-Boer War) in order to prevail.

In an age of instant satellite communication, it is frequently overlooked that colonial military actions were often regarded with suspicion by the metropolitan rulers in London, Paris or Lisbon. In South Africa, two of our selected battles were the result of unauthorised – indeed disobedient – actions by the men on the ground:

Sir Bartle Frere (Isandlwana) and General Sir George Colley (Majuba). Even in the cases of Colenso, Delville Wood and El Alamein, the tactics of commanders on the spot were hardly influenced at all by distant politicians. Cuito, however, saw the other extreme: although it was indeed deemed necessary by Pretoria to fight certain battles, a tight rein was kept on the field commanders to ensure that policy remained the master of war.

The indigenous response to imperial aggression was not monolithically hostile. Fissures in local polities were often exploited to recruit substantial numbers of black allies to the British cause, and sympathetic Zulu chiefs were often rewarded with land and cattle. An advantage was that local black recruits were cheaper to pay than imported British regulars; the disadvantage was that their loyalty was superficial and they were usually poorly armed and trained, and therefore of little use in a major engagement. The understandable desertion of the Natal Native Contingent was a key factor in the British defeat at Isandlwana.

The involvement of black auxiliaries and soldiers provokes the observation that, even in warfare, the white South African takes his servants with him. Even inside the laager at Blood River there were many black grooms and helpers, as was the case with the British in their advance to Majuba. Black people were drawn into the Anglo-Boer War on both sides as non-combatants, and as communities they were among that conflict's most disadvantaged victims, in terms of land dispossession, loss of cattle and massive loss of life (20,000) in the concentration camps. When the political settlement came in 1910, it excluded black people, thus igniting a struggle for rights that was to last another 85 years before the advent of democracy.

In the two world wars, 'natives', Cape Coloureds and South Africans of Indian descent joined up in their tens of thousands, generally for the money. The fact that they were officially non-combatants and placed in humble musterings as labourers and stretcher-bearers did not guarantee them any protection from the dangers of battle, and some were to distinguish themselves by their bravery under fire – despite being unarmed. When they returned to South Africa, after 1918 and 1945, it was with a broader awareness of human rights and an expectation that the gratitude of the white ruler would be expressed in political concessions. That this reasonable expectation was dashed (to the embarrassment of many white returning soldiers) made the subsequent black struggle for equal rights more intense, untrusting, uncompromising and bitter.

White South Africa was also adept at fighting wars by proxy. The brunt of the war in Angola was born by Jonas Savimbi's Unita movement, while much of the SADF's hard fighting was done by the feared 32 Battalion, officered by whites but consisting mainly of black Angolans.

Two of our seven battles, Cuito and El Alamein, were on territory that was in itself barely populated and of little consequence. At the other extreme, Delville Wood showed what devastation could be wrought by huge firepower in a relatively small area. In South Africa and southern Africa, the multiplication of firepower through artillery and aircraft has always been subordinate to distance and therefore logistics. One reason why the 'garden province' that is now known as KwaZulu-Natal hosted so many battles was that it offered plentiful water and grazing, by contrast with the vast arid areas of the Cape and Transvaal – but even in Natal, mountains and rocky valleys made military advances difficult. There have been few major conventional battles in southern Africa. Arguably, the relationship in this country between firepower, logistics and ground has helped us to avoid the physical devastation experienced by Europe in two major wars. The political effects of subjugation – of the Boers and the Zulus, and then of blacks by whites – are another matter.

What is heartening about the South African military tradition is that it has always depended on citizen armies. Although the Zulu culture was militaristic, with prowess in battle integral to the status of men, the Zulu army was not a standing one; it was called up as necessity dictated, and like any citizen army there were limits in time and space to its deployment. The old SADF always depended on a small core regular force, with full-time professionals in highly skilled arms like the air force and navy. Its manpower came mostly from conscripts and volunteers. Similarly, the new SANDF strategy is to rely essentially on the Reserve Force (formerly the Citizen Force) to expand its very limited regular fighting capability when needed.

The tradition of a citizen army has served as a brake on militarism and recklessness. Yet in the seven battles we have chosen, there are more than enough tales of bravery on all sides to suggest a military culture informed by ideas of service and sacrifice. It has thrown up remarkable individuals who, in their time and place, served their people admirably: Dingaan and Andries Pretorius; John Chard and Cetshwayo; Ian Hamilton and Piet Joubert; Louis Botha and Jan Smuts; Dan Pienaar and Jannie Geldenhuys.

NOTES

1. Helmoed-Römer Heitman, *War in Angola – The Final South African Phase*. Gibraltar: Ashanti, 1990.
2. Douglas Porch, *Wars of Empire*. London: Collins, 2004.

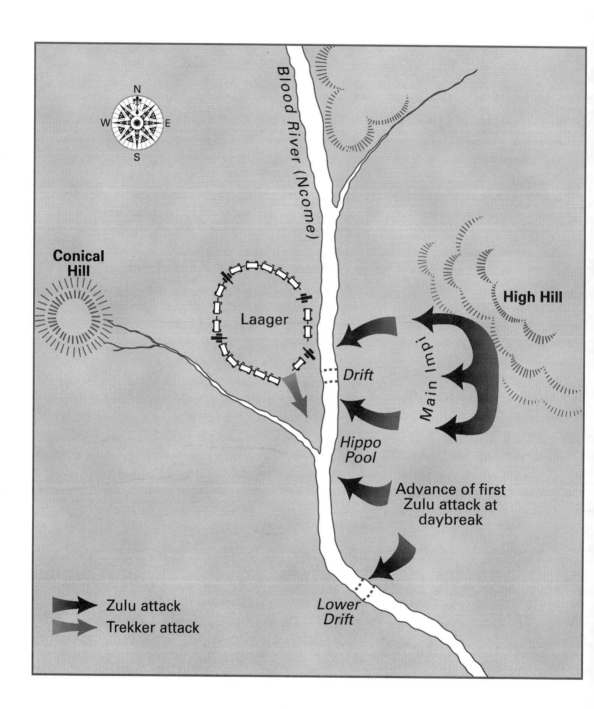

An ancient battle that casts a long shadow

The Battle of Blood River
16 December 1838

Few battles can have had such enduring influence on the attitudes of a people over generations. The Battle of Blood River, fought on the morning of 16 December 1838, came to be seen by many Afrikaners as a literally sacred event.

Militarily, it was a crucial victory for the Boer Voortrekkers over the Zulus, at a time when the trekkers in Natal faced extinction. Spiritually, the battle was seen as a sign of divine approval of the Boers' cause and of their justified retribution for Zulu treachery. Politically, the event would be skilfully employed by politicians more than a century later to rally support for the Afrikaner nationalist cause and, more crudely, to remind their people of the continued existence of the swart gevaar ('black danger').

Culturally, Blood River remains an emblem of an embattled and 'civilised' white minority prevailing, through superior tactics and firepower, over hordes of brave black 'savages'. That emblem (there are other battles in colonial history that express it, but few as powerfully) was a kind of shorthand for the power relationships between black and white in South Africa until 1990.

What sets Blood River apart is the distinctive covenant (or promise, or vow) that the Boers made in late 1838 in anticipation of a major and decisive battle with the Zulus:

'Mijn broeders en medelandgenoten

'Hier staan wij tans op een ogenblik voor een heilige God van hemel en aarde om een belofte aan Hem te belowen, als Hij met Zijn bescherming met ons zal wezen, en onze vijand in onze handen zal geven dat wij overwinnen, dat wij

23

die dag en datum elk jaar als een dankdag zoals een Sabbat in Zijn eer zal voorbrengen, en dat wij een tempel tot Zijn eer stichten zal; waar het hem sou behagen, en dat wij ook aan onzen kinderen zal zeggen, dat zij met ons erin moeten dele, tot gedachtenis ook voor ons opkomende geslachten. Want de ere van Zijn Naam daardoor zal verheerlikt worden, dat de roem en eer van overwinning aan Hem zal worden gegeven.'

('Here we stand before the Holy God of Heaven and Earth, to make Him a promise that if He will protect us, and deliver our enemy into our hands so that we prevail, we will observe the day and date each year as a day of thanks, like a Sabbath, and that we will erect a temple in His honour wherever He may choose, and that we will also tell our children to join with us in commemorating this day, also for coming generations. For His name will be glorified by giving Him all the honour and glory of victory.')[1]

No original text of the covenant survives, but three versions in Dutch have been handed down: those by H J Hofstede (1876), F L Cachet (1892) and G B A Gerdener (1919). Afrikaner scholars over the years have been anxious to ensure, by assessing eye-witness and other contemporary accounts, that the words are accepted as being very close to the original. It is also clear that the search for accuracy was prosecuted with the kind of zeal normally found in the analysis of holy texts.

To understand what was in the minds of the Boers when they made their vow, we first need to understand the context.

Those who fought at Blood River had originally been among the Dutch-speaking farmers in the Eastern Cape whose deep discontent with British rule had induced them to migrate in a north-westerly direction to Natal and the highveld, the high-altitude grassland region that would be known as the Transvaal. This migration became known as the Great Trek. By 1840 over 6,000 Boer men, women and children – about a tenth of the white population of the Cape Colony – had left for the interior. Some of these Voortrekker parties moved to the areas now known as Gauteng, Limpopo and Mpumalanga (formerly the southern, northern and eastern Transvaal respectively). The parties that concern us here are those that crossed the Drakensberg into Natal under several different leaders, the most important of whom was Piet Retief.

In October 1837 Retief went ahead of the trek with a small party to Port Natal (now Durban) to meet British traders in an attempt to stave off any British intervention. While the traders appeared to welcome the presence of the trekkers because it would increase their security, they showed little interest in what was happening in the interior. This was dominated by the warrior nation of Zulus under their king, Dingaan (as contemporary accounts spell his name), descendant of the great Zulu nation-builder Shaka. Retief also made contact with Dingaan, to head off a possible Zulu attack and to ask him for a grant of land.

Dingaan apparently stalled, asking Retief and his men to demonstrate their good faith by recovering some cattle that had been stolen from the Zulus by a Sotho chief, Sekonyela. Retief did so, and in February 1839 he went back to Dingaan's royal kraal at Mgungunhlovu ('place of the great elephant'), accompanied by 70 trekkers and 30 coloured servants, all men. According to the orthodox version in Afrikaner historiography, a treaty had been prepared according to which Dingaan would cede to the trekkers all land between the Tugela and Umzimvubu rivers. A photograph of the original document appears in one Afrikaans history, providing this text (in English, not Dutch):

'Know all men by this that whereas Pieter Retief, Governor of the dutch Emigrant South afrikans has retaken my Cattle which Sinkoyello had stolen which cattle the said Retief now deliver unto me. I Dingaan, King of the Zoolas as hereby certify and declare that I thought fit to resign unto him the said Retief and his countrymen (on reward of the case hereabove mentioned) the place called Port Natal together with all the land annexed that is to say from Dogeela to the Omsoboebo River westward and from the Sea to the north as far as the Land may be useful and in my possession which I did by this and give unto them for their Everlasting Property.'

At the bottom of the document, dated Sunday, 4 February, attention is drawn to 'the mark' of 'Koning Dingaan', who was illiterate, with witnesses listed as trekkers M Oosthuyse, A C Greyling and B J Liebenberg, and senior Zulu councillors Maoro, Joelawoesa and Manonda.[2]

The trekkers were due to leave on Tuesday, 6 February, but that morning they were invited by Dingaan to attend a final farewell ceremony. They accepted, but were instructed to leave their weapons outside the gate of the kraal. Retief sat on the ground beside Dingaan's carved chair to watch a display of dancing. Also present was the missionary Francis Owen, who seems to have been an occasional courtier of Dingaan and who lived on a hill near the kraal.

The warriors danced closer and closer. Suddenly Dingaan jumped up and shouted: 'Bulalani abatagathi!' ('Kill the wizards!'). The trekkers were immediately overpowered, bound with rawhide thongs and taken into the valley and up the slopes of KwaMatiwane, a hill that served as Dingaan's place of execution. There they were clubbed to death or their skulls were crushed with rocks; a few were impaled and left to die more slowly. Retief was spared till last, in order that he might see the agony of the others (including his own son). After his death, Retief's chest was opened with an assegai, and his heart and liver were placed in a cloth and taken to Dingaan.

The missionary Owen's journal entry for that day begins: 'A dreadful day in the annals of the Mission . . . At present all is as still as death: it is really the stillness of death, for it has palsied every tongue in our little assembly'.

Worse was to come. The next day, Owen looked across at the royal kraal from his dwelling on a nearby hill: 'I have seen by my glass that Dingaan has been sitting most of the morning since this dreadful affair in the centre of his town, the Army in several divisions collected before him. About noon the whole Army ran in the direction from which the Boers came.'[3]

The Zulus were headed for trekker encampments around the sources of the Tugela River, in the area near the modern town of Colenso. They waited until the night of 17 February, when there was no moon, and attacked the settlements at about 1am. Close on 500 people were killed – about 40 white men, 56 white women and 185 white children, and over 200 coloured servants – and the Zulus seized 35,000 cattle and sheep. A Mevrou Steenkamp said it was 'unbearable for flesh and blood to behold the frightful spectacle the following morning. In one wagon were found fifty dead, and blood flowed from the seam of the tent-sail down to the lowest part . . . On all sides one saw tears flowing and heard people weeping by the plundered wagons, painted with blood; tents and beds were torn to shreds; pregnant women and little children had to walk for hours together, bearing the signs of their hasty flight.'[4] The events of that night became known as the Bloukrans Massacre, a hardly less emotive event

Above: Dingaan's royal enclosure at Mgungunhlovu. (*SANMMH*)

Left: The alleged signing of the treaty, as depicted in stone relief at the Voortrekker Monument. (*DB*)

Below: Andries Pretorius, leader of the Boer forces at Blood River. (*SANMMH*)

for Afrikaners than the murder of Retief, and there were other similar attacks at Moordspruit ('the stream where murder was committed') and Weenen ('place of weeping').

However, the Zulus had underestimated how dispersed the trekker camps had been, which meant that many Boers were spared. Within six weeks the trekkers had mustered their forces for revenge. A trekker commando led by Hendrik Potgieter and Piet Uys moved in two columns towards Dingaan's kraal. But on 10 April the Zulu commander Mhlela lured them into an ambush that ended with many trekkers killed (including Uys and his 14-year-old son Dirkie, who refused to leave his dying father's side) and the rest retreating in disarray. This was the battle of Mtaleni and it was a third disaster for the Boers.

In August Dingaan sent an impi of warriors to attack a trekker camp at Gatslaer ('laager where the hole is'), so named because

it was situated between the Bushmans River and a deep donga. Here the Boers adapted their tactics and formed a laager of their wagons, with the gaps between them blocked by felled thorn trees and other thick branches. In a battle lasting three days, just 75 men armed with muskets and a small cannon fought off 10,000 Zulus, who failed to penetrate the defences. (Gatslaer was later renamed to the more dignified Veglaer, 'fighting laager'). Laagering was a tactic that had first been used in 1836, and the Boers would remember it a few months later. But they had been seriously weakened by defeat and disease, by the loss of their cattle and much internal dissension, and their very survival in Natal was now at stake.

The trekkers were reinforced from the Cape, and their new leader was Andries Pretorius, one of those remarkable individuals who stand above the impersonal forces of history be-

Above: The attack on Retief and his men whilst inside Dingaan's enclosure, as depicted by Con Burton. (*DB*)

Right: An artist's impression of the killing of Retief. (*SANMMH*)

cause he was able to shape events. Tall and physically strong, with a powerful personality, he became known to the Zulus as Ngalonkulu ('brawny arms'). Pretorius imposed unity on the bickering Boers and by November 1838 he was able to set out from the area around the present-day town of Estcourt, headed for Dingaan's kraal at Mgungunhlovu. He had 64 wagons, 900 oxen, two muzzle-loaded guns and about 470 fighting men and 100 black servants. There were no women and children. All the Boers were mounted, with extra horses in reserve. The revered early twentieth-century Afrikaner historian, Gustav Preller, who served as a gunner in the Anglo-Boer War, judged that Pretorius's commando was 'the most remarkable example in our history of coaching an unorganised force whose morale, through numerous setbacks and disappointments, was very low, to a nearly perfect war unit, ready to execute miracles.'[5]

The expedition moved north-west towards Colenso, Ladysmith and Dundee, after which it made a 90-degree turn to the south-west,

heading for Dingaan's stronghold. The Zulus – whose spies kept the trek under constant surveillance – called it 'the moving of the white houses', after the canvas on the wagons. The trekkers had crossed the Ncome River, a tributary of the Buffalo, when their scouts reported that a large Zulu force was approaching. Pretorius realised that he should go back to the Ncome, which presented an ideal tactical defensive position, reminiscent of the conditions at Gatslaer.

To the east of the position chosen was a large, deep hippo pool – about 50 yards long, with the water more than three yards deep (as measured by a trekker's whip). To the south, running at a right angle to the pool, was a large dry donga at least four yards deep. Between these two natural obstacles, the laager was formed in less then an hour (we are told that the trekkers had practised laagering every day for the previous two weeks). Wooden barricades (veghekke, 'fighting gates') were placed between the wagons, and underneath the wagons between the wheels. There were three narrow openings that could be closed quickly by moving wagons lengthways into them from inside the laager. A cannon was placed in two of the openings. Inside the laager there were also hundreds of oxen and horses.

The main line of attack for the Zulus would have to be from the land on the north-westerly side of the laager. In this area, then as now, there is no high ground to enable manoeuvre, nor dead ground to offer concealment. It was simply a wide, flat grassy plain. Sarel Cilliers, one of the spiritual leaders of the trek, later wrote: 'I must particularly mention how the Lord, in His watchfulness over us, brought us to the place where He ordained the battle had to be fought.'

It seems that the trekker's covenant was not formulated at Ncome for the first time, but at least a week earlier on 9 December at Dans-kraal, site of the present-day railway marshalling yard near Ladysmith. According to one account, the Englishmen in the party also took part in the vow ceremony, but five Boers abstained 'for fear of God's vengeance on their descendants if in years to come they broke the promise'. The ritual was repeated each day after that until the laagering at the Ncome site.

On the afternoon of Saturday, 15 December, Pretorius left the laager at Ncome with a large mounted group to do reconnaissance. In the east near Nqutu they encountered a Zulu army that they estimated at 15,000. The Zulus moved towards the Boers, then suddenly retreated – a classic tactic from the time of Shaka, aimed at luring the enemy on towards the 'chest' of the Zulu army, while outflanking and then surrounding them with the two 'horns'.[6] Sarel Cilliers urged Pretorius to attack, but that was how the Boers had gone wrong at Mtaleni in April. This time they resisted the temptation. 'Do not let us go to them, but let them come to us,' said Pretorius, and he led his men back to the laager at Ncome. At dusk, cannon shots were fired to signal to all the Boer scouts to return. A thick mist rose from the river.

Mhlela, the Zulu commander, moved his men quickly to positions near the Ncome. His attempt to lure the Boers into battle in the open had failed. In theory there were two other tactical possibilities: lay siege to the laager and starve out the Boers (and their animals), or attack the laager. But it would seem that the aggressive traditions of Zulu warfare did not allow for anything but an immediate offensive.

Indeed, it is not certain why Mhlela did not attack that very evening. A theory is that the Zulus perceived wizardry in the eerie glow through the fog of the Boer candle-lanterns, one lantern hanging from the front of each wagon. Another is that the Zulus, who had some knowledge of firearm technology, were expecting the thick fog to dampen the defenders' gunpowder and so render their rifles useless. In the end, on a night with fog and no moon, it was probably too dark to prepare, launch and control an attack. It seems that Mhlela simply needed more time to get his men into position. The eyewitness account by J G Bantjes, personal secretary to Pretorius, mentions that even at sunrise the next day, some Zulu regiments were still moving into position.

Estimates of the size of the Zulu attacking force range from 10,000 (several historians) to 15,000 (Andries Pretorius) to 30,000 (M W Pretorius, son of Andries). The regiments of unblooded young warriors, carrying black shields and eager to kill in battle for the first time, would attack first from the north-west, deployed at distances between 40 yards and 1,000 yards from the edge of the laager. The veteran regiments (with white shields) would wait on the eastern banks of the Ncome until the Boers ran out of ammunition and then move into the laager to finish off the defenders.

The Afrikaner historian Victor D'Assonville described the scene on the eve of battle: 'Before evening prayers it was quiet in the laager at Ncome and the atmosphere was very tense. Inside the laager, orders were given and carried out in whispers. Lanterns were moved around in silence. In the light of huge fires near the hippo pool and the donga, the human bodies looked ghostlike . . . outside the laager, a noise of thousands of feet, mixed with the voices of the Zulus, evolved – an invisible, mysterious, awesome massive noise . . . a noise like thunder, a strong wind blowing or the roaring of waters.'[7]

There was singing. The Zulus must have been mystified by the sound of nearly 500 Boer voices singing verses in Dutch, derived from Psalm 38. The historian Preller later recorded the memory of an old Zulu that 'it sounded as if the Boers were all weeping together. Our young men heard it and said to each other: Keep on weeping, the sun of tomorrow you will never see to set.' And the Boers, not knowing when an attack would come, could not avoid listening through the night to the martial singing of thousands of Zulus.

When dawn came on Sunday, 16 December, wrote Bantjes, the day 'was as if ordained for us – the skies were open, the weather bright and clear . . . although awesome, the arrival of the last Zulu regiments with their captains was a beautiful sight.'

Accounts differ on how the battle started. D'Assonville writes that Pretorius had given the order that nobody was to fire before he himself had loosed two shots. When those shots were heard, 'within two seconds the Boer fusillade created a perfect sheet of fire along the whole semicircle from the river to the donga. Before they could stand up, hundreds of the brave young warriors who sat 40 yards from the wagons were dead.' In response, the Zulu

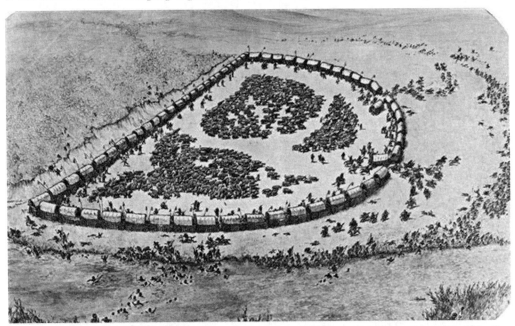

The lay of the land, showing how the Zulus were caught between the Ncome and the laager. It is said that after the battle, the Zulus vowed never to drink from this river again. (*SANMMH*)

commanders gave the signal to attack, sounded on the *icilongo* – a kind of trumpet made from a tube of bamboo and the horn of an ox. That set off the warriors shouting and screaming, and drumming with their stabbing assegais on their shields.

The English historian Oliver Ransford does not mention the *icilongo*, and says the Boers started firing when they saw the Zulus already charging in the light of early dawn.

Either way, the effect was incontrovertible. Ransford reconstructs the scene: 'It was impossible for a single shot to miss such a target . . . The shock of the concentrated fire was devastating and almost at once the first wave of Zulus reeled back in disorder. Then for two mortal hours these regiments mounted a wild chain of doomed charges on the north and west faces of the laager, and one after the other they were smashed and flattened . . . Each charge was followed by a lull with the battle smoke hanging in the thin morning air, during which the fighting regiments received a trickle of reinforcements from across the river, and the only noise was the rattling of spears on shields, the shuffling of naked feet on the ground as the warriors nerved themselves for another rush, and the moaning of the wounded.'[8]

The initial Zulu advance failed to break through and their renewed attacks became steadily weaker. The central tactical problem for the Zulus was that they could not build up momentum. Too many of them were packed together in a limited space, as they tried to attack the narrow front presented by the wagons. Increasingly their path was cluttered with their own dead and wounded. The Boers were using buckshot, so that they could discharge ten or more little lead balls with each pull of the trigger. This proved lethal at short range.

The Zulu historian Credo Mutwa wrote in *Indaba My Children* that it was 'the only battle in human history where more people were killed than there were shots fired'.[9]

Ironically, the main danger to the Boers turned out to be their own oxen and horses, upset by the noise of battle. There was a danger that they would stampede and break the wagon line. Ransford continues: 'Sarel Cilliers seems to have been the first to appreciate the danger; he promptly led some men to the southern flank of the laager and began firing into the dense mass of Zulus crowded within the donga. The din, as was intended, drove the animals back into the centre of the laager, but the raking of the donga also did dreadful execution. Here indeed the worst killing of the entire action took place. The very number of Zulus there was a disadvantage: they stood so tightly packed together that they were unable to climb the steep sides, unable even to throw their assegais, and when Cilliers called for volunteers to leave the shelter of the wagons and approach the donga, every single warrior who had stood there was shot dead.'

The Boers each had two or three muskets, a vital surplus considering that barrels became to hot to hold from the constant firing. One defender, Bezuidenhout, recalled: 'Of that fight nothing remains in my memory except shouting and tumult and lamentation, and a sea of black faces; and a dense smoke that rose straight as a plumb line upwards from the ground.'

At one point the muskets and guns had created so much smoke that Pretorius called on his men to cease fire. As the air cleared, the Boers were surprised to see that the Zulus had retreated to a line about 500 yards from the laager. Pretorius needed to entice them back into battle. He ordered one Flip Coetzer, who was fluent in Zulu, to stand on a wagon and

Many of the Boers had two muskets, a vital surplus considering that barrels became too hot to hold from the constant firing. They also had 'Ou Grietjie', one of three cannon used at Blood River. (*SANMMH*)

shout a challenge to the enemy: 'What is your idea now, men of Dingaan? We have arrived here to fight – and not against defenceless women and children but against tough men. This is no more a case of Bloukrans. Are you afraid to start the attack?'

But the Zulus resisted the provocation, and revised their tactics for a fresh charge. This time they started at a line about 200 yards away, and they were more spread out. Immediately the tactical advantage shifted. The Boer shooting was having much less effect because of the enemy's dispersal; the Zulus still had vastly superior numbers (including elite regiments still in reserve) to enable them to keep fighting until the Boers ran out of ammunition.

Pretorius knew this. 'We will have to take care that this fighting is not dragged out too long,' he told his men, and he accepted he would have to take risks.

First, realising that the veteran warriors on the east bank of the river would soon be called in, Pretorius trained his two guns on those regiments. The weight of fire provoked some

of them into attacking prematurely in a dense mass, and these rushes were also broken up by musket fire, or by the natural obstacle of the hippo pool.

Second, Pretorius decided he must switch over to the attack by taking the fight to the Zulus. 'You will scarcely be able to form an idea of the sight presented around us,' he later wrote. 'It was such as to require some nerve not to betray uneasiness in the countenance. Seeing that it was necessary to display the most desperate determination, I caused four gates of our enclosed encampment to be simultaneously thrown open, from whence some mounted men were to charge the enemy, at the same time keeping a heavy fire on them.'

Under covering fire, the wagons were wheeled back from the prepared openings, and Bart Pretorius (the leader's younger brother) led out a mounted commando of about 100 men in an attempt to divide and confuse the Zulu forces. After initial resistance, they succeeded in their third attempt, dividing the Zulus and then attacking them from behind. From being a set-piece attack on a defensive position, the battle now changed suddenly into a fluid contest between cavalry and infantry. 'The warriors at last began to waver,' says Ransford. 'Led by Pretorius himself, the greater part of his force now deployed north and south along both banks of the full Ncome River, shooting down the Zulus who approached or tried to hide among its reeds. These warriors could only cower helplessly in the water as the Boers came riding slowly down the banks, picking them off at leisure. The water was deeply stained that morning with their life-blood, and ever since the Ncome has gone by the name of Blood River. Some of the Boers believed that far more Zulus were drowned at Blood River than shot to death.'

It was only then – and too late – that the remaining Zulu reserves were ordered into battle. Their arrival confused the battle scene further, and they were impeded by the many warriors now trying to escape. 'They were quite unable to affect the issue of the fight,' says Ransford, 'and in a queer, slow stumbling flight, because they were simply too tired to run fast, an immense disorganised rabble of men streamed off in defeat in every direction with the Boer horsemen in pursuit.'

The Battle of Blood River was over. One of the participants, J H Hattingh, later recalled that he had been told by the Zulus that they would never again drink the water of the Ncome. An estimated 3,500 Zulus had been killed. None of the Boers was killed and only three were lightly wounded (one was Pretorius, stabbed in his left hand during the mounted pursuit).

The next day, Monday, 17 December, Pretorius ordered his men to Dingaan's royal kraal at Mgungunhlovu, 100km distant as the crow flies. They arrived four days later, only to find that Dingaan had pre-empted them by setting fire to the kraal and fleeing. But they did find the remains of Retief and his men, slaughtered by Dingaan eight months before. Retief's skeleton was identified by the satin waistcoat he had worn, and by a leather pouch which contained the piece of paper in which Dingaan had pretended to cede territory to the trekkers. The document was so well-preserved, wrote Bantjes, that it could have been written that very day.

However, there seems to be some doubt over the authenticity of the cession document. Leonard Thompson says it 'may' have been signed by Dingaan, and also says briefly in a footnote to his general history that 'it is possible that no such treaty existed'. Does this mean that the photographed document is a forgery? Such doubts are certainly not entertained in the Afrikaner version of events, which also uses as evidence the presence as witnesses (at the meeting between Retief and Dingaan) of the missionary Francis Owen and a translator, William Wood.

Beyond the legalistic aspects, there is the immense force of the belief in divine vindication of the Boer cause. As one ardent Afrikaner nationalist, Morgan Gregory of Utrecht, asserted recently in a pamphlet on the battle: 'For us, the descendants of the people of the Covenant, no doubt exists that God Almighty answered the prayers of the Trekkers. God let the meeting between the two sides take place during a dark moon. God destined the battle to take place in daylight. God destined the (Pretorius) Trekkers to follow an unusual, unexplained route, to allow them to find the choice of the most suitably situated place for setting up laager. The gunpowder remained dry, despite the thick fog of the night before.'[10]

Was Dingaan simply guilty of treachery? Judging by the writings of both Gustav Preller

POTGIETER'S CERTIFIKAAT

Affidavit by the Voortrekkers who found Retief's bones and who swore that they found the signed treaty, almost brand new, in his pouch. (DB)

and Credo Mutwa, the Zulu king may have been angry at the white men because an English trader, Thomas Halstead, was caught looking over the fence enclosing the king's wives and concubines – an act that any Zulu knew was punishable by death. Perhaps this merely exacerbated Dingaan's hostility towards Retief and his men. Through his spies he knew that some trekkers had already claimed farms before any agreement had been reached. Intimidation was probably felt when trekkers openly showed off their horsemanship and firearms in a ceremonial display, during their three-day stay at the royal kraal. And Zulu oral history recalls that after two of those nights, hoofprints were found around the kraal, provoking suspicion that the Boers wanted to attack Dingaan. In that light, his 'treachery' might be seen simply as a preventive strike against an enemy with superior firepower.[11]

Boer and Zulu relations at the time of Blood River tend to be presented in Afrikaner 20th-century accounts as those between negotiating equals, one of whom acted in innocent good will and the other with cunning and deceit. This would accord with the National Party ideology of the 1950s to 1980s of 'separate but equal' nations. But there were other aspects to the relationship, aspects which must have caused great bitterness among the Zulus. For instance, the Boers in Natal, like those who had trekked further north, badly needed labour to work their farms. Hermann Giliomee writes: 'The easiest way in which to acquire labour was to seize (black) women and children . . . Before the Battle of Blood River, Andries Pretorius had warned the burghers not to catch Zulu children and women during the battle, since it would be a distraction, and to seize them only after the battle. In the follow-up expedition against Dingaan, the trekker military council authorised every member of the commando to seize four children . . . In 1841 the Volksraad in Pietermaritzburg expressed dismay over a reported trade in Zulu children, but lacked the power to stamp it out'.[12]

In terms of military tactics, Pretorius succeeded at Blood River because he was able to counter the Zulus' traditional strengths – mobility, speed, surprise, reckless courage and massive numerical superiority – by inducing them to fight on ground of his choosing, against a compact defensive position and superior firepower. Pretorius was also able to judge to a nicety when he needed to break out and switch over to the attack.

As for the Zulus, they erred in launching their initial attacks from a position too close to the Boers' laager, thus offering a concentrated target; and they were too slow in changing their tactics and in bringing in their reserves. Like their counterparts 80 years later in World War I, the Zulu commanders instinctively preferred attrition in a set-piece battle. And like the British 40 years later at Majuba, and 60 years later in the 1899–1902 war, the Zulus struggled to find an answer to the exceptional shooting and horsemanship of the Boers.

The strategic outcome of Blood River was, briefly, the establishment in Natal of a Boer republic, which acknowledged Zululand as a sovereign independent state. Both these entities would fall victim, sooner or later, to aggressive British colonialism. But the Zulu nation split: Dingaan's half-brother Mpande became an ally of Pretorius in follow-up operations against Dingaan. According to Hermann Giliomee, 'Afrikaner nationalists of the next century considered Blood River the battle that "saved" the Great Trek and secured the victory of Christianity and "civilisation". But the victory itself at most secured only a temporary beachhead.'

Despite the fervent words of the Boer covenant and the emotional impact of the crushing victory at Blood River, it seems that 16 December was hardly marked at all for nearly three decades. In 1866, however, there was a commemorative gathering at the battlefield, attended by many aged voortrekkers and their children. The Zulu king at the time, Cetshwayo, attended the ceremony with several Zulu veterans, and apparently spoke of the good relations that had developed between Boer and Zulu. It was at this event that the first memorial cairn of stones was built, and to this day it can be seen in the centre of the ox-wagon laager.

In the 1880s, the Transvaal Boer leader Paul Kruger showed that he understood the political potential of Blood River. According to Giliomee, it was Kruger who first 'turned the Great Trek into a heroic myth . . . the Battle of Blood River and the vow made before the battle were to him the symbol of the will of the Transvaal burghers to survive as an independent people against overwhelming odds.'

Half a century later, 1930s Afrikaner nationalists shrewdly used the symbolism of the Great Trek, and Blood River in particular, to mobilise support. There were commemorative ox-wagon treks to the Transvaal and to the site of the battle. The liberal writer Alan Paton recalled being impressed by the force of Afrikaner nationalism in the 1930s, and by the commemorative treks, which he said 'evoked indescribable emotion. There was an upwelling of Afrikaner pride and sentiment such as South Africa had never known.'[13] The celebrations climaxed in Pretoria on 16 December 1938 with the laying, before a crowd of 100,000, of a foundation stone for what would become the Voortrekker Monument.

Paton himself grew a beard and travelled to

Inauguration of the Voortrekker Monument in 1949. Nationalists shrewdly exploited the symbolism of the Great Trek and Blood River to mobilise support. A decade earlier the foundation stone of the monument had been laid in a festive ceremony. *(DB)*

Pretoria to show solidarity with the Afrikaners. Yet such was the hostility towards English-speakers, he said, that 'what I had done in such good faith and such good will turned to ashes. I wanted only that the celebration should end. It was a lonely and terrible experience.' He went back to his wife and told her: 'I'm taking off this beard and I'll never grow another.'

Both the political giants of the 1920s and 1930s, J B M Hertzog and Jan Smuts, were marginalised by these events that expressed an increasingly fervent and exclusive Afrikaner nationalism. Paton later noted that the events of 1938 were a major factor in the coming to power of D F Malan's Nationalists in 1948. Blood River had cast a very long shadow.

After the formation of the Union of South Africa in 1910, 16 December was made an official (and semi-religious) public holiday, known for many years (with unintended irony) as Dingaan's Day. After sustained protests from

some Afrikaner nationalists, the holiday was renamed the Day of the Covenant in the 1960s. This gave rise to an interesting theological debate. Was it desirable (or possible) for men to make a covenant – a deal – with God? To say: if you give us victory, only then will we honour you . . . was this legitimate? The answer that prevailed was that the worship of God could not be conditional, and therefore the trekkers could not in principle have made a deal with the Almighty (even if they, in early December 1838, thought they had). But it was permissible for men to make a promise to honour God, and so the public holiday became known as the Day of the Vow.

Such philosophical disputes may seem arcane, now that the anniversary of Blood River has been subsumed in a broader holiday known as Reconciliation Day. Paton believed that many Afrikaners had always found the triumphalism of Blood River celebrations distasteful. But

35

the date of the public holiday remains 16 December – a tacit acknowledgement by the new rulers of South Africa of the importance of Blood River in the political consciousness of Afrikaners, and indeed in the development of the country's history.

The definitive *Harbottle's Dictionary of Battles*, first published in London in 1904, lists thousands of minor and major military engagements across all countries and cultures in history – but it ignores Blood River. Perhaps that is as it should be. It was, in a peculiarly intimate way, a very South African battle, remote from the imperatives of European expansionism and colonialism. At its worst, Blood River is about treachery, revenge and naked racial aggression; at its best, courage in adversity and the survival of a people.

Above: The view from the Voortrekker Monument after its inauguration in 1949. (*DB*)

Left: Granite memorial at the Blood River site. (*RW*)

CEMETERIES, MEMORIALS AND VISITOR CENTRES

The Boer memorial at Blood River was established essentially as an Afrikaner shrine, and the triumphalist sculptures of ox-wagons in granite (outside the museum) and bronze (in the huge realistic laager) are intriguing. The museum at the Visitor Centre, completed in 1996, has a professionally compiled, informative and reasonably balanced survey of the battle and events around it, with a range of souvenirs and literature linked to the battle and Afrikaner nationalism. There is an exhaustive list of the trekkers who took part in the battle.

The single granite wagon by sculptor Coert Steynberg was unveiled in 1947. When the laager of bronze wagons was completed in 1971, the Steynberg wagon was moved to its present position outside the museum. Inside the laager is a stone cairn constructed in 1938 for the centenary celebrations of the Great Trek. Near the cairn, two sets of wagon tracks are set in concrete: those of the 'Johanna van der Merwe' wagon used in the 1938 centenary celebrations, and those of the 'Natalia' wagon arranged by Afrikaans cultural organisations for the 150th anniversary in 1988. The oldest commemorative monument is the stone pile that was built during the memorial gathering of 1866.

The small staff at the Visitor Centre are friendly, helpful and knowledgeable. The museum also offers home-cooked meals. Nearby is a small conference centre, and it is possible to book self-catering overnight accommodation in the caravan camp and chalets. There is a nominal entrance fee to the site. For more information contact Dawie and Elbie Viljoen (034) 632-1695 or PO Box 2194, Dundee 3000.

On the other side of the laager is a more modest Zulu memorial, established in the 1990s, presumably as an attempted corrective to the Boer interpretation of events. The road signs directing visitors to this memorial refer pointedly to 'Ncome' rather than 'Blood River'. However, while this small exhibition is of interest, it is too limited in scope to make any substantial historical statement, and unlike the other memorial it is poorly staffed. The most memorable aspect is the row of outsize Zulu shields outside the building, bleakly facing the laager. For some reason the direct footpath between the two memorials was in 2005 blocked by a locked gate, seeming to suggest that racial reconciliation has some way to go in South Africa.

Because the battlefield is so isolated, it is not built up and there is no vehicular traffic. Only the wind and the faint voices of distant villagers disturb the silence. The wagons are broodingly impressive at dusk, in particular, when their shapes seem to hunch and harden in the fading light, as if to refute any attempt to undermine the importance of this battle in Afrikaner and South African history.

HOW TO GET THERE AND WHERE TO STAY

From Johannesburg (five hours): Take the N3 highway to Durban and exit at Villiers. Follow the R103 and then the R34 to Vrede, Memel and Newcastle. (If you want to take in the Majuba battlefield on the way, from Vrede take the R546 to Standerton, then the R23 to Volksrust and the N11 to Newcastle.)

From Newcastle take the N11 to Ladysmith, then the R621 left to Dundee. From Dundee take the R68 for 6km and then the R33 for about 25km. The turnoff to Blood River is to the right, and the battle site is about 30km from the turnoff on a good dirt road.

From Durban (four hours): Take the N3 highway to Johannesburg and then the N11 to Ladysmith. About 27km after Ladysmith take the R602 right to Glencoe and Dundee. From Dundee take the R68 for 6km and then the R33 for about 25km. The turnoff to Blood River is to the right, and the battle site is about 30km from the turnoff on a good dirt road.

WHERE TO STAY

For those interested in staying close to the battlefield, the **Blood River caravan camp** with chalets are near the Visitor's Centre and museum. For more information contact Dawie and Elbie Viljoen (034) 632-1695.

Battlefields Country Lodge (034) 218-1641 is on the road to Vryheid and offers 3-star accommodation for 50 to 60 guests with access to a pool, lapa-pub and conference centre.

The Royal Country Inn (034) 212-2147 (until recent renovations known as the Royal Hotel) in Dundee is recommended for its tranquil garden setting and good restaurant.

Dundee is geared for battlefield visitors, with many lodges and bed & breakfast establishments (and the excellent Talana Museum). Nearby Glencoe also has accommodation.

Dundee Tourist Information: (034) 212-2121.

REFERENCES AND FURTHER READING

Victor d'Assonville, *Blood River*. Roodepoort: Marnix, 2000.

Hermann Giliomee, *The Afrikaners: Biography of a People*. Cape Town: Tafelberg, 2003.

Morgan Gregory, *The Battle of Blood River*. Utrecht: self-published pamphlet, date unknown.

Alan Paton, *Towards the Mountain*. Cape Town: David Philip, 1980.

Oliver Ransford, *The Great Trek*. London: John Murray, 1972.

Leonard Thompson, *A History of South Africa*. Sandton: Random Century, 1990.

T V Bulpin, *Natal and the Zulu Country*. Cape Town: T V Bulpin Publications (Pty) Ltd, 1977 (3rd ed).

NOTES

1. Document distributed by Blood River museum.
2. Victor d'Assonville, *Blood River*. Roodepoort: Marnix, 2000, p.10.
3. Quoted in Oliver Ransford, *The Great Trek*. London: John Murray, 1972, chapter 6.
4. *Ibid*, chapter 7.
5. Quoted in D'Assonville, *op cit*, p.32.
6. Ian Knight, *The Anatomy of the Zulu Army from Shaka to Cetshwayo 1818-1879*. London: Greenhill Books, 1999.
7. Quoted in D'Assonville, *op cit*, p.31.
8. Ransford, *op cit*, chapter 7.
9. Quoted in D'Assonville, *op cit*, p.47.
10. Morgan Gregory, *The Battle of Blood River*. Utrecht: self-published pamphlet, date unknown, p.12.
11. James Stuart Archive, Vol. III.
12. Hermann Giliomee, *The Afrikaners: Biography of a People*. Cape Town: Tafelberg, 2003, p.263.
13. Alan Paton, *Towards the Mountain*. Cape Town: David Philip, 1980, p.174.

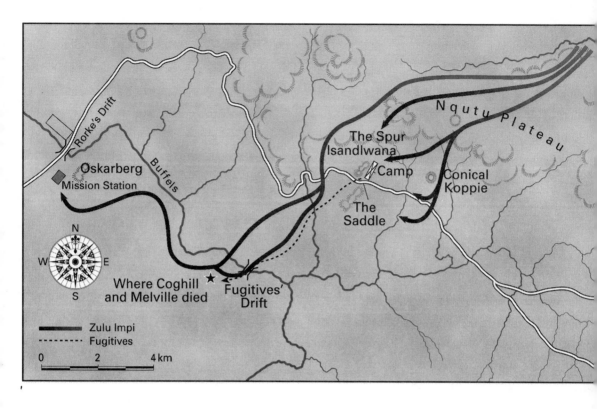

Rorke's Drift

Buffels

Oskarberg
Mission Station

N
W   E
S

Where Coghill
and Melville died

Fugitives'
Drift

The Spur
Isandlwana

Camp

Conical
Koppie

N q u t u   P l a t e a u

The
Saddle

Zulu Impi
Fugitives

0   2   4 km

Isandlwana and Rorke's Drift

22–23 January 1879

It has been said that the British Empire was acquired in a fit of absence of mind. Perhaps it would be more accurate to talk of a series of changes of mind and emphasis, based on a swirling blend of commercial interests, missionary zeal and military strategy. The British had first occupied the Cape in 1795, more than 140 years after the first Dutch settlers, then again in 1806. In 1820 the first English settlers were located in the Eastern Cape, and in 1824 a colony was established in Natal. In the era before the discovery of diamonds and gold, and before the 'Scramble for Africa' by the European powers, South Africa was of interest to the British mainly for the way it fitted into the broader strategy of the first global superpower.

'By the 1870s,' writes the Anglo-Zulu War historian John Laband, 'imperial policymakers in Britain were looking to consolidate rather than extend the empire.' India was the jewel in the crown of that empire, and the Cape sea route was seen as vital to the security of India. 'The difficulty in maintaining Britain's traditional paramountcy of the African sub-continent lay not so much with the ambitions of rival colonial powers as with the politically and economically fragmented nature of the region itself,' says Laband. 'The uncoordinated activities of British colonies, Voortrekker republics and the surviving independent black polities made for inefficient and incomplete management.'[1]

In pursuit of more efficient and complete management, British imperial policy had become more coherent from 1875 onwards under the activist Lord Carnarvon, Foreign Secretary in Benjamin Disraeli's Conservative

41

Above: Fugitives' Drift from Rorke's Drift side of the Buffalo River. (*RW*)

Right: King Cetshwayo. He lamented in the aftermath of Isandlwana that the 'British have thrust a spear deep into the belly of my beloved Zulu people'. (*SANL*)

government. Inspired by what had happened in Canada, which had been formed into a federal British dominion in 1867, Carnarvon imagined the southern African colonies and republics uniting in a self-governing, white-controlled entity under Britain. To execute this vision, Carnarvon appointed the Indian colonial administrator Sir Bartle Frere to South Africa as High Commissioner and military commander-in-chief.

Frere arrived in South Africa in March 1877. He perceived the Zulu kingdom, divided from the colony of Natal by the Buffalo River, as the chief obstacle to confederation, not least because it inspired other black peoples to resist encroachment on their lands and cultures by the British and the Boers. As Donald Morris puts it, Frere 'determined to pick a preventative war with the Zulus.'[2] His strategy was in effect to make demands on the Zulus that he knew King Cetshwayo could not accept.

First Frere tried to limit Zulu power by setting up a commission to investigate a boundary dispute to the north-east between the Zulus and the Boers. When his own commission disap-

pointed him by finding in the Zulus' favour, he kept its decision secret, perceiving that he could not afford to provoke the Boers into rebellion. Eventually Frere announced the decision of the commission. But linked to it was a demand that the Zulu army must disband, using as a convenient pretext a series of otherwise insignificant incidents on the border between Natal and Zululand. Says Laband: 'The ultimatum was primarily a means of forcing war on the Zulu, and only secondarily an instrument whereby the kingdom could be emasculated without a struggle.'

Even after Carnarvon had left office, Frere continued to pursue the vision of his former patron. It is worth noting that London was not informed of Frere's ultimatum, and the slow communications of the time meant that Frere was able to evade the instruction in October by the Colonial Secretary, Sir Michael Hicks Beach, that any military action by British forces should be limited to defending Natal. 'I cannot really control Frere without a telegraph,' admitted Hicks Beach. 'I don't know that I could *with* one.'[3]

On 11 December 1878 the terms of the ultimatum were read to representatives of the Zulu king, Cetshwayo, who was given a month to reply. The British expected nothing other than a rejection of the terms – which in effect demanded that the Zulus must give up their independence – and the generals were ready to begin their advance into Zululand as early as 13 December, just two days after the terms were issued. Historians are unanimous that the British were the aggressors, and that Cetshwayo did not want war. But by the time London heard of the invasion, it was too late to prevent it.

At dawn on 11 January 1879, the 4,850 men of the Centre Column started their crossing from Natal into Zululand at Rorke's Drift. They were commanded by Lord Chelmsford, an aristocrat who had been Eton-educated and spent much of his military career in India. He is judged today to have been worthy but unimaginative. There were two other columns,

making a total invasion force of 18,000 men, including 7,000 regular British troops. The force had been divided in order to prevent outflanking by the Zulus and to deter raids on settlers in Natal, thus maintaining security along the long border with Zululand. It was planned for the three columns to converge on the Zulu capital, a large collection of kraals at Ulundi to the north-east.

Chelmsford's column consisted of 2,000 infantry regulars, mainly of the 1st and 2nd battalions of the 24th Regiment of Foot; about 1,000 white colonial volunteers from Natal, many of them militarily competent and mounted; and over 2,000 men of the Natal Native Contingent (NNC). Some of these men were from other tribes; many were Zulus disaffected with Cetshwayo's rule or that of his predecessors. The NNC was poorly armed with just one rifle for every ten men, although most had traditional weapons. They were referred

Troops crossing the Tugela under the inspection of Lord Chelmsford. (*SANL*)

to with contempt by British officers as the 'untrained untrainables'.

The next day, in what now seems like a practice match for the real thing, a force from Chelmsford's column attacked the kraal of the clan of a local Zulu chief, Sehayo, and destroyed it. The operation was led by a young subaltern and enthusiastic beetle collector, Lieutenant Henry Harford, and it seems that this attack was seen as a way of testing the capability of the NNC. The ease of this success enhanced the British sense of confidence and complacency.

What the British did not realise was that the Zulu army itself, the descendant of that great instrument forged by the military genius Shaka half a century before, was an altogether different proposition to taking on isolated clans – or, indeed, any other southern African native force (such as the Xhosa in the Eastern Cape) that the British had previously encountered. Although the Zulus were actually a citizen army, called into action by the king as events required, they had a highly developed warrior culture. They were brave, physically tough and – in a military culture where mercy and the taking of prisoners were not contemplated – feared for their ruthlessness in battle.

The Zulu army had great mobility. Lightly clad and carrying spears and meagre rations, the warriors could cover up to 50 miles a day in extreme circumstances. They could live off the land, or from the supplies carried by the women and young boys who often moved with the warriors. By contrast, the British had to move and supply an army entirely from the coast. Chelmsford needed over 600 wagons to move 1,500 tons of tents, food, ammunition, engineering equipment, medical stores and much else. Sixteen or more oxen were needed to pull each wagon and they might average five miles a day. When Chelmsford moved from the mission station at Rorke's Drift towards what was to become the battlefield of Isandlwana, it took him eight days to move ten miles.

British lack of mobility was partly offset by superior and potentially devastating firepower. They possessed modern rapid-firing rifles, Gatling machine-guns and artillery. However, the variable accuracy of the Martini-Henry rifles and the tendency of Gatling guns to jam meant that concentration and coordination of fire was vital.

It is often wrongly assumed that the Zulus had no firearms. It is estimated that 10,000 firearms were entering Zululand every year in the late 1870s, even though the Natal government had prohibited their sale. There were stores of ammunition in Zululand; the king employed Sotho gunsmiths and ensured that the skills were available to make gunpowder. But many of the

Isandlwana battlefield: heavy wagons made the British slow and vulnerable. (*SANMMH*)

44

weapons imported illicitly were obsolete, such as muskets from the 1830s, and those that were in working order were generally not well looked after. Probably no more than a few hundred Zulu warriors were both familiar with modern firearms and proficient in their use. There seems to have been little knowledge or practice of rifle drill, so reloading and marksmanship were poor.

The main Zulu weapons were still spears, the most important of which was the short-handled stabbing spear or *iklwa* (so named because of the suction noise it made when removed from a victim's abdomen). There were also long-shafted throwing spears (*izijula*) and knobkieries (*iwisa*). Protection was afforded by a shield of stiffened cattle-hide, often marked to signify regimental identity and personal seniority.

Conservative Zulu military sensibilities also limited the effective use of firearms. Rather like those British officers in the early years of the 20th century who thought the use of the machine-gun ungentlemanly, the Zulus of the 1870s seemed reluctant to allow technology, however efficient, to disrupt their customs.

As John Laband puts it, the Zulus 'continued to favour the traditional tactics practised since the time of Shaka. As was well known to all their neighbours, these consisted essentially of surrounding the enemy and finishing him off in hand-to-hand combat. The British may have been under the mistaken impression that the Zulu favoured night attacks and ambushes, but in reality they preferred attack by day, in the open (unless heavily outnumbered), and according to an ordered and predictable formula.'

Chelmsford knew that there was no point in merely occupying territory. In Zululand there were no equivalents of medieval castles that might be besieged. If a royal kraal was burned down, it could be quickly rebuilt elsewhere. To impose British will, Chelmsford needed to bring the main Zulu army to battle, and he could only do that if it attacked him – because he did not have the mobility to chase after it. Ideally, he would want to be attacked on ground of his own choosing, in a prepared defensive position that would maximise the effect of British firepower, especially artillery, while preventing the Zulus from exploiting their great and fearsome skills in hand-to-hand fighting.

After the deceptively easy victory over Sehayo, Chelmsford moved ahead with some officers and mounted infantry. He needed a temporary camp on his way to Ulundi, now some 60 miles to the north-east. What he was looking for was commanding high ground on which to establish lookout pickets; he needed water for 4,850 men, 4,500 oxen and 500 horses and mules. He needed grazing for the animals and, if possible, firewood. He found all these things 12 miles into Zululand from Rorke's Drift, at an isolated place known to the Zulus as Isandlwana, 'the mountain that looks like a little house' (or, according to other linguistic interpretations, 'a man's fist' or 'a cow's stomach'). Some of the British soldiers uneasily perceived in the shape of the mountain the likeness of the Egyptian sphinx – an uncanny coincidence, because that mythical creature was incorporated in the cap badge of the 24th Regiment, ever since it had served in Egypt during the Napoleonic wars.

Omens aside, the practicalities of the site were favourable. There were several springs in

Summit of Isandlwana, containing the cave where the last British soldiers were killed. (*RW*)

45

Chelmsford's chosen camp site: the rocky outcrop's similarity to the Egyptian sphinx unsettled many British soldiers. (*RW*)

the vicinity, with acres of open grassland and clumps of trees in an area that was otherwise unwooded. Militarily, the site was certainly defendable. A deep donga guarded the front of the camp, with the mountain blocking another side and offering high ground for observation; and there was limited cover for attackers.

So the camp was established on 19 and 20 January, and it was necessarily a massive, sprawling affair. The 850 white canvas tents covered an area half a mile long and three hundred yards across, with space for over 250 wagons and carts.

It was a standing order of the British army that in enemy territory a camp must be entrenched on all sides. But the ground at Isandlwana is mainly coal-bearing shale. It would have taken more than a week to dig in around a perimeter of that size, and the supremely confident Chelmsford planned to be there for only two days. So no orders were given to entrench.

Nor were the wagons laagered. This was an understandable omission. Unlike the relatively light and compact covered wagons made famous by the Boers and American settlers, the long transport ox-wagons of the British army had to be moved by up to 120 men on level ground. Fully loaded, they might weigh 6,000 pounds (2,700kg). There would also be the difficulty of disengaging the oxen and then pushing the wagons end-to-end, an enormous effort for the sake of only two days. The British were clearly of the view that it would simply not be worth the trouble.

On that first night at Isandlwana, canvas was drawn up to make a rudimentary officers' mess. The toast in the mess that night expressed the hope that the regiment would not get into the predicament against the Zulus that they had against the Sikhs in India in 1849 (when the 24th Regiment had charged the Sikh guns and the Queen's colour was lost).

Whilst the officers were having their dinner, a Zulu scout working for the British came into the camp. He informed them that the Zulus had been deployed to repulse the British from Zululand. This was true. After Frere's ultimatum expired, Cetshwayo assembled 30,000 warriors at Ulundi and told them that 'I am sending you out against the whites, who have invaded Zululand and driven away our cattle. You are to go against the column at Rorke's Drift, and drive it away into Natal . . . You will attack by daylight, as there are enough of you to "eat it up", and you will march slowly so as not to tire yourself.'[4]

Marching slowly for the Zulus, of course, entailed covering 'only' 40 miles in a day instead of 50 or 60. The army moved out of Ulundi on January 17, and four days later, on January 21, reached the area around Isandlwana. They hid themselves in a ravine, behind the lip of a plateau that can be seen from the plain where the British were encamped. The king had not only instructed his men to husband their strength, but also to resist fighting on 'the day of the dead moon' – for Wednesday 22 January happened to be a day when the sun and moon would be in eclipse, and such days were deeply inauspicious in Zulu culture. He also ordered them to be the defenders in repulsing the invasion, but not aggressors – they were not to cross into Natal. And Cetshwayo, mindful of the terrible lessons of Blood River, warned his men to avoid battle if the British were in prepared positions, but rather to attack them in the open.

Chelmsford and his officers knew none of this. While the British accepted that the main Zulu force must have advanced, there had been no indication that it was anywhere near. But there had been reports of Zulus moving into the hills away to the east. As a result, the British readily assumed that the main Zulu army was ahead on the route to Ulundi, not on their left to the north – as was, in fact, the case.

With that perspective, Chelmsford was concerned that as he proceeded to Ulundi from Isandlwana, the Zulus would move behind the mountain range on the east (on his right), on the other side of a deep valley covered with steep bush, and threaten his right flank. He was also worried that the Zulus would not stand and fight. He wanted to push them into a corner. So he sent out reconnaissance patrols to the east and southeast into the mist to look for the Zulus. But it now seems clear that he was being tempted into a classic mistake of generalship: expecting the enemy to fit in with your own plans, and then unconsciously seeking evidence to confirm that expected compliance.

On the afternoon of 21 January, Chelmsford sent out a much bigger force of 150 colonial volunteers and over a thousand members of the NNC, under command of the competent Major John Dartnell, to search the foothills ahead. They did find small parties of Zulu warriors who would skirmish, but not stand and fight. These encounters seemed to confirm to the British the movement of the enemy across to the south-east that Chelmsford had seen with his field glasses. Later in the day Dartnell's force encountered a mass of several hundred Zulus, who then employed the classic tactic of withdrawing with the intention of luring the enemy onto the 'chest' formed by the warriors, only to encircle him with the fast-moving 'horns' of the buffalo. Thanks only to the fact that his men were on horseback, Dartnell was able to withdraw just in time. He was forced to set up camp for the night at the Hlazakazi heights, across the valley from the Zulus, who lit fires that remained menacingly visible through the night.

Dartnell's experiences of the day had convinced him that he was facing a large force with hostile intentions: the main Zulu army. And he concluded that this force would threaten Chelmsford's route to Ulundi. So he sent an urgent message to Chelmsford calling for reinforcements. Dartnell's pencilled note reached the camp at 01h30, and Chelmsford was roused with the words: 'My lord, my lord, these people want to fight!'

Chelmsford took the communication as confirmation that Dartnell had located the main Zulu army. He immediately ordered one of the two 24th Regiment infantry battalions to prepare to move out, to be accompanied by four of his six seven-pounder guns and all the remaining mounted troops. He also sent orders to Colonel Anthony Durnford, in command 12 miles back at Rorke's Drift, to come up to reinforce the camp at Isandlwana. In Chelmsford's mind, all that had happened was that his camp had proved to be more temporary than he had expected. At dawn he moved out with 1,100 men to support the 1,600 he'd sent out the previous day. That left about 30% of the force, or 1,800 men, in the camp at Isandlwana, where he clearly believed there was no threat from the Zulus.

'Chased by haste,' as historian Rob Caskie puts it, Chelmsford even neglected to leave orders for the officer left behind in command, Colonel Henry Pulleine. This task was undertaken by a staff officer junior to Pulleine, Major Francis Clery. Pulleine was told little beyond that he must act 'strictly on the defensive'. Clearly little was expected of him. He was a regular officer of over 20 years' experience, but had never seen action.

Chelmsford reached Dartnell's position at about 06h00, intent on bringing the main Zulu army to battle. But by the time he got there, the force that had so disturbed Dartnell had entirely disappeared. Some Zulu warriors were seen to the north-east, and they were chased. There were further skirmishes, but no decisive action. Chelmsford became increasingly frustrated and irritable.

Back at Isandlwana, Pulleine was joined in mid-morning by Durnford, the more senior of the two officers. The military importance of this disparity in rank, particularly while on operations in the field, does not seem to have registered with Chelmsford and his staff, in their haste to advance. But the disparity inevitably caused some tension and confusion between the two men. Was Pulleine to command the camp, in view of the fact that Chelmsford had appointed him to the role; or was Durnford supposed to take over, being the senior man?

Colonel Durnford was unusual among British and Colonial officers in his empathy for the Zulus, and loved by the black soldiers he commanded. He had served on Frere's boundary commission and, supported by the Governor of Natal, Henry Bulwer, had found in favour of the Zulus. When conflict became inevitable, Durnford had said: 'As a soldier I should delight in the war, but as a man I condemn it.'[5] However, as a soldier, he had not been pleased at being ordered by Chelmsford to remain at Rorke's Drift – and he was eager for action. The confusion over seniority was resolved when Durnford, not long after arriving and meeting Pulleine, decided to move out across the plain with 200 mounted men to support Chelmsford. After all, that was where the enemy was.

Pulleine remained in command at the camp. Having received intelligence reports of enemy movements on the plateau to the north, he correctly ordered his men to fall in as a precaution. They were not pleased, because their breakfast had been interrupted, but four of his six companies were duly deployed in a line about a mile long in front of the camp. Eventually they were allowed to return to their food, but ordered to keep their webbing on and their rifles at hand.

At midday a patrol led by Captain George

Shepstone was some five miles away from the camp to the north. While chasing a group of Zulus foraging for food and driving a small herd of cattle, this patrol stumbled upon the enemy. Their appalled eyes saw 40,000 human beings in the ravine beyond the plateau, resting silently and (we know now) prepared to sit out the inauspicious 'day of the dead moon'. Most of them had indeed been out to the east of the camp the night before, but under cover of darkness had moved around to the north and were now sitting in silence, waiting to attack in the dawn, when the British would be in the open and on the move to their new camp.

Shepstone's men fired some shots in panic and then withdrew. But now the Zulus had been discovered and their advantage of surprise was lost. The Zulus began to move and, in the words of Donald Morris, 'came boiling out of hiding'.[6] Their commanders had difficulty keeping them under control, but managed to get them into battle order. They were running barefoot and in 40-degree heat, and they covered the six miles to Isandlwana in little more than an hour. Behind them were 10,000 teenage boys carrying sleeping mats, food and weapons for their brothers and fathers; and 8,000 women who at the height of this battle would stand along the escarpment, and scream and ululate.

Back at Isandlwana, Pulleine had been standing by his tent when he was brought a message from Chelmsford by Captain Alan Gardiner of the 14th Hussars, to say that a new site had been identified and that Pulleine must strike camp. Pulleine had barely put this message in his pocket when he and Gardiner saw another lone horseman galloping down towards them from the plateau. It was Captain Shepstone. David Rattray takes up the story:

'Shepstone blurted out the unbelievable news that the main Zulu army was not off to the south and south-east, where Chelmsford was blundering around looking for it, but to the north. And that at this very instant, there were 25,000 Zulu warriors in full regalia and full formation, about to hit that camp at Isandlwana. Pulleine's reaction was one of lack of reaction. He simply sat down at his portmanteau and pencilled another note to Chelmsford: "Heavy firing to the left of our camp. Cannot move camp at present." Almost in an act of insubordination, Captain Gardiner penned a second note to Major Clery (out with Chelmsford) that Shepstone had come in for reinforcements . . . and that the whole remaining British force was turned out about a mile in front of the camp – in other words, the line was too far out. These messages were given to a despatch rider . . . they were to reach Chelmsford only after the Battle of Isandlwana was over. The dust from that despatch rider's hooves had yet to settle, when Pulleine and Gardiner looked up again at the plateau. They saw a thin, black snake coming over the skyline at the notch in the plateau. They picked up their glasses, and they saw that the snake was made up of Zulus.'[7]

And the snake thickened and then divided. The Zulu 'right horn' headed round the mountain in order to strike at the camp from behind. This intention was not evident to the British soldiers deployed along the ridge, who were puzzled by these Zulus running away across their front. One of them reported to Pulleine: 'Good God, Sir. There are thousands of Zulus now, behind the mountain on our wagon-track back to Rorke's Drift.' Meanwhile the 'left horn' of 5,000 men moved across to outflank the right of the British line. It was this part of the force that would catch Durnford on the open plain, where he was still advancing to link up with Chelmsford.

With the two horns deployed across a front of more than three miles, the senior Zulu regiments stepped out onto the high ground facing the camp. Their commander, mTshingwayo kaMahola Khoza, was 70 years old and he'd been at the head of his army throughout the 60-mile advance from Ulundi, running with his warriors. Down in front of him was the thin, red British firing line, again deployed after finishing their breakfast. They had been moved so far forward from the camp – the tactic that Gardiner had deplored in his note to Chelmsford – in order to be able to fire into a depressed area of dead ground, which otherwise would have afforded the Zulus much cover. But the line was indeed too far out from the camp, and too thinly spread.

Over 15,000 Zulu warriors swept down in perfect order towards the extended British defence line. This 'chest' of the Zulu army attacked the left-centre of the camp. Despite their massed numbers, they were almost stopped by the concentrated British fire. 'Yet the Zulu did not seem dismayed,' says John Laband, 'but filled up their gaps in perfect silence, and pressed on with the utmost bravery. Not that they were absurd in their courage. As they rushed forward, they threw themselves upon the ground whenever the fire became too hot . . . It was easier for them to avoid the shells from the seven-pounders than the rifle volleys. When they saw the gunners stand clear, they either fell down or parted ranks, allowing the shot to pass as harmlessly as wind, and leaving the British unsure as to whether their fire had taken effect. They took this evasive action with no hurry or confusion, as if they had been drilled to it.'[8]

'The volleys had stopped the Zulus a hun-

dred yards away,' wrote Donald Morris, 'and the entire mass had thrown themselves down, humming in anger like a gigantic swarm of bees.'

Out on the British right flank, Durnford had managed to execute a fighting retreat back towards the camp, as far as the large donga to the east of the camp. Here he was reinforced by other colonial mounted soldiers sent by Pulleine, but this had the effect of further dissipating the British defensive capability. Durnford's force of 200 then held off the Zulu left horn with disciplined rifle fire, supported by two seven-pounder guns in the centre of the extended British line. But Zulu reinforcements prevented the attack by the left horn from stalling, and increased the pressure on Durnford.

It was now early afternoon and Durnford's men were running short of ammunition. He sent messengers across to the main camp for more cartridges, kept in two wagons a quarter of a mile apart and watched over by the quartermasters of the two infantry battalions. The legend is that the wooden cartridge boxes were bound with copper straps screwed onto the wood, and that they could not be opened for the want of a screwdriver. But this seems unlikely, because research has proven that it was relatively easy to smash the boxes open on nearby rocks. The main problem was one of military bureaucracy: while men were dying in the heat of battle, the quartermasters refused to issue rounds to men who were not of their own battalion. Eventually boxes were seized and some were broken open, but precious time had been lost.

The lull in firing gave the Zulus the initiative and Durnford was forced to retire towards the main camp. But this movement exposed the right flank of the main British defence line. To prevent it being surrounded and cut off, Pulleine had to order the men in the forward position to stop firing and to fall back on the camp to set up a new defence line. When the Zulu commanders on the high ground saw this withdrawal begin, they ordered one of the senior indunas, Ndlaka, to run down the hill to encourage the Zulus of the 'chest' who had until now been pinned down and demoralised by the intense British rifle and artillery fire.

'You did not say you were going to lie down,' Ndlaka roared at his warriors, 'the little branch of leaves that beats out the fire (Cetshwayo) did not order this!' The Zulu were roused (though Ndlaka fell dead almost immediately with a bullet in the head) and began to advance at a steady walking pace. About 100 metres from the British line, they began to run, inspiring one another with the chilling war-cry '*Usuthu!*' and then letting loose a volley of throwing spears. At this point, understandably, the mostly unarmed members of the Natal Native Contingent fled, leaving a gaping hole in the British defences.

Within a minute the men of the Zulu 'chest' were among the retreating British, who were forced to fight in disarray, trying to retreat into their camp and then severely hampered by the obstacles presented by their own tents, wagons and livestock. Of course the camp should have been struck before the fighting, but there had been no time. In the camp itself now, brutal hand-to-hand fighting took place amid thick smoke and dust, with many of the British soldiers unable to fire a shot before being overwhelmed by hordes of Zulus. And at 14h29 the battlefield was suddenly turned dark by the partial eclipse of the sun.

Lieutenant Horace Smith-Dorrien wrote afterwards in a letter to his father: 'Before we knew where we were they came right into the camp, assegaying everybody right and left.

Everyone who then had a horse turned to fly. The enemy were going at a kind of fast half-walk and half-run. On looking round we saw that we were completely surrounded and the road to Rorke's Drift was cut off.'[9]

While Durnford's men fought to the last man at the southern corner of the camp, the Zulu right horn had come round the base of the Isandlwana mountain to completely encircle the camp. One British company made their last stand on the slope of the Isandlwana hill itself, until eventually the last man holed up in a cave near the summit and continued resistance for an hour until the Zulus finished him off. As was customary, no prisoners were taken by the Zulus and no mercy was granted to the wounded or those who wished to surrender. By 15h00 the battle was over.

Lieutenant Henry Curling, a survivor, wrote to his mother of the British soldiers at Isandlwana: 'They behaved splendidly in this fight. They were all killed in the ranks as they stood. Not a single man escaped from the companies that were placed to defend the camp. Indeed, they were completely cut off from any retreat and could not, as we did, gallop through the Zulus. When I last saw them, they were retreating steadily but I believe a rush was made and they were all killed in a few minutes.'

Only about 60 whites survived the carnage, all of them because they had managed to escape before the camp was completely encircled. On the British side, 52 officers, 727 white troops and 471 black troops were killed. Corpses were routinely disembowelled, a practice which appalled the British but was part of the traditional Zulu ritual of spiritual purification after battle, as well as being a tribute to a brave adversary.

Most of the men who fled back towards Rorke's Drift were hunted down by the Zulus, who managed to catch even mounted soldiers, because the ground down to the river was so bad. Some fugitives reached the Buffalo River, swam across and escaped into Natal; others, like Lieutenants Melvill and Coghill, were killed halfway up the hill on the far bank after famously trying to save the Queen's colour of the 24th. (They failed, thus making the regiment the only one ever to have lost its colours twice in battle, but the standard was washed away and later recovered.) Some who survived owed their lives only to the Zulus' aversion to swimming.

But Chelmsford had first received news of the attack on Isandlwana in the early afternoon. War correspondent Charles Norris-Newman, who had gone out with Major Dartnell, reported that when Chelmsford got this message he 'at once galloped up to the crest of the hill, accompanied by his staff, and on arrival every field-glass was levelled at the camp. The sun was shining brightly on the white tents, which were plainly visible, but all seemed quiet. No signs of firing or of an engagement could be seen, and although bodies of men moving about could be distinguished, yet they were not

Far left: Memorial to Coghill and Melville. (*RW*)

Left: Where Coghill and Melville were killed. (*RW*)

The Zulus were to say they had never met a braver adversary than the red-coated British soldier at Isandlwana – 'He fought like a lion and he fell like a stone.' The British dead were left where they had fallen, to be buried only four months later (after the series of vengeful battles that led to the final defeat of the Zulu nation at Ulundi). The victors looted the camp, dragged away their dead, and did not return.

'I can't understand it. I left a thousand men here.' That was the appalled reaction of Lord Chelmsford when he eventually returned to the scene late in the afternoon of the battle, having been alerted by a fleeing survivor.

unnaturally supposed to be our own troops. The time was now 1.45pm and not the faintest idea of disaster had occurred to us. It was believed that an attack on the camp had been made and repulsed . . .' But by then the battle was, in fact, nearly over.

Chelmsford was now in an unenviable position. Standing in the dark among the ruin and slaughter of what he had expected to be a temporary camp, he did not know where the victorious enemy was and he could not risk being attacked if he moved. And his men were hungry and tired. Although there was an ominous glow of fire in the sky in the direction of

Rorke's Drift, and the faint sound of rifle fire, he decided he would have to spend the night where he was, on the battlefield – and a ghastly night it was, as a report in the *Natal Mercury* was to recall:

'Oh! How dreadful to all were those fearful hours, knowing that we were standing and lying among the bodies of our own comrades, though how many we little knew then. Many and deep were the sobs ... at discovering, even in the dim morning light, the bodies of dear friends brutally massacred, stripped of all clothing, disembowelled, and in some cases with their heads cut off. How that night passed, I fancy few of us knew ...'[10]

But when 'the day of the dead moon' ended at Isandlwana, the fighting between British and Zulus was not over. The reserve of the Zulu force at Isandlwana, between 3,000 and 4,000 strong, had not taken part in the battle and had proceeded to the high ground north of the camp. Some of these warriors, anxious also to 'wash their spears' in the blood of an enemy, were among the Zulu who ran down the fleeing British who had managed to escape the encirclement at Isandlwana.

This reserve force was commanded by Prince Dabulamanzi kaMpande, King Cetshwayo's half brother. 'Tired and hungry as they were after their long march,' says John Laband, 'it seems certain that they had no plans for a serious incursion into Natal. Their intention was simply to scour the countryside as far as the Helpmekaar heights, burn the farms, lift what cattle they could, and then return to Zululand with honour salvaged. In other words, what they had in mind was a limited but destructive raid across the middle Thukela River ...' When they came across the mission outpost at Rorke's Drift, continues Laband, 'it seemed a tempting and prestigious prize, to be snatched up lightly on the way.'

Lieutenant John Chard of the Royal Engineers surrounded by a group of his men.
He had to take over after Durnford's departure and distinguished himself for his bravery. (*SANMMH*)

The men left behind at Rorke's Drift by Chelmsford consisted of a company of the 2nd/24th Regiment under the partially deaf Lieutenant Gonville Bromhead; a company of the Natal Native Contingent (the 'untrained untrainables'); and various other support staff. In the 12 rooms of the mission hospital were 35 men, some of them delirious with fever and too ill to be moved. The most senior officer, following the departure of Colonel Durnford, was Lieutenant John Chard of the Royal Engineers, and it was he who took command.

At about 15h30 on the afternoon of 22 January, the skeleton garrison at Rorke's Drift was stunned to hear of the massive defeat at Isandlwana, and were told that a large Zulu force was already on its way. Chard realised there was no time to load the sick into ox-wagons, which would in any case be overtaken by the fleet Zulu warriors; he decided that he would have to stand and fight until relieved.

The contrast in scale is stark. Isandlwana was fought on a large plain under a huge sky, enveloped by mountains and marked by dongas and rivers; the Battle of Rorke's Drift took place on an area no larger than three tennis courts. There were two buildings, the hospital and a storehouse, that formed the core of the defensive position. The perimeter was completed by moving two wagons into position and piling up bags of mealies and boxes of army biscuits, which created a low wall around the position. Volunteers were posted in each room of the hospital to protect the sick (each room opened outwards, with no interlinking doors between most of the rooms). Loopholes were knocked in the walls to facilitate efficient rifle fire by the defenders. Reserve ammunition was put in position and bayonets were fixed.

By 17h00 the Zulus had managed to ford the deep, fast-flowing river by linking arms and forcing one another across, and it was reported that they were approaching the mission station. At that point the men of the NNC deserted en masse, accompanied by their commanding officer, Captain Stevenson, and his white non-commissioned officers. One of these deserting NCOs, Corporal Anderson, was shot in the back by one of the British soldiers of the 24th.

The battle of Rorke's Drift as depicted by the French oil painter A. de Neuville. (*SANMMH*)

This desertion meant that the garrison strength was suddenly reduced from 450 men to 139 (including the 35 sick). Within half an hour the Zulus had appeared on the side of the nearby Oskarberg mountain, and they then launched their first attack on the southern defences. This was contained, but successive waves of Zulu attacks meant that the defenders would soon be forced to move out of the hospital into the yard. Chard saw that he had to abandon the first perimeter and withdraw to the second line of defence.

This left the hospital isolated. Inside, Privates Henry Hook and John Williams retreated room by room, breaking holes in the walls with a pickaxe and dragging the sick and wounded behind them. But before they could get out the Zulus set fire to the roof – a frightening development, but also a tactical error, because for some hours the flames would illuminate the attackers for the rifle sights of the defenders. Eleven patients were passed and pulled through a small window, with the aim of somehow getting them across ground now left undefended following Chard's order to withdraw to a new barricade. Amazingly, nine of the patients made it. One was speared after he had refused, in his delirium, to leave his bed; the other was stabbed as he tried to move across the unprotected gap. Other British soldiers escaped by suddenly charging out of the hospital, past the surprised Zulus and into the protection of the night, where they hid in bushes undetected. Hook was the last to leave the hospital, at about 21h00.

Donald Morris describes how the battle surged on: 'Over-used gun barrels glowed in the dark, their heat firing off rounds before the defenders had time to pull the trigger. The men lost all count of the charges and all sense of time. They existed in a slow eternity of noise and smoke and flashes, of straining black faces that rose out of the darkness, danced briefly in the light of the muzzle blasts, and then sank back out of sight. It was after midnight when the rushes began to subside, and after two o'clock in the morning when the last charge was over.'

During that endless night the British were forced to withdraw twice to set up new and more compact defences. Eventually they established themselves behind a wall which joined onto the storehouse building. There could be no further retreat, because there was nowhere else to go. But after 04h00 there were no more attacks – although the defenders remained on the alert, taut with adrenalin and exhaustion. If the Zulus had known that the British were down to less than two boxes of ammunition, they would surely have attacked again.

By dawn the Zulus had gone. They left behind 600 of their comrades, dead and dying, and even the unscathed attackers were worn out, having eaten very lightly since their march started from Ulundi six days before.

By 08h00 the garrison was relieved by Chelmsford and what was left of his Central Column – the column that had crossed at the drift so confidently just a few days before. He found 15 of the defenders dead and two dying, eight wounded and another 70 men still on their feet. Defences were immediately strengthened because it was feared that the Zulus would attack again – but they did not.

The British found in the heroic defence of Rorke's Drift some compensation for the humiliation of Isandlwana. Eleven Victoria Crosses were awarded to recognize the valour of the defenders that day, the most ever given for a single action. Among them was Lieutenant John Chard.

But both battles represented a postponement of the final reckoning. Cetshwayo was to lament that at Isandlwana 'the British have thrust a spear deep into the belly of my beloved Zulu people,' because he knew that none of his senior regiments would fight again at full strength, such had been their losses – some 3,000 killed. And he was angry and distressed that so few British soldiers had been able to hold off thousands of his warriors at Rorke's Drift – angry, because his orders not to enter Natal had been disobeyed and because the mission had no strategic value; and distressed, because he knew that British tactics and firepower would prevail in the long run.

Historian Rob Caskie has asserted that it is time the Battle of Isandlwana is recognised for what it was: not a British blunder, but a great Zulu victory. Militarily, that may have been so, but not strategically. As John Laband points out, 'the very degree of Zulu success at Isandlwana (only partially negated by the subsequent fighting at Rorke's Drift) had ensured that the British must proceed until the Zulu army was crushed, and the Zulu king had acceded entirely to their demands.'

That is precisely what happened. In July 1879 at Ulundi, Chelmsford finally smashed the Zulus by using the traditional British device of overwhelming firepower delivered from a huge hollowed square. It marked the end of the Zulu nation as an independent entity and the start of 110 years of largely unchallenged white domination in southern Africa.

CEMETERIES, MEMORIALS AND VISITOR CENTRES

The entire battlefield of **Isandlwana** is itself a brooding memorial, evocative of an ancient clash of arms. This mood prevails whether the day is cold and misty, or oppressively hot. (As it is possible to experience extremes of weather on the same morning, whatever the season, it is best to dress accordingly; a hat is essential.) Many cairns of whitewashed stones are dotted about the battlefields, marking the places where several men were buried together. There are regimental memorials, as well as one marking the site of Durnford's fight to the death, and a more recent circular Zulu memorial in metal, modelled on the necklace fashioned of lion's teeth that was awarded to Zulu warriors for bravery.

Rorke's Drift is much more compact and accessible. Allow a full day to explore both sites. As with Blood River, these battlefields are far from the main roads and towns, and so look much as they did in the nineteenth century. Both are accessible by good dirt roads.

Although it is possible to visit the battlefields privately, it is strongly recommended that you employ the services of a professional guide, preferably one who is a specialist. Some of these battlefields guides are raconteurs of note, able to make history come alive with anecdote and emotion, while standing on the spot where men fought and died. Guides can usually be organised through the hotels and bed & breakfast establishments in and around Dundee, or those near the battlefield itself.

Top: The Zulu memorial at Isandlwana. (*RW*)

Left: Cairns at Isandlwana. (*RW*)

Below: Isandlwana – looking across the battlefield to Durnford's last stand. (*RW*)

HOW TO GET THERE AND WHERE TO STAY

From Johannesburg (five hours): Take the N3 highway to Durban and exit at Villiers. Follow the R103 and then the R34 to Vrede, Memel and Newcastle. (If you want to take in the Majuba battlefield on the way, from Vrede take the R546 to Standerton, then the R23 to Volksrust and the N11 to Newcastle.)

From Newcastle take the N11 to Ladysmith, then the R621 left to Dundee. From Dundee take the R33 towards Greytown for 14km. Turn left onto the gravel road to Rorke's Drift. For the site of the Rorke's Drift defence, continue straight. For Isandlwana, turn left at the Isandlwana sign, cross the Buffalo River over the single lane bridge. Turn right at the T-junction. (If you also want to visit Blood River, go north towards Vryheid on the R33 for about 25km, then turn right to Blood River on a good dirt road.)

From Durban (four hours): Take the N3 highway to Johannesburg and then the N11 to Ladysmith. About 27km after Ladysmith take the R602 right to Glencoe and Dundee. From Dundee take the R33 towards Greytown for 14km. Turn left onto the gravel road to Rorke's Drift. Continue as described in the previous paragraph.

WHERE TO STAY:

David and Nicky Rattray's **Fugitives' Drift Lodge** (034) 642-1843, email: fugdrift@trustnet. co.za is the ideal venue at a very reasonable R600 p.p. It is ten minutes' walk away from a magnificent vantage point over the place in the Buffalo River where so many British soldiers tried to escape, and from the graves of Melvill and Coghill. It is wise to arrange to stay at least two nights, so that an entire day can be spent on the guided tours of both battlefields, expertly conducted by Rattray and his colleagues. The Isandlwana tour takes about five hours, Rorke's Drift about three, divided by lunch back at the lodge. These tours are intense experiences, cerebrally and emotionally. The main lecture at Isandlwana is presented near the summit of the hill that dominates the battlefield, a few metres from the cave where the last survivors holed up on the afternoon of the battle. At Rorke's Drift the visitor is taken through the battle, literally moving from room to room in the building used as the hospital, now a museum.

The other main venue nearby is the exclusive **Isandlwana Lodge** (034) 271-8301/2/3/4, email: lodge@isandlwana.co.za, which overlooks the battlefield of Isandlwana (about 1km away). This purpose-built luxury lodge sleeps 24 people and prices include dinner, bed and breakfast (approx. R1,300 p.p.). The lodge also offers specialist tours to Isandlwana and Rorke's Drift, lead by battlefield experts.

Dundee is geared for battlefield visitors, with many hotels, lodges and bed & breakfast establishments (and the excellent Talana Museum). Nearby **Glencoe** also has accommodation. **Dundee Tourist Information:** (034) 212-2121

REFERENCES AND FURTHER READING

Ken Gillings, *Battles of KwaZulu-Natal*. Johannesburg: Art Publishers, 2004.

Ian Knight, *The Anatomy of the Zulu Army from Shaka to Cetshwayo 1818–1879*. London: Greenhill Books, 1999.

Ian Knight, *The Sun Turned Black: Isandlwana and Rorke's Drift – 1879*. Johannesburg: William Waterman, 1995.

John Laband, *Kingdom in Crisis: The Zulu Response to the British Invasion of 1879*. Pietermaritzburg: University of Natal Press, 1992.

John Laband, *Rope of Sand: The Rise and Fall of the Zulu Kingdom in the Nineteenth Century*. Johannesburg: Jonathan Ball, 1995.

John Laband and Ian Knight, *The War Correspondents: The Anglo-Zulu War*. Johannesburg: Jonathan Ball, 1996.

Ron Lock, *Isandlwana: Zulu Battlefield* (DVD).

Donald Morris, 'War on the Veld', pages 813–831, *The British Empire*. London: BBC/Time-Life, 1971.

James Morris, *Heaven's Command: An Imperial Progress*. London: Faber & Faber, 1973.

Thomas Pakenham, *The Scramble for Africa*. Johannesburg: Jonathan Ball, 1991.

David Rattray, *The Day of the Dead Moon: The Story of the Anglo-Zulu War 1879* (CD). Rorke's Drift, 1997.

David Rattray and Adrian Greaves (eds), *Guidebook to the Anglo-Zulu War Battlefields*. Johannesburg: Jonathan Ball, 2003.

NOTES

1. John Laband, *Kingdom in Crisis: The Zulu Response to the British Invasion of 1879*. Pietermaritzburg: University of Natal Press, 1992, p.6.

2. Donald Morris, 'War in the Veld', in *The British Empire*. London: BBC/Time-Life, 1971, p.815.

3. John Laband, *Kingdom in Crisis: The Zulu Response to the British Invasion of 1879*. Pietermaritzburg: University of Natal Press, 1992, p.12.

4. David Rattray, *The Day of the Dead Moon: The Story of the Anglo-Zulu War 1879* (CD). Rorke's Drift, 1997.

5. Ian Knight, *The Anatomy of the Zulu Army from Shaka to Cetshwayo 1818-1879*. London: Greenhill Books, 1999, p.83.

6. Morris, *op cit*, p.818.

7. Rattray, CD3.

8. Laband, *op cit*, p.82.

9. Knight, *op cit*, p.208.

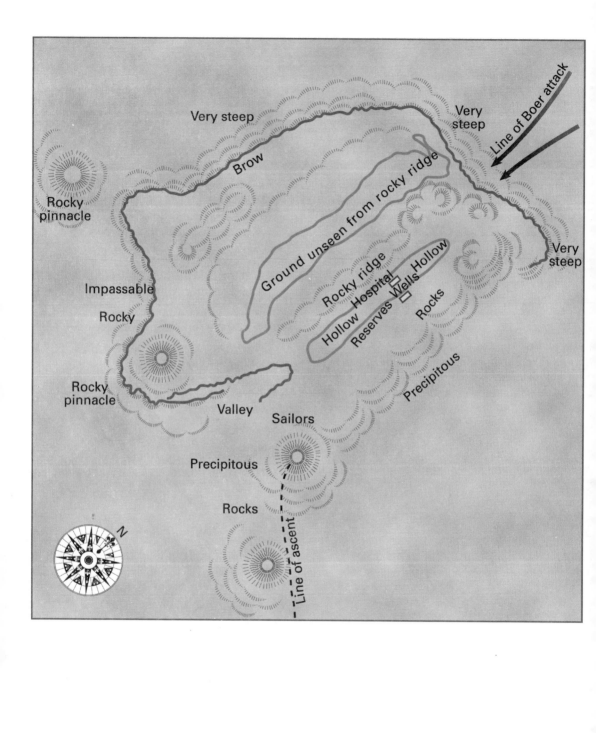

The Battle of Majuba
27 February 1881

It is hard to believe that the Victorian British army – vanguard of the most powerful empire the world had seen – experienced its two worst disasters within two years of each other, and both in South Africa. Military sins that were evident against the Zulus at Isandlwana in 1879 – complacency, flouting of standing orders, poor intelligence, underestimation of the enemy, confusion in the command structure, poor appreciation of ground – were to be repeated against the Boers at Majuba soon after in 1881. Indeed, 'it was the only occasion in the history of Queen Victoria's Empire,' noted the historian James Morris, 'when the British negotiated a peace settlement from the losers' side of the table.'

Morris describes Majuba mountain as being 'as distinctive as Isandlwana itself. It rose massively flat-topped above the pass, and could be seen from far across the Natal border like a sentry guarding the inner fastness of Afrikanerdom. Majuba was 6,000 feet high, but looked higher, and had a majestic if brooding presence.'[1]

The Boer victory at Majuba was not only a crushing blow to British prestige – and therefore an important influence in the Boers' willingness to take on the Empire again in 1899–1902 – but also a reminder that this was a battle that should never have taken place.

The background to the battle lay in the British pursuit of a more aggressive foreign policy for southern Africa in the 1870s. When Lord Carnarvon, the British Foreign Secretary, failed to get support for his confederal vision of southern Africa he resorted to arbitrary action. Using concerns about the weakness of the Boer government of President Burgers as a pretext,

61

The distinctive Majuba mountain which, at 6,000 feet high, could be seen for miles. Here British soldiers view the battle from the hill above Mount Prospect Camp. (*NARSSA*)

he authorised the annexation of the Transvaal in 1877 by Sir Theophilus Shepstone. This violated the Sand River Convention of 1852, in which Britain had promised the Transvaal burghers 'the right to manage their own affairs without any interference.'

The annexation was not resisted but it was deeply resented, and poor British administration alienated the burghers further. Ironically, the ruthless defeat by British forces of the Zulu and Pedi nations had eased Boer concerns about their own security, and they felt more confident about challenging the British. If the Free State could be independent, why should the Transvaal remain a British colony? Protest meetings were held by the Transvalers at Wonderfontein and Kleinfontein in 1879.

In 1880, in defiance of the British High Commissioner at the Cape, Sir Garnet Wolseley, 3,000 Boers assembled at a protest meeting under the old republican flag. When he heard of the meetings, Wolseley did not take them seriously. 'I feel I could walk all over them,' he told his wife. He reported confidently to the Colonial Office in London that the Boers would 'renounce all further disturbing action and return to the peaceful cares of their rural life.' But that year also saw a change of government in London, with the Tory Benjamin Disraeli replaced as Prime Minister by William Gladstone, the Liberal leader. Gladstone had described the 1877 annexation of the Transvaal as 'dishonourable' and he recalled Wolseley to London, replacing him with Major-General Sir George Colley.

Active Transvaal resistance to British rule came in late 1880, when a tax dispute involving a Potchefstroom farmer sparked an armed uprising by the Boers. One Piet Bezuidenhout refused to a pay a 27-pound tax, and his wagon was seized for sale by public auction. Over 100 Boers, led by the future general Piet Cron-

Piet Cronjé (*NARSSA*)

George Colley (*NARSSA*)

jé, intervened and returned the wagon to Bezuidenhout; the small local British military detachment was ignored when it attempted to restore British authority. There followed a protest gathering of over 10,000 Boers at Paardekraal, near the present-day Krugersdorp. Here it was decided to re-establish a Boer republic, with Heidelberg as the interim capital. It is said that every person present at Paardekraal placed a stone on a pile, as a mark of their determination to regain independence. The pile still exists at the Paardekraal Monument, one of the shrines of Afrikaner nationalism.

Colley, who landed in Natal rather than at the Cape in order to deal with the Boers' restiveness, claimed to be puzzled: 'I cannot conceive what can have so suddenly caused the Boers to act as they have.' But he nevertheless had to act against them. A few days after the formation of the rebel government, its forces attacked or laid siege to British garrisons all over the Transvaal – at Pretoria, Potchefstroom, Rustenburg, Lydenburg, Wakkerstroom, Standerton and Marabastad.

The first battle of what Afrikaners call the First War of Independence was at Bronkhorstspruit on 20 December 1880, four days after the end of the Paardekraal gathering. Boer forces attacked a column of mounted men and infantry under Colonel Philip Anstruther, on its way from Lydenburg to Pretoria. After Anstruther ignored an ultimatum from General Piet Joubert ('I have orders to march to Pretoria, and to Pretoria I will go!') and his band struck up 'God save the Queen,' a brief battle left 57 British soldiers dead and 100 wounded, for Boer casualties of just two killed and five wounded. Anstruther died of his wounds. All the British officers were casualties and across all ranks the average number of wounds per man was five. The dead soldiers were buried on a local farm; the men had bought peaches at a recent halt, and the legend is that a small orchard grew from the peach-stones that had been in their pockets and knapsacks.

In the same week Colley dispatched a force of 235 men, including the elite Connaught Rangers regiment, from Pietermaritzburg to Pretoria. Before it came near to the Natal border, this column was attacked by concealed Boers who killed or wounded more than half the Connaughts; the rest surrendered. On 1 January 1881, the upset Colley wrote to his sister in England:

> This is a sad and anxious New Year for us all here, as you may imagine. The last of the troops I have available, including some drafts only three days arrived from England, are marching this morning, and I start in a few days to take command and try to bring the Boers to battle, and relieve our garrisons at Potchefstroom and Pretoria. The disaster to the 94th Regiment (at Bronkhorstspruit) has not only been a painful loss to us of many good officers and men, but has changed the whole aspect of affairs – a sort of Isandlwana on a smaller scale.

In early January Colley advanced towards the Transvaal with 1,000 men and six guns. Enemy scouts watched his progress constantly. The Boers understood the strategic value of the mountain passes between the present-day Newcastle and Volksrust. Over 1,500 of them dug in on a 3km line near one of these passes, on the hill known as Laing's Nek, east of the mountain of Majuba. When Colley's force arrived he ordered the Boers to disperse. They replied firmly that such an action would be conditional:

> We declare that we would be satisfied with a rescinding of the annexation, and the restoration of the South African Republic [the formal name of the old Transvaal] under a protectorate of Her Majesty the Queen, so that once a year the British flag shall be hoisted . . . If your Excellency resolves to reject this, we have only to submit to our fate; but the Lord will provide.

So Colley decided to attack the Boer position. On 28 January 1881, after a 20-minute artillery bombardment that had little effect, the hill was attacked by the 58th Regiment under Colonel Bonar Deane, supported by cavalry on the Boer left flank. In a scene that must have been reminiscent of European warfare from the eighteenth century, the infantry detachment in their red and blue jackets advanced in perfect line. Orders were given to fix bayonets, and then to charge – but the Boer rifle fire cut down nearly all the officers, including Colonel Deane, and the surviving troops had to be recalled. Colley had lost 73 men killed and 111 wounded, the Boers 14 killed and 27 wounded. For the Boers, relatively speaking, the Lord had indeed provided. It was at Laing's Nek that British regimental colours (of the 58th Regiment) were carried into battle for the last time.

The English author H Rider Haggard, who farmed in the district, had this to say of Laing's Nek:

> What Sir George Colley's real object was in exposing himself to the attack has never transpired. It can hardly have been to clear the road, as he says in his despatch, because the road was not held by the enemy, but only visited occasionally by their patrols. The result of the battle was to make the Boers, whose losses were trifling, more confident than ever, and to greatly depress our soldiers. Sir George had now lost between three and four hundred men out of his en-

tire column of little over a thousand, which was thereby entirely crippled.[2]

To make matters worse, a supply column from Pietermaritzburg was then overrun and looted by the Boers.

On 8 February Colley again tried to hunt down his elusive enemy, this time at nearby Ingogo (also known as the Battle of Skuinshoogte) with a force of 300 men, including 38 cavalrymen and four guns. The correspondent for *The Times* of London, Thomas Carter, wrote that 'everyone was in good spirits at the prospect of an outing.' But again the English were no match for the mobile Boers, under command of General Nicolaas Smit. Their accurate fire from the saddle killed all the gunners, and in all the British lost six officers, with 70 men killed and 63 wounded. Just eight Boers were killed and six wounded – and their forces at Laing's Nek still blocked Colley's path.

Colley's gallant instincts (he wrote to Smit after Laing's Nek, offering medical help 'should you not have skilled assistance at hand') are impressive in a loser, but the British commander was now desperate. He had thrice been humiliated, twice in ten days, with casualties amounting to close on half his force.

On 23 February he was reinforced with another 2,000 men, comprising the 92nd Regiment (Gordon Highlanders), a Naval Brigade with two Gatling machine-guns, two nine-pounder guns and a cavalry troop from the 15th Hussars. General Sir Evelyn Wood VC had accompanied the fresh units from Durban and he persuaded Colley to agree to wait for more reinforcements from Britain before taking any further action. Wood moved back to the Tugela River, unaware that Colley did not intend to honour his undertaking.

Colley badly needed to gain the initiative, and he saw a solution in gaining the high ground – indeed, the highest ground in the area – the summit of the *aMajuba* mountain (Zulu for 'hill of doves'). The consensus is that he was also anxious to restore British honour (as well as his own reputation) after the disasters of Laing's Nek and Ingogo – and to get on top of the Boers before political interference from London might halt operations.

'One hill, Majuba, dominated all the Laing's Nek area,' writes the British historian Brian Roberts. 'From it the Boer lines were clearly visible and their flank endangered; if it were taken, the enemy might well be obliged to withdraw without firing another shot. Colley assembled his force, about 600 strong, at night. Security was so intense that many of the officers did not know of his intentions.'[3]

On the night of Saturday 26 February, Colley wrote to his wife: 'I am going out tonight to try and seize the Majuba Hill, which commands the right of the Boer position, and leave this behind in case I should not return.' He led his force out from the main British camp at Mount Prospect at about 21h30. No lights were carried and strict orders were given to move silently, so as not to alert the Boers. They passed farmer R C O'Neill's house (still there today), where the barking of O'Neill's dog made some officers anxious that the Boers would be roused. They headed up the slopes of the Nkwelo Mountain (where men of the 60th Rifles were left in position) and along a linking ridge (where two companies of the 92nd Regiment were placed), then onto the south side of Majuba and up the very steep, rocky approach to the summit. Zulu scouts helped show the way – and got lost at one stage. For many soldiers the last part of the climb had to be pursued on hands and knees.

It would not have been an easy ascent even

Colley's midnight ascent of Majuba (*NARSSA*)

in daylight. Each soldier had to carry a rifle, bayonet and 70 rounds of ammunition, as well as a greatcoat, blanket, waterproof sheet, water bottle and rations for three days. In addition each company had to take picks, shovels, axes, hammers and pliers. Medical assistants transported equipment for a field hospital. Lieutenant Ian Hamilton of the Gordon Highlanders wrote in old age: 'I remember, as if it were yesterday, the tense excitement of that climb up with a half-dozen of shadowy forms close by, which were swallowed up and disappeared if they got further away from me than half a dozen paces.'

The first troops got to the summit between 03h00 and 04h00, the last of them just before dawn. In the dark, and heavy-laden as they were, many of the men had lost contact with their comrades. As the stragglers came in, they tended to be sent to places that seemed short of men, rather than to their own units. This meant that significant parts of Colley's force were now not deployed under their own officers, and that would make command and coordination more difficult.

The total force that actually reached the top of Majuba numbered some 370 men – half an infantry battalion. The ground on the summit of this extinct volcano resembles a rough triangle, about 400 yards long and 300 yards at its widest, with a slight indentation towards the centre that creates the effect of a saucer. At the lowest part it is often filled with water, and on that Sunday morning the men were ordered to dig a well. Water was struck at a depth of about five feet.

Colley was satisfied. He had gained the commanding high ground he needed without being detected by the Boers. 'We could stay here forever,' he said – but his confidence made him careless. The men were not ordered to dig trenches or to build breastworks, even though 80 picks and 80 spades had been carried up the mountainside. No serious reconnaissance was carried out, which meant the defenders had no sense of how the ground might be used by attackers. For instance, men were posted unnecessarily to defend a side that was protected by a sheer cliff. And, most mystifying of all, the guns were not brought up – an omission which largely nullified the advantage of possessing the high ground in the first place.

At dawn the Boers at Laing's Nek were still unaware of the occupation of Majuba. Carter wrote: 'Looking down from our position right into the enemy's lines, we seemed to hold them in the palm of our hands.' On the western side of the mountain was the Boer republic of the Orange Free State, and near the border was the homestead of the farm owned by the De Jager family. The story goes that Mrs De Jager happened to see from her kitchen door the flare that Colley lit to signal his success to his forces back at Mount Prospect. She immediately rode on horseback to alert the Boers. And in the Boer laager it was Hendrina Joubert, General Piet Joubert's wife (she always went with him on commando), who first noticed the British and ran to wake her husband: 'Piet, come here. There are people on the kop.'

Joubert called his officers together and stated simply: *'Daar's nou 'n klomp Engelse op die berg. Julle moet hulle ondertoe bring.'* ('There are Englishmen now on the mountain. You must bring them down.') General Nicolaas Smit called for volunteers and about 180 were chosen for the initial assault. As early as 06h30, they moved up slowly in small groups, expertly using the ground to remain out of sight of the British. By 08h00 the first shots were fired. The Boers used the technique of fire-and-movement (*skiet mekaar los*) whereby half a group

Hendrina Joubert always went on commando with her husband, Piet. It was she who alerted her husband to the presence of men on the 'kop'. (*NARSSA*)

The assault on Majuba endured some hours, but Colley seems never to have been aware of the grave danger to his position, despite repeated and anxious reports from officers like Hamilton. In mid-morning Colley sent off a heliographed morse signal to Mount Prospect: 'All comfortable. Boers wasting ammunition. One man wounded in foot.'

At about 10h30 Colley and his officers were casually inspecting the south-western perimeter of the summit, with a view to identifying defensive positions in case of a Boer attack that night. 'All of a sudden,' writes the Afrikaner historian Victor d'Assonville, 'a bullet from a lone Boer marksman hissed close to the heads of the officers. They saw this Boer sneaking through the undergrowth behind a rock near the foot of the mountain. Colley turned to Colonel Stewart and asked: 'I wonder what the distance is?' Stewart looked through his binoculars and noted that this man was aiming from about 900 yards, virtually out of range. At that moment the Boer fired again.' This time the bullet hit one of the officers: Colley's second-in-command, Commander Romilly of the Naval Brigade. He was mortally wounded in the back and stomach.

The unexpected loss of Romilly was a blow to morale as well as to the command structure. The British soldiers were beginning to tire in the mid-summer sun after a sleepless night, and they were not properly deployed. By noon the Boer attackers were getting close to the summit of Majuba; on the northern side, some were exploiting dead ground to pin down with heavy fire the Gordon Highlanders under Hamilton. On the eastern side, the Boers – including the future General Christiaan de Wet – did much the same to the 58th Regiment.

This might have been the opportunity for the British to restore the position with a bayo-

would advance 15 or 20 yards while the other half provided covering fire. The roles would then be reversed. Older Boer men, all superb marksmen, were stationed on a nearby ridge to give further covering fire, whose effect was no less than if the Boers had used artillery. The angle and accuracy of this fire ensured that the British soldiers on the ridge had to keep their heads down – which made it even more difficult for them to see the Boers scrambling up the slopes. In any case, some of the officers later asserted, British marksmanship was poor – and this was exacerbated (it was later discovered) by the fact that many soldiers were aiming according to rifle sights that had been incorrectly set.

It is clear that the British never realised that the Boers were launching a concerted attack.

General De Wet (DB)

net charge. Colonel George Duxbury, director in the 1980s of the SA National Museum of Military History, recounted in a paper on Majuba that at this crucial stage,

> Hamilton, now wounded, ran down to General Colley and, saluting, said: 'I do hope, General, you will let us have a charge, and that you will not think it presumptuous on my part to have come up and asked you.' To which Colley replied: 'No presumption, Mr Hamilton, but we will wait until the Boers advance on us, and then give them a volley and charge.' It is on record that other appeals were made, but to all the General returned non-committal replies.[4]

By now the perimeter of the summit was threatened. Duxbury continues:

> The Boers had quietly slipped around under cover of the crest-line to the right of the Brit-

ish and soon were pouring heavy fire into their backs at almost point-blank range. A fresh body of Boers now threatened the left front flank and things got out of hand. Discipline was fast on the wane but what could be expected when the men belonged to three different regiments and the personal influence of their officers was missing? It was not long before the defence wavered and finally broke with a wild rush into the basin and up the slope to the south-east perimeter. Hamilton described the bullets as pitting on the ground like hailstones. Many of the men who reached the perimeter flung themselves wildly over its precipitous edge. Some paused long enough to see the sheer drop and attempted to veer round to the south, but few covered the fifty or seventy metres without being hit.

'Men began to slide and slither down the slope,' says Brian Roberts. 'Boers stood openly on the edge of the escarpment and picked the British off like wild game.' According to one officer, 'a general funk had become established.'

At about 13h00 Colley himself was killed instantly by a single bullet which entered his head above his right eye and exited behind the left ear. Several Boers later claimed to have shot him. Just before Colley was hit, Hamilton remembered, he called on his men to hold the ridge. According to another account his last words were: 'Oh my men, do not run.'

Carter, the man from *The Times*, wrote:

> Five, six, seven, eight men broke from the ranks in front of us and fled . . . It was not long before I was on my feet and running with the rest. Right in our path was the hospital, and we had to go round it to avoid jumping over the bodies of the wounded . . . A terrible volley from the stone ridge we had

just left let us know the Boers were there already. It told horribly on the fugitives, for I saw several in front and right and left of me stopped in their flight. After delivering this first volley the Boers kept up a terrible fire, and every moment their number increased as they swarmed up the hill, now on all sides except that we were running for. It was cruel work; our poor fellows dropped by the score.[5]

Although the battle was effectively lost, there were still the two groups Colley had left on the ridge between Majuba and Nkwelo. But the 92nd Regiment troops under Captain Robertson had not even committed fully to battle before they were ordered to withdraw, taking some casualties. The companies left on the Nkwelo mountain were not engaged by the Boers at all and silently withdrew to Mount Prospect without attempting to assist either Colley's or Robertson's forces. Duxbury says that 'neither group had been given orders by Colley as to what was expected of them should they be attacked.' Yet Robertson later maintained that if he had not been ordered to withdraw, and had been able to fight with the support of the forces still at Mount Prospect, the outcome of the Majuba battle would have been different.

One of the British officers to emerge from Majuba with some credit was Lieutenant Hector MacDonald, who with 19 men held the strategic hill now known as MacDonald's Koppie. Only when the rest of the British force had collapsed did MacDonald order his men to escape, but all were shot except for MacDonald and one other, who were taken prisoner. D'-Assonville tells the story of what happened when MacDonald's sword was brought to General Piet Joubert:

He read the inscription on the weapon which mentioned the bravery of this officer in Afghanistan, and told how he had risen from the ranks. General Joubert, with the sword in hand, went straight to the prisoners and asked for Lieutenant MacDonald. Immediately he responded with a salute and Joubert gave him his hand, and handed back the sword, saying: 'A man who has won such a sword should not be separated from it.'

In another conversation on the summit after the battle, Lieutenant Hamilton (who had been wounded by a bullet through his left wrist) observed to Joubert: 'This is a bad day for us'. The general replied: 'What can you expect from fighting on a Sunday?' Hamilton's wound was dressed by one of the Boers, J H J Wessels, using his own red handkerchief. Thirty years later

Hector Macdonald, one of the few to survive Majuba, was later wounded at Paardeberg, and succeeded General Wauchope. He won respect and a salute from a Boer general. (*NARSSA*)

Peace negotiations on Gert O'Neill's farm, Mount Prospect, on 23 March 1881.
The representatives are M W Pretorius, Paul Kruger, Sir Evelyn Wood, Pres J H Brand, P J Joubert,
E J P Jorissen, Major Fraser, C J Joubert, Major Clark, Lt. B Hamilton, T Cropper, D Uys, J P Maré.
Hamilton, survivor of the battle, is in the front, third from left. (*NARSSA*)

the two men happened to meet again and Hamilton (by then General Sir Ian) presented Wessels with a new handkerchief in a silver box.

The British losses at Majuba were 92 killed, 134 wounded and 59 taken prisoner. The Boers lost one man killed (Johannes Bekker of Middelburg) and five wounded, one of whom subsequently died from his injuries. 'Majuba, although a small affair,' wrote the historian Byron Farwell, 'was particularly mortifying for Britain; never before in its long history had British arms suffered such a humiliating defeat: a group of unsoldierly farm boys had completely routed a British force containing elements of the Royal Navy and regulars from some of the most famous regiments in the British army, and

a force, moreover, that was six times larger than that of the Boers and in what ought to have been an impregnable position.'[6] And, unlike at Isandlwana in 1879, this time there was no heroic Rorke's Drift to compensate for the thrashing. No battle honours were awarded by the British army to regiments that fought at Majuba.

The sad irony of the humiliating defeat was that it came at a time when Gladstone had already decided to make peace with the Boers. The British Prime Minister was against 'shedding more blood,' even though Queen Victoria wrote that 'I do not like peace before we have retrieved our honour.' Sir Evelyn Wood, now commander in Natal following Colley's death, also wanted to continue the war. 'Now that we have so many troops coming,' wrote Wood, 'I recommend decisive though lenient action; and I can, humanly speaking, promise victory.'

But Gladstone had his way, and the first peace talks were held on 23 March in O'Neill's cottage near Majuba. The overtures were accepted. The Boers agreed to withdraw and the British promised not to follow them into the Transvaal. This finally finished off Carnarvon's vision of a voluntary confederation of colonies, protectorates and republics in southern Africa. By August 1881 the negotiations were completed and the Pretoria Convention recognised the Transvaal's independence, while retaining influence over its foreign affairs through an ill-defined 'suzerainty'.

The British army was understandably out-raged. As Lieutenant Colonel Hugh McCalmont of the 7th Hussars wrote in a letter home: 'Why have Colley and all his men been sacrificed if there was a foregone conclusion of the government that there was nothing worth fighting about?'

This bewilderment in a serving officer is understandable, but history is not sympathetic to Colley's motives. When London heard the news of the earlier defeats at Ingogo and Laing's Nek, the Gladstone government was already digesting a report from the governor of the Cape Colony, Sir Hercules Robinson, about Boer restiveness in the Transvaal, the Orange Free State and even the Cape. The Colonial Secretary, Lord Kimberley, suggested to Gladstone that peace talks should be opened with the Boers – 'better surely to negotiate, even

O'Neill's cottage where the armistice was signed after the First Anglo Boer War of 1880–1881.
(NARSSA)

after three defeats, than to turn the whole of South Africa into another Ireland,' as the historian Thomas Pakenham expressed it. Gladstone, who was preoccupied at that time with the Irish question, agreed.

On 16 February (ten days before his occupation of Majuba) Colley had been ordered by cable to offer the Transvaal president, Paul Kruger, a ceasefire and an invitation to talks. Kimberley had told him to inform Kruger that 'if the Boers will desist from armed opposition, we shall be quite ready to appoint commissions with extensive powers . . . Add that, if this proposal is accepted, you are authorised to agree to suspension of hostilities.' In a second cable, Kimberley had said that 'if the arrangement proceeds' (that is, if Kruger accepted a ceasefire) Colley was not to make another attempt on Laing's Nek or try to proceed into the Transvaal; and that Kruger had to be given 'a reasonable time' in which to reply. All the evidence from before and after Majuba indicates that the Boers would have accepted the British government's terms without more fighting.

But, Pakenham argues, Kimberley's instructions were 'just vague enough to be misinterpreted.' Colley decided that 48 hours was 'a reasonable time' in which to reach Kruger and get his reply, though Colley was warned that Kruger was at Heidelberg and that a round trip could take six days. (In fact it took twelve days, because Kruger was much further west at Rustenburg.) Two days was indeed 'a most reasonable time,' says Pakenham tartly, 'if the aim was to sabotage the armistice.'

So Majuba was a most unusual military event in terms of diplomatic objectives, because both sides would probably have got what they wanted if the battle had not been fought. It had been entirely unnecessary. Strategically, the decisive battles of that war were Laing's Nek and Ingogo. These victories finally induced London to seek the settlement that was duly achieved after Majuba – and indeed extended in favour of the Boers three years later, when the British backtracked again. According to the London Convention, the British ceded the right to march troops through the Transvaal or to influence treatment of the republic's black population. Even the reference to suzerainty was removed, at the insistence of Kruger.

The Boer gains from the First War of Independence, then, were considerable and satisfying – but they would be utterly undone in the course of events sparked by the 1886 discovery of gold that created Johannesburg, culminating in the devastation of the Anglo-Boer War, also called the Second War of Independence, of 1899–1902. In the harsh light of that much greater conflict, names like Bronkhorstspruit and Laing's Nek seem to fade into the margins of history.

But the impact of the Majuba victory endured (and endures) in Boer mythology. It was here that the British Empire was utterly humiliated, and the memory of this was a comfort to many Afrikaner nationalists for much of the next century. The Nazi-aligned Afrikaner movement of the 1940s, the Ossewabrandwag, established a refuge on a ridge adjoining Majuba. One senses in the more rightwing Afrikaner writings a *schadenfreude* about Majuba that is not evident in the cultural response to most other battles between Boers and British.

CEMETERIES, MEMORIALS AND VISITOR CENTRES

A stone on the **summit of Majuba** marks the spot where Colley was killed, and 76 of his men were buried on the mountain. There is also a monument to the 58th Regiment. Colley is buried in the **cemetery at the site of the Mount Prospect camp**, with others who were brought down from Majuba and from the battles of Ingogo and Laing's Nek. Although some of the graves are anonymous, more than 50 of the fallen are identified, including Commander Romilly. The cemetery is on private land owned by Dr Paul Waite, but permission can be obtained by contacting the manager of **Mt Prospect bush camp**, Mr Jan Pretorius, on (034) 325-0521 (tel/fax) or 072 7077 057. (For accommodation details, see **Where to stay** section.)

It is also possible to explore the **battlefield** itself, which is not far from the national road and therefore more accessible than Isandlwana, Rorke's Drift and Blood River. It is easy to trace the steep route taken up the mountain by the British on the night of 26 February, and at least two hours should be set aside for this ascent. Many of the Boer fortifications are still visible and it is worth arranging a guide in advance. The climb is well worth the effort even if you are not interested in battlefields: the view from the top in all directions is superb.

There is a commemorative working farm at the foot of Majuba – a sensible arrangement, because it means the site is secure and cared for, but without the need for an expensive permanent staff. Overlooking Majuba is a small but informative **museum**, made from an old corrugated-iron railway worker's house transported from nearby Volksrust. The museum contains a very useful model of the Majuba topography, showing the routes taken by defenders and attackers. There is also a youth centre and a picnic and camping ground, and the large rondawel occupied by the Ossewabrandwag is still identifed as such. Contact the manager of the farm at (017) 735-1962/3401, or PO Box 1071, Volksrust 2470.

O'Neill's Cottage, where the peace negotiations took place, is a proclaimed national monument and can be accessed on a rough track from the main road, about 10km south of Majuba. But it is derelict and deteriorating fast. The reason for this disgraceful neglect, apparently, is a classic instance of bureaucratic muddle. In 1983 the National Monuments Commission insisted on expropriating the land on which the cottage stands from the owner, but having failed to maintain the property, now wants to restore it to him. The dispute between them continues.

GEORGE POMEROY COLLEY was 45 years of age when he was sent to Natal. He was then regarded as one of the most brilliant officers of his generation, and had served in the Cape, in China and in Africa in the Ashanti War in present-day Ghana under Sir Garnet Wolseley. Colley had also been private secretary to the Viceroy in India. 'But he was also a kind, sensitive and imaginative man,' wrote James Morris, 'who took his watercolour sketchbook wherever he went, and whose heavily bearded soldier's face was given grandeur by a dreamy look in the eyes.' He was an expert ornithologist, and fluent in French and German.

Colley's appointment as British High Commissioner in South Africa was his first independent command, and he seemed to lack confidence. He wrote home: 'Whether I shall find that South Africa is to me, as it is said to be in general, "the grave of all good reputations", remains to be seen.' He was extremely secretive in his planning at Majuba, as if he did not want to involve his senior officers in case they refused to support him.

There were rumours that Colley did not, in fact, succumb to a Boer bullet, but committed suicide. There is no evidence for this, but it seems clear that if he had survived the battle, disgrace awaited him. As Pakenham notes, 'Colley had much to answer for.' He had disobeyed orders and prevented an armistice when he knew that one was desired by his own government. Before advancing on Majuba, he did not consult his senior officers. On Majuba, by not bringing up his guns, or digging in or doing proper reconnaissance, he failed to protect his men and the ground he had taken.

The purely military errors were so elementary that we have to ask whether Colley really expected to have to defend Majuba at all. Was his assault on the mountain something quixotic, an attempt to salve his soldierly vanity while waiting for the London-initiated peace process

to take its course? Having achieved a strong position on high ground, he evidently did not expect to attack the Boers again, or even to be attacked by them. How else does one explain his neglect of the artillery, without which (he must have known) occupation of the summit was tactically meaningless?

Whatever his motivation, there can be no doubt about Colley's bravery. He may well have been 'a disastrous commander, rash in assuming battle, but timid in the conduct of the battle itself' (as one military website puts it), but he did not run from the enemy.

In his last letter to his wife before the battle, he had written: 'Think lovingly and sadly, but not too sadly or hopelessly of your affectionate husband . . . How I wish I could believe the stories of meeting again hereafter.'

General Colley's grave showing the Majuba mountain.
(*NARSSA*)

HOW TO GET THERE AND WHERE TO STAY

From Johannesburg (four hours): Take the N3 highway to Durban and exit at Villiers. Follow the R103 and then the R34 to Vrede, then the R546 to Standerton, then the R23 to Volksrust and the N11 to Newcastle. The right turn onto the dirt road to Majuba is a few kilometres outside Volksrust ('people's rest,' so named because of the relief given to the Boer people by Majuba). The left turnoff to Laing's Nek and the right turnoff to O'Neill's Cottage are about 10km after the Majuba turnoff, but are easy to overshoot on the winding road.

From Durban (three hours): Take the N3 highway to Johannesburg and then the N11 to Ladysmith, Newcastle and Volksrust. The left turn onto the dirt road to Majuba is a few kilometres outside Volksrust, preceded by the left turnoff to O'Neill's Cottage and the right turnoff to Laing's Nek.

WHERE TO STAY:

Majuba Lodge is about 9km from Majuba itself and is the only lodge which offers views of this beautiful mountain from all its bedrooms. In 2005 prices ranged from a very reasonable R150 to R180 per day, exclusive of breakfast. Owner-manager, Cathy Booysen, also runs an a la carte restaurant at the lodge. Tel: (017) 735-2550.

Mt Prospect bush camp and chalet is 20 km from Volksrust, and within close view of Majuba. The bush camp is about 800m from the British cemetery, Colley's grave and the site of the British camp, all accessible on foot or otherwise by ordinary or 4x4 bakkies only. Day visitors strictly by appointment: phone manager Mr Jan Pretorius (034) 325-0521 or 072 707 7057. The bush camp offers a lapa, bar, playroom, splash pool, trampoline, braai area and accommodation for 18 people. There is also a chalet sleeping eight people, offering fully equipped self-catering accommodation. Prices in 2005 were R200 min. for two persons per night and R75 p.p.p.n. for additional guests.

Newcastle Tourism: (034) 315-3318. Phone them to arrange for Battlefields Route tour guides as well as accommodation in the various lodges, B&Bs, guestfarms and campsites in the area.

Amajuba Publicity and Tourism Association: (017) 734-6135 in Volksrust will likewise arrange tour guides and accommodation in and around Volksrust.

The tiny village of **Wakkerstroom**, close to Volksrust and 30km from Newcastle, also offers accommodation in more than 20 guesthouses and B&Bs, on top of being a popular wetlands bird-watching destination.

O'Neill's cottage at the foot of Majuba today. The memorial in the foreground is to the King's Royal Rifles. (*GM*)

REFERENCES AND FURTHER READING

Victor d'Assonville, *Majuba*. Roodepoort: Marnix, 1996.

George Duxbury, 'The Battle of Majuba', *SA Military History Journal*, Vol 5 No 2.

Byron Farwell, *The Great Boer War*. London: Allen Lane, 1976.

Hermann Giliomee, *The Afrikaners: Biography of a People*. Cape Town: Tafelberg, 2003.

James Morris, *Heaven's Command: An Imperial Progress*. London: Faber & Faber, 1973.

Thomas Pakenham, *The Scramble for Africa*. Johannesburg: Jonathan Ball, 1991.

Brian Roberts, 'The Boers Rebel', pages 832–840, *The British Empire*. London: BBC/Time-Life, 1971.

NOTES

1. James Morris, *Heaven's Command: An Imperial Progress*. London: Faber & Faber, 1973, p.74.
2. Quoted in Donald Morris, 'War in the Veld', in *The British Empire*. London: BBC/Time-Life, 1971, p.834.
3. *Ibid*, p.837.
4. George Duxbury, 'The Battle of Majuba', in *SA Military History Journal*, Vol.5 No.2, p.14.

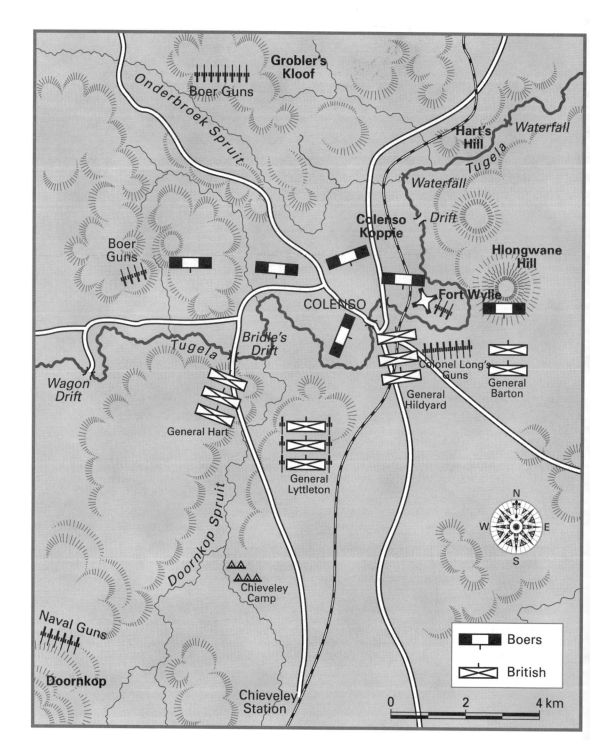

Grobler's
Kloof

Boer Guns

Onderbroek Spruit

Hart's
Hill

Waterfall

Tugela

Waterfall

Colenso
Koppie

Drift

Boer
Guns

Hlongwane
Hill

Fort Wylie

COLENSO

Bridle's
Drift

Colonel Long's
Guns

Tugela

General
Barton

Wagon
Drift

General
Hildyard

General Hart

General
Lyttleton

Doornkop Spruit

N

W   E

S

Chieveley
Camp

Naval Guns

	Boers
	British

Doornkop

Chieveley
Station

0   2   4 km

*'No end of a lesson'**

Colenso and Black Week, 1899

No water, not a breath of air, and not a particle of shade and a
sun which I have never felt hotter, even in India
British Tommy at the Battle of Colenso, 15 December 1899[1]

The 1899–1902 Second Anglo-Boer War – also called the 'South African War' or 'Second War of Independence' – is sometimes portrayed as the 'last of the gentleman's wars' and the 'first of the modern wars'. It was both and it was neither.

This war lasted just under three years and, apart from the countless lives lost, involved considerable cost to British prestige and finances. The largest mobilisation since the Crimean War (1853–56) cost the British exchequer £223 million. Over 22,000 of the 364,693 Imperial troops and 82,742 colonial soldiers died, with over 100,000 casualties (dead, wounded and missing) overall. Some 7,000 deaths were recorded among the 87,365 Boer burghers. But the Boer hardship did not end there. An estimated 28,000 Boers – mostly women, one in five children and the aged – died in the con-

centration camps due to dysentery, typhoid and starvation. Moreover, 20,000 black South Africans also died in these camps – a fact until recently given scant attention. Many of these black victims had been servants and labourers on Boer farms; others were from local tribes who were either suspected of aiding the Boers or who had to be prevented from doing so.

Apart from these considerable human losses, material losses included over 400,000 mules, donkeys and horses along with several million Boer and African livestock. Even more devastating to Boer and black farmers and villagers alike was the loss of their homes, sheds and outhouses, farming implements and all their crops – indeed in many instances, their entire livelihood.

The long-term cost of the war was equally extreme. Its legacy was to cast a shadow over

79

Boer gun emplacement at Colenso. Note the absence of trees and cover compared to today. (*BKZN*)

the following century of South African history and politics. Afrikaners emerged from the war with a profound sense of grievance, coupled with an intense need to preserve and protect their own culture, rights and survival. Such was the negative impact of the war on Afrikaner sentiment towards their English counterparts, that most post-Boer War decision-making was dominated by attempts to consolidate the fragile unity between these two white groups – at the expense of all other racial and political groupings.

With hindsight, it is noteworthy that around 100,000 black, Indian and coloured people participated in the war on the British and Boer sides – a greater number than the total of Boers in the field. Most worked as drivers, scouts, stretcher-bearers and labourers and were to suffer heavy losses during the war – a fact also underplayed by apartheid historians. Ironically the civil rights of this 'invisible majority' were to be ignored and eventually trampled underfoot in the aftermath of the war.[2]

In terms of its contribution to modern warfare, the Anglo-Boer War brought about a number of innovations. The American Civil War 35 years earlier had offered a glimpse into the future by demonstrating the impact of modern weaponry such as artillery and the machine gun on the battlefield, and revealing the gulf between technological advancements and tactical thinking. The South African War helped to confirm the impact of such technological developments, exacerbated by the introduction in this war of smokeless powder and the repeater rifle, so that the defensive and offensive cover of the trench and the use of field craft and camouflage (such as the employment of khaki) became paramount. The war also saw the end of the use of the cavalry, at least in the British Army. Indeed, one of the last cavalry charges on record is that made by the Dragoons and Lancers at the battle of Elandslaagte on 21 October 1899.

But it was perhaps only after the fall of Pretoria to the British on 6 June 1900, that the greatest, ongoing contribution of the war to military tactics was made. At that point, a Boer *Krijgsraad* held in the capital decided that the war would continue and that guerrilla tactics would substitute for conventional war. The use of guerrilla hit-and-run tactics, epitomised by the term 'commando', was the forerunner of many similar struggles elsewhere in the world up until the present day.

At that initial stage of the war the Boers were technically defeated inasmuch as they had lost their capitals, which, apart from loss of prestige and centres of administration, affected supplies of all kinds. Conditions were exacerbated by a lack of supplies for their horses caused by a dry summer. Even so, after those first eight months the British already recognised that to counter ongoing Boer resistance, they would have to 'drain the sea in which the Boer guerrilla lived' – to paraphrase Mao Zedong – or the war could drag on indefinitely. Hence the use of a 'scorched-earth' policy, coupled with the establishment of concentra-tion camps to limit the succour offered to the Boer insurgency.

There are many battles in the Anglo-Boer War which reinforced this impression of the Boers as daunting and determined adversaries but arguably none more so than the defeat of the British at the first battle of Colenso on 15 December 1899. This – along with Stormberg and Magersfontein – was the final battle in a series of three British reversals during what became known to the British here and abroad as 'Black Week'. So seriously did the mother country regard these losses, that General Sir Redvers Buller VC was replaced as commander-in-chief of the British forces by Field Marshal Lord Roberts, then already known as Lord Roberts of Kandahar, following his success in the Second Afghan War of 1878–80. His appointment and particularly that of Kitchener as

The charge of the Lancers at Elandslaagte, the last cavalry charge in the world. (WF)

Roberts's Chief of Staff, was to radically shape the course of the war, to the detriment of the Boers. The tough-minded Roberts saw the war through to the conclusion of the conventional phase in 1900, whereupon he was replaced by Lord Kitchener who was primarily responsible for the 'scorched-earth' tactics used to combat the Boer guerrilla operations.

The destruction caused by such tactics meant that the peace process did not end with the conclusion of the Treaty of Vereeniging in Pretoria on 31 May 1902. For the British, there was work to do. In the years after the war, the two republics had to be rebuilt, basic infrastructure recreated and industries developed. The decisions made at this time, particularly by the British High Commissioner to the Cape, Lord Milner, whose antipathy towards the Boers was well known, had a number of longer-term political and economic implications which further alienated Afrikaners.

The Milner administration set about rebuilding the Transvaal and Orange Free State (OFS) along British colonial lines, importing Indian and Chinese indentured labour for this purpose. The largely English-speaking immigrants or *uitlanders,* whose lack of political rights in the Transvaal had been the *cause célèbre* for the war in the first instance, were resettled with greater rights. With the accelerated development of the mining industry, the importance of black labour on the mines also increased. All of this rubbed salt in Afrikaner wounds, as they had not only lost say in the land that they had gained with difficulty and fought for bitterly, but also they felt threatened by what they perceived as increased and unwanted competition in the labour market. Consequently they felt marginalised, angered and financially dispossessed. This resentment eventually found expression in the rebellion against

the Union's involvement in the Great War of 1914–18, for it was inconceivable to those who had lost the war, to be fighting on the British side so soon after. Likewise there was intense Afrikaner resistance to the Smuts-led participation in the Second World War on the Allied side. Ultimately the National Party election victory in 1948 can be said to have had many of its roots in the Afrikaner experience of the Anglo-Boer War and its post-war period.

Indeed, it would not be overstating the case to argue that the fissures created by the outbreak of war in 1899 and the effect of the tactics employed by the British after Colenso were only resolved politically in South Africa with the advent of non-racial government in 1994, though individual grudges still live on.

The Background to the Anglo-Boer War

The origins of the Second Anglo-Boer War resided in the clash between Afrikaner nationalism and British imperialism. Such tensions were exacerbated by the personalities involved, from the dour 'Oom' Paul Kruger to the expansionist Cecil Rhodes, then head of the British South Africa Company, and the imperious British High Commissioner to the Cape Sir Alfred (later Lord) Milner.

At the heart of the issues that led to war was the combination of politics, power and, critically, money. The discovery of diamonds in Kimberley in 1870 and the discovery of gold on the Witwatersrand in 1886 had given South Africa's interior a new significance and interest for the British. The role of the new industrialists – termed 'gold-bugs' – led by Rhodes and Alfred Beit, was key in Milner's precipitation of the war.[3] Coupled with the threat of German imperial territorial expansion into

The dour 'Oom' Paul Kruger, who clashed violently with the expansionist Cecil Rhodes and imperious Lord Alfred Milner. (*SANMM*)

chial Kruger administration, the gold industry was monopolised, posts were reserved for Dutch speakers, and *uitlanders*, while bearing the brunt of an onerous taxation regime, possessed no political rights nor access to services and schools. Tensions were raised after the Rhodes-sanctioned Jameson raid on 29 December 1895, which was intended to be a catalyst for the *uitlanders'* rising in revolt against the ZAR government and in support of the British. But the mission of 600 armed Rhodesian policemen and other volunteers led by Dr Leander Starr Jameson, failed dismally.

Jameson's rebels were all captured by 2 January 1896, and Rhodes forced to resign as Prime Minister of the Cape. Many Afrikaners, including future Prime Minister Jan Smuts, moved to the Transvaal in support of the ZAR, believing that Britain had breached their undertaking in the London Convention of 1884 not to interfere in the domestic affairs of the Transvaal.

Jameson's action had, ironically, served to bolster Kruger's faltering support in the Transvaal. The autocratic, headstrong and tactless[4] methods of the 73-year-old Boer leader had exacerbated what many of the younger progressives in the Raad, led by the hero of Majuba, General 'Slim' Piet Joubert (the runner-up to Kruger in three presidential contests), saw as the anachronism and inefficiency of 'Krugerism'. The raid also rallied Boer support for the cause of independence outside of the Transvaal, especially in the Orange Free State.

The Bloemfontein Conference from 31 May to 5 June 1899 led by Cape Afrikaners William Schreiner and Jan Hofmeyr, was a final attempt to settle the tensions growing between Milner and the ZAR. But Milner, believing that war was the best route to safeguard Britain's interests, rejected Kruger's offer of limited reform including partial, conditional franchise.

southern Africa and Germany's growing friendship with Kruger's *Zuid-Afrikaansche Republiek* (ZAR) which Britain could not ignore, the stage was set for war.

But this war had its origins, too, in the failure of the British to resolve decisively their interests through military intervention 20 years earlier, when the Transvaal Boers defeated them at Majuba in 1881. (See pages 61-77 for an account of this battle).

Pretext and Politics

The pretext for the 1899 war was essentially the *uitlander* question – to resolve the issues surrounding the franchise for and other rights of those 'outsiders' – mostly British immigrants – who had settled in the ZAR after the discovery of gold in 1886. Under the paro-

The British cabinet reacted by sending 10,000 troops to Natal. Kruger's ultimatum for the withdrawal of British troops near to the border with his South African Republic was ignored, and on 11 October war broke out.

Strategy and Overview

Essentially the conventional phase of the war (1899–1900) can be divided into two sectors: The Eastern Front – Natal – and the Western and Central Fronts – from Kimberley to Mafikeng.

The Eastern Front

The plan of the Boers at the outset of war was to clear the Northern Cape and Northern Natal of British troops which threatened the Transvaal and Orange Free State. The Boers concentrated their efforts against the main British troops in Natal using a force comprising 11,000 ZAR burghers under the hero of Majuba, General Piet Joubert; 3,000 burghers under Lukas Meyer; and 6,000 OFS burghers under Marthinus Prinsloo. Opposing them were 4,000 troops under Major-General Sir William Penn-Symons based at Dundee, and 8,000 troops of the main Natal Field Force under the command of Lt.-General Sir George White VC (he had won his Victoria Cross in the Afghan War of 1879–80) at Ladysmith.

Joubert's forces occupied Newcastle, before heading down the railway line towards Dundee and Ladysmith. The battle at Talana Hills on 20 October 1899 was a tactical victory for the British, but resulted in the death of their commander, Major-General Sir W Penn-Symons, and the British were nonetheless forced to fall

back from Dundee towards Ladysmith. Instead of the knockout blow that they sought against the Boers, the British were now on the backfoot. Boer attacks on British positions east of Ladysmith led to a tactical defeat on Monday 30 October 1899 – known as 'Mournful Monday' – and retreat in defence of the key railway junction town of Ladysmith, as a result of which the Boers surrounded Ladysmith and the siege began, trapping 13,000 British troops, their 2,500 servants, and 5,400 civilians.

In response, the British assembled 18,000 troops at Frere and Estcourt, including four brigades of infantry, a brigade of mounted troops, five batteries of field artillery, and a number of naval guns. A new commander arrived in Cape Town on 30 October 1899, General Sir Redvers Buller[5] VC, GCB. Buller's appointment reflected the tensions between the two foremost British soldiers of their generation, Lord Wolseley and Lord Roberts. Buller was a senior general within the 'Wolseley ring' of 'Africans' (senior British soldiers who had distinguished themselves in wars fought in Africa) as opposed to the 'Roberts ring' of 'Indians'.

According to all accounts, Buller was a man immensely cool under fire and one who often put the well-being and safety of his troops before his own. He 'stood watching the artillery fire [at Colenso] while the bullets dropped all about him', observed one British private, 'and when he was hit in the side with one, the doctor, Captain Hughes . . . rode up to him and asked him if he could do anything for him. He calmly replied that it had only just taken his wind a bit . . . He is as brave as a lion.'[6]

On arriving in South Africa, Buller decided to divide his 47,000-strong Army Corps between the Western and Natal theatres, with the General himself taking command in the field in Natal. At his disposal were four infan-

Born in 1839, REDVERS BULLER was commissioned into the 60th Rifles (King's Royal Rifle Corps) in May 1858. He served in the Peking Expedition of 1860, in the Red River Rebellion (Canada) of 1870, and the Ashanti War (Ghana) of 1873–74, where he came to the notice of General Garnet Wolseley. He then served in South Africa during the 'Kaffir War' of 1878 and the Anglo-Zulu War in 1879, where he commanded a regiment of irregular horse. During the last-mentioned war, Buller lost approximately 90 men of his force in the retreat from Hlobane, though he was awarded the Victoria Cross for rescuing three of his men from the Zulus.

From General Officer Commanding at Aldershot in 1899, Buller became Commander-in-Chief of the South African Army Corps, and later of the field force for Natal. Despite his 'reversals' at Colenso, Spion Kop and Vaal Krantz and his resultant replacement by Lord Roberts, he returned to a hero's welcome in Aldershot in January 1901. A disagreement over policy led to his retirement in October 1901 and he died in Devon in June 1908, aged only 68. Given his key role in its development, he is remembered as the 'father' of the Army Service Corps (now incorporated in the Royal Logistics Corps). The Royal Logistics Corps barracks, in Aldershot, bear his name.

Lt.-Colonel Buller was awarded the VC for his rescue of Captain D'Arcy and others at Devil's Pass during the battle of Hlobane. (*BKZN*)

Buller watches the battle from Clouston where the memorials are today. The emplacement for the naval gun is still visible today. (*WF*)

try brigades, a mounted brigade, five field artillery batteries, two 4.7 inch and 12 'Long 12' 12-pounder naval guns, totalling 20,000 men and 44 guns. The main challenge immediately facing Buller in Natal was to find a place to cross the Tugela River (known now as the 'uThukela') to relieve Ladysmith. The Boers, realising this, had fortified the likely crossing points such as those at Colenso, where they had also blown the railway bridge and dug

The Colenso bridge destroyed by the Boers. (*NARSSA*)

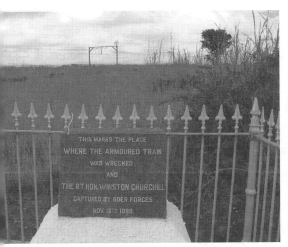

The memorial plaque at Chieveley (above) where the train carrying Winston Churchill was derailed and the future British prime minister captured, and the gravesite (right) further down the track. Note the spent cartridge cases used in the wording of the grave. (*GM*)

emplacements on the range of hills on the northern banks of the river.

Following their success in besieging Ladysmith, the Boers moved southwards further into Natal with a force of around 2,000 led by Commandant-General Piet Joubert and Louis Botha with the intention of damaging the railway to slow any British relief effort towards Ladysmith. On 15 November they attacked a British armoured train reconnoitring from Estcourt towards Colenso. This train had left Estcourt the day before with 164 officers and men of the Dublin Fusiliers and Durban Light Infantry in three armoured trucks, including a young war correspondent by the name of Winston Spencer Churchill. Just south of Chieveley the train was attacked, and some trucks derailed after hitting a pile of stones laid on the track by the Boers. Although the engine and tender made a successful dash to Estcourt, several men were left behind, including Churchill. Buller described these events as 'inconceivable stupidity'.[7]

Churchill was taken to Pretoria from where he made his escape on 12 December 1899 via train to Delagoa Bay (now Maputo) in Mozambique. He returned to Durban by steamer on 23 December and by the end of the month had been given an honorary commission as Lieutenant Churchill into an irregular unit, the South African Light Horse, and rejoined the Natal operation in time for the British attack on Spion Kop in January 1900. His reporting of his activities leading up to the ride into Ladysmith with the relief column on 28 February 1900 helped to launch his political career.

Although the Boers pushed on towards Estcourt, they did not press home their advantage and instead dug in on the hills north of the

Tugela River at Colenso in order to prevent the British from crossing in their attempts to relieve Ladysmith. Joubert decided to occupy the highground north of the Tugela with the knowledge that Buller's force was preparing to advance from Durban. However, the hero of Majuba withdrew from the theatre after falling from his horse, passing command to a 37-year-old Volksrust farmer, General Louis Botha, viewed as one of the 'most brilliant

LOUIS BOTHA[8] (1862–1919) became a member of the parliament of Transvaal in 1897, representing the district of Vryheid. Born in Natal near Greytown, he was made a general in the Second Boer War, and led the Boers at Colenso and Spion Kop. On the death of Piet Joubert, he was made commander-in-chief of the Transvaal Boers, and soon demonstrated his abilities again at Belfast-Dalmanutha. After the fall of Pretoria, he led a concentrated guerrilla campaign against the British, together with Generals de la Rey and de Wet. He later worked towards peace with the British, representing the Boers at the peace negotiations in 1902.

Botha's distinguished war record made him prominent in the politics of the Transvaal so that he became a major player in the post-war reconstruction of that country, becoming Prime Minister of Transvaal in 1907.

In 1910, together with another Boer war hero, Jan Smuts, he formed the South African Party (SAP). Widely viewed as too conciliatory with Britain, Botha faced revolts from within his own party and opposition from J B M Hertzog's more conservative National Party. When South Africa obtained dominion status in 1910, Botha became the first Prime Minister of the Union of South Africa. Although Botha's SAP was not as radical in its racism as Hertzog's National Party, Botha was seen by some as being complicit in the first steps of the South African government toward the tradition of apartheid.

After the First World War started, Botha in his capacity as Prime Minister, sent troops to take German South West Africa on behalf of the Allied forces, a move unpopular among Boers, and which provoked the revolt led by Koos de la Rey and Christian de Wet. Later, when he and Smuts participated in the peace treaty of 1919, Botha argued presciently that the terms of the Versailles Treaty were too harsh on the Central Powers, but signed the treaty anyway. He died soon afterwards on 27 August 1919.

Above: The brilliant strategist Louis Botha, who was appointed commander of the Boer forces at the age of 37 years. (*WMBR*)

strategists to emerge from the Boer ranks.'[9] The stage was set for the first of Buller's 'reversals', Colenso, on 15 December 1899.

Colenso, Boers, God and the Mauser[10]

Facing Buller's force of around 20,000 men were about 4,500 Boers under Botha's command. Around 3,000 of these Boers were engaged at Colenso.

The men under Buller's and Botha's commands could not have been more different though they faced the same hardships.

The British Army reflected to a degree some of the reforms undertaken from 1870 as a direct result of the experience gained in the Crimean War. These included the disappearance of the old numbered regiments of the line to be replaced by those recruited from a geographical area. But the Army remained small by the standards of Britain's European rivals, with a total of 340,000 regulars and reservists compared to the three million of Germany, ten million of Russia and four million of France. There were only around 70,000 men available for overseas 'demonstrations', and in virtually every part of the globe, given Britain's colonial reach.[11] The Secretary of State for War, the Marquess of Landsdowne, had also to deal with serious shortages of artillery, cavalry and essential supplies for this task.

The core of the Army remained the fighting ability of the average soldier – or 'Tommy Atkins' – those whom Wellington referred to as 'articles', the men who formed the backbone of the army but were often out of public sight and mind. As Kipling wrote in 'The Absent-Minded Beggar':

When you've shouted 'Rule Britannia'
When you've sung 'God Save the Queen'
When you've finished killing Kruger with your
* mouth*
Will you kindly drop a shilling in my little
* tambourine*
For a gentleman in Kharki [sic] ordered
* South?*

South Africa in the heat of summer must have seemed distressingly alien. The heat, flies and disease contrasted with the heavy woollen tunics and inadequate pith helmets. The officer cadre were a gentlemen class, well-fed on all manner of delicacies compared to their troops' staple of bully beef and biscuits, and schooled in the set-piece traditions of European conflict: first softening up by the artillery; second, the insertion of infantry in close order; and finally, the use of the cavalry to finish off the job. In colonial battles – such as in Afghanistan, Egypt and the Sudan – the battles against a poorly-armed if brave enemy were usually, as Pakenham notes, one-day affairs 'as practised on Salisbury Plain.'[12] It would not be overstating the case to say that even experienced British troops were ill prepared for the conditions and intensity of skilled resistance they were to encounter in South Africa.

By comparison, Kruger had prepared well for the war, importing modern technology for his citizen army, including 23,000 rifles from 1894–95, Maxim machine guns, and artillery pieces from Krupp and Creusot. By 1899, the two Boer republics had an estimated 80,000 rifles in store. The Boers were, first and last, riflemen.[13]

At Colenso, the Boers had only four guns and one 37mm Maxim-Nordenfelt 'pom-pom' to the 44 of the British (including 15-pounders, 12-pounders and two naval 4.7s). To an

The Boer and his Mauser. (*WF*)

extent the quality of the Boers' two 75mm Creusot field guns, the one 75mm Krupp field gun and one 120mm Krupp howitzer, was superior to the 12- and 15-pounders used by the British. More important than superior technology, however, were the different tactics adopted by both sides, and how that influenced the outcome of the war.

In contrast to the orderly British regiments, the Boers were a citizen army who assembled without uniform. They were organised along democratic lines following leadership they had voted in, and were products of an electoral district-based commando system. Each of the 22 Transvaal and 18 Free State electoral districts produced a commando ranging in size from 300 to 3,000. Key in the organisational structure of each commando was the Field Cor-

net who was responsible for securing supplies and ammunition. The men themselves were usually riders and hunters, and lived easily on a staple of maize, biltong and coffee. There were few European military conventions adhered to, even though this citizen army included the 1,800 men of the Transvaal and Swaziland police, plus a number of foreign contingents including Germans, Irish, Scandinavians, Americans and Frenchmen.

Their use of the ground, the superior range of their Mauser rifles and their familiarity with the environment stood the Boers in good stead, just as their lack of discipline and related shackles of their own democratic system ultimately detracted from their efforts. But this was to come later, after Colenso and a series of near-calamitous British defeats.

The Colenso Battle

In the weeks leading up to the Colenso battle, Buller was faced with a conundrum. He needed to cross the racing Tugela to relieve Ladysmith, but there were only a few places where this might likely occur: the iron road bridge and Bridle's Drift at Colenso, and, 30km to the west under the shadow of Spion Kop, Potgieter's Drift and Trichardt's Drift.

Buller's plan was to attack Colenso and to take over the Colenso Koppie and Fort Wylie, which he believed were the main positions held by the Boers. However, as it turned out, the Boers had dug deep trenches and used camouflage to remain virtually invisible and safe from the British offensive and decoys to deceive the enemy, and had already placed their small number of cannon strategically on the high ground.

Buller was to rely on a three-pronged attack. One infantry brigade totalling 3,500 men would occupy the town of Colenso and then cross the river by the road bridge.

Another brigade, the 5th Irish Brigade, was to cross the river to the west of the village at Bridle's Drift, and then move eastwards to support the main attack. The third prong comprised the mounted attack on the hill of Hlongwane, which dominated the Boer position and the town.

With all these strategies in place, the naval guns commenced bombardment of the Boer positions from 05h00 in the morning of 15 December 1899. However, things started badly when the Irish Brigade under the command of Major-General Hart, instead of crossing at Bridle's Drift further upstream, were led by a local guide into the loop of the river where they came under intense fire from the Boers.

An advance guard of the Boers at Colenso. (*WMBR*)

They were quickly annihilated. The Irish suffered more than 500 casualties including nearly 100 dead, and the attack had to be called off. To the sound of firing, the British field guns under the command of Colonel C J Long of the Royal Horse Artillery, unlimbered virtually on the banks of the Tugela, near to where the cooling towers are today. The naval guns were moved approximately 500m forward, though these never came into action during the engagement.

Fifteen minutes after the Irish Brigade had come under attack at 06h30, the field guns opened fire. The Boers replied with a single shot from their howitzer on Colenso Koppie, the signal for a fusillade of artillery and rifle fire. Conan Doyle described the scene:[14]

> Officers and men fell fast. The guns could not be worked and yet they could not be removed, for every effort to bring up teams ended in the death of the horses . . . One gun was still served by four men who refused to leave it. They seemed to bear charmed lives as they strained and wrestled with their beloved 15-pounder amid the spurting sand, and the blue wreaths of the bursting shells. Then one gasped and fell against the trail and his comrade sank beside the wheel with his chin upon his breast. The third threw up his hands and pitched forward on his face, while the survivor, a grim, powder-stained figure stood at attention looking death in the eyes until he too was struck down.

With the ammunition supply 90m away, it was impossible under the withering fire to replenish or to remove the guns. The main infantry attack entrusted to the 2nd English Brigade attempted to advance at 08h00, but was too late to synchronise with the Irish on the left flank. The third prong, that of the cavalry of the Natal Carbineers, Imperial Light Horse and the South African Light Horse, had commenced their attack on the hill of Hlongwane. But this was too little too late.

In the first attempt to bring the guns out, two of the 12 guns were safely brought back at the cost of seven of 13 men and 13 of 22 horses. Buller, badly bruised by a shell splinter which had killed his staff surgeon, Captain Hughes, and in all likelihood suffering from shell-shock, made the decision to withdraw with fewer than half of his troops having seen action and 'not one in a hundred' a Boer.[15]

Seven Victoria Crosses were awarded after the battle of Colenso, six in connection with saving the guns (Captains H N Schofield, H L Reed and W N Congreve, Lieutenant F H S Roberts, Corporal G E Nurse, and Private G Ravenhill) and a seventh for Major W Babtie for his bravery in attending to the wounds of those injured. In a twist of fate, Captain Walter Congreve went on to command XIII Corps at the Battle of the Somme in July 1916, which included the South African Brigade under his command. It was Congreve who ordered the South Africans to take Delville Wood 'at all costs.'[16]

The impact of the defeat at Colenso was profound and paradoxical. It highlighted the ponderous tactics of the Victorian army and the ineptitude of many of its generals, even though there has been some revision of the initially scathing criticism of Buller. Furthermore, the crushing Boer victory ensured that London now ceased to think in terms of a six-month 'sideshow' and began to understand the commitment that would be needed. As in 1914, there was now a realisation that this war would not be over by Christmas. Indeed, immediate resolve was needed not to surrender the besieged Ladysmith.

Buller was shaken by the defeat. He cabled a pessimistic note to the Marquess of Landsdowne, the Secretary for War in London, on the evening of 15 December: 'My failure today raises a serious question. I don't think I am now strong enough to relieve White . . . I do not think either a gun or a Boer was seen by us all day . . . My view is that I ought to let Ladysmith go, and occupy good positions for the defence of South Natal, and let time help us . . .'[17] Landsdowne did not agree, appointing not Buller's patron Lord Wolseley as the new Commander-in-Chief in South Africa, but rather Wolseley's bitter rival, Lord Roberts, with Lord Kitchener as his Chief of Staff.

Roberts and Kitchener, in their different ways, turned the conflict into a major war and without a doubt influenced the nature of its legacy on South African domestic politics. The impact on military practice was likewise profound, with the Boers and the British developing their respective commando *versus* counter-insurgency tactics. The latter included the 'scorched earth' practice developed under Kitchener, which is as old as war itself, but also added the use of concentration camps – the first war in which this tactic was used, and with devastating effects.

When Roberts arrived in South Africa, he was already a celebrated soldier, hard in battle but loved and respected by his troops. Proof of his popularity is the term 'Bob's your uncle' which originated amongst troops under his command as a term of endearment and trust, indicating that all was well with the world while the capable 'Uncle Bob' was in charge.

FREDERICK SLEIGH ROBERTS[18] – Lord Roberts of Kandahar, Pretoria and Waterford VC (born 30 September 1832, Cawnpore, India, died 14 November 1914, Saint-Omer, France) – is remembered as being an 'outstanding combat leader' in the Second Afghan War (1878–80) and the South African War (1899–1902), and also the last Commander-in-Chief of the British Army (1901–04; after which time the office was abolished). Roberts first distinguished himself during the suppression of the Indian Mutiny (1857–58). Perhaps his most noteworthy military accomplishment was the march he led on Kandahar to relieve Lt.-General James Primrose in 1879. It took Roberts 22 days to move his army 313 miles across Afghanistan's hostile terrain. At the end of it, he defeated his enemy, to date the only general to have emerged with flying colours from an expedition into Afghanistan in the last 200 years. On 1 September 1880, he scored the decisive victory of the Second Afghan War, defeating Ayub Khan's Afghan Army near Kandahar.

Lord Roberts of Kandahar. (WF)

From 1885 to 1893 Roberts was commander-in-chief in India, where he served for a total of 41 years, at a time when the Indian Army (consisting mainly of Indian soldiers and British officers) was both unfashionable and unadvantageous. Yet he rose from Horse Artillery subaltern to Commander-in-Chief of the Indian Army. He served with distinction in the Indian Mutiny, winning the VC for repeated acts of heroism, though he will chiefly be remembered as the man who wiped out the memory of British defeats and brought (at least temporary) peace to the North-West Frontier. His march from Kabul to Kandahar was viewed as a remarkable feat of both strategy and administration. Beset by Sir Garnet Wolseley's jealousy of all Indian officers, 'though the Indian Command was by far the most enlightened and experienced'[20] Roberts nonetheless succeeded in rising through the ranks, making it to Commander-in-Chief of the British Army before the post was abolished.

As the second British commander-in-chief in South Africa in (December 1899 to November 1900) in the South African War, he ended a succession of British defeats; captured Bloemfontein, capital of the Orange Free State Republic (13 March 1900), and annexed that Boer state as the Orange River Colony (24 May 1900); took the cities of Johannesburg (31 May 1900) and Pretoria (5 June 1900); and defeated Boer commandos at Bergendal (27 August 1900). A field marshal from 1895, he was replaced by Kitchener as commander-in-chief in South Africa in November 1900. With Kruger having fled over the border with Mozambique in October and following the annexation of the Transvaal, proclaimed on 25 October, Roberts, believing that the war was practically over, returned to England in December 1900 to fill the office of Commander-in-Chief of the Army in succession to Lord Wolseley. In 1905 he resigned his post on the Committee of National Defence, and devoted himself to attempting to rouse his countrymen to the necessity of cultivating rifle shooting and of adopting systematic general military training and service. As an author he is known by his *Rise of Wellington* (1895), and his *Forty-One Years in India* (1897), an autobiography which has passed through numerous editions.

True to character, Roberts died of natural causes while visiting his beloved soldiers on the Western Front in 1914, aged 83.

Roberts became known as 'Kipling's General', as the personification of what Kipling thought best in a soldier. He was immortalised in Kipling's poem 'Lord Roberts 1914' in which the opening lines evoke Roberts's dying moments during his visit to the British troops on the Western Front:

He passed in the very battle-smoke
Of the war that he had descried.
Three hundred mile of cannon spoke
When the Master-Gunner died.
He passed to the very sound of the guns;
But, before his eye grew dim,
He had seen the faces of the sons
Whose sires had served with him.

Or, as the historian W H Hannah observes:[19]

His life was jewelled and upheld by those ideals the poet himself sought to glorify – courage, faith and honour. But . . . to Kipling's 'Tommy Atkins' he was just 'Bobs', a well-loved commander who had been with them since most of them were recruits, a shrewd tactician, yet careful of his men's lives and solicitous of their welfare. Nothing endears a leader to his men more than sparing them needless hardship, and for this reason his men would follow Bobs through all necessary perils, partly for their belief in him, and partly to see that no harm befell him.

News of his appointment to South Africa came the day after Roberts received a telegram from Buller which read: 'Your gallant son died today. Condolences. Buller.'[21]

His son, Freddie Roberts, was buried at Chieveley two days after the battle of Colenso. The wounds to his abdomen and groin would, from accounts, not be life-threatening today, but were beyond the field medical facilities of that time. Three of his six pallbearers were not to make it through the war: Prince Christian, grandson of Queen Victoria, who died of enteric in Pretoria; Colonel Buchanan Ridell, killed at Spion Kop; and Captain the Hon. Reginald Cathcart, a descendant of an early Governor of the Cape, who was killed on the Tugela Heights.

The final tally of Colenso on the British side was 143 killed, 756 wounded and 240 prisoners or missing. The Boers lost seven dead including one man who was drowned, and 30 wounded. But that was not to be the end. As the fate of young Roberts's pallbearers indicates, Buller's attempts to relieve Ladysmith were to continue to cost the British dearly.

Spion Kop, Vaal Krantz and Beyond

Buller, now relegated to command of the Natal front only, decided to march upstream to cross the Tugela near Spion Kop and from there to advance on Ladysmith. He arrived at his headquarters at Mount Alice on 12

Above: Field Marshall Lord F S Roberts with his wife Nora, daughter Aileen and son Frederick (Freddie), who died in the battle of Colenso. Note Lord Roberts's advanced years. He was sent to South Africa after spending 41 years in India and had to depart for the South African front just one day after news of his son's death had reached him. (DB)

Right: The gun saved by Freddie Roberts. He lost his life in the attempt. (WF)

January 1900, where he decided to split his force. His second-in-command, Lt.-General Warren, would take 15,000 men and 36 guns and cross the Tugela at Trichardt's Drift, while Buller would remain with 9,000 troops at Mount Alice. After some delay, compounded by a failed frontal attack on the Boer positions on the Ntabamnyama mountain which gave the Boers, again under the command of Louis Botha, opportunity to organise, Warren launched his attack on Spion Kop under cover of darkness on 24 January.

A British force of around 1,700 men under the command of Major-General Edward Woodgate were initially successful in clearing the Boer picket off Spion Kop early in the morning of 24 January. The Boers immediately reinstated a small force on the slopes of Spion Kop and, once the morning mist had cleared, poured rifle and artillery fire from the nearby Aloe Knoll and Twin Peaks onto the exposed British position on the summit.

The battle, comprising artillery fire attack and counter-attack, raged the whole day. Around midnight, in the confusion of battle and command, the decision was taken for the British to withdraw their forces from the summit, despite having gained control of the Twin Peaks to the west of Spion Kop. Another way across the Tugela would have to be found. British losses amounted, over the course of the day, to 322 dead, 563 wounded and 300 prisoners. In contrast, the Boers lost some 58 dead and 140 wounded.

With hindsight one notes that a stray bullet or two at Spion Kop would have changed the course of, not only South African, but also international history, for present that day was Winston Churchill, *Morning Post* correspondent and, by then, lieutenant in the South African Light Horse; Louis Botha, as commander of the Boer forces and Mohandas Gandhi, then a 28-year-old barrister cum stretcher-bearer. Gandhi led members of the Indian community in Natal in this humanitarian task – a strange role for an arch-anti-imperialist and pacifist[22] to be providing support to imperial Britain. Gandhi's stretcher-bearers worked tirelessly, bringing down the wounded, and assisting in burying the dead on the hill during a truce the next day. The shallow trenches in the rocky soil, used to provide scant cover to the British soldiers, became mass graves.

On 25 January, Buller – by now denigrated as 'Sir Reverse' Buller and the 'Ferryman of the Tugela' – ordered his troops back across the Tugela. Before he finally managed to break through the Boer lines at Colenso during the battle for Pieter's Hill on 27 February and before he succeeded in relieving Ladysmith by the end of that month, Buller would suffer another defeat at Vaal Krantz (5–7 February).

The Western-Central Front

The other major front of the Anglo-Boer War was also dominated by the imperative to relieve sieges. In the west, Mafikeng, the original source of Jameson's raid on the ZAR, was laid siege to by Boers for seven months, commencing on 14 October 1899. Its garrison was defended by Colonel Robert Baden-Powell, later famous for his role in the scouting movement. Mafikeng was relieved on 17 May 1900 by Lt.-Colonel Hubert Hunter's force of colonial irregulars and members of the Rhodesian Police, joined by a 'flying column' of General Sir Archibald Hunter.

To the south, Kimberley was also laid siege to in October 1899, defended under command of Lt.-Colonel Robert Kekewich. On the Central Front, the British forces commanded by Lt.-General Sir William Gatacre suffered a defeat at Stormberg Junction (near Molteno in the Northern Cape) and in the Kissieberg Hills on 10 December 1899, with nearly 700 British casualties and POWs.

In the meantime, Lt.-General Lord Methuen's advance to relieve Kimberley was punctuated by engagements at Belmont and Graspan. On 23 November 1899, the area around Thomas' Farm in the Belmont district was turned into a British campsite on account of its natural spring water source (sufficient for 10,000 men and horses), the only source of water between the Orange and Modder Rivers on the British route to Kimberley. Julian Ralph, the Special War Correspondent of the *Daily Mail* reported on this reprieve in lyrical terms:

> At the head of the glen where we had camped was an oasis of green trees toe-deep in the edges of a pond. Nearby was a stone tank full of crystal clear water, and beside it our people [the Royal Engineers] had constructed another of white canvas in which the same pure liquid shone like melted diamonds, touched with emerald shadows by some sprays of foliage above. Lines of men were standing beside the tanks dipping in their

bottles, a line at a time. Other men in scores sat in the shade beside the water. Under the trees, in the invigorating coolness of their shelter, the bullet-riddled, shell-mangled wounded were laid in rows upon stretchers, with the doctors in attendance ministering to them.

From this campsite, British troops under the command of Lt.-General Lord Methuen attacked Boer positions along a range of hills – Table Mountain, Gun Hill, 'Kaffirkop' and Sugarloaf Mountain.

On 21 November 1899, Methuen's Kimberley Relief Column left the Orange River Station (base camp) by rail with some 8,500 troops. Upon reaching Witput (alternatively known as Witteputs) about 13km to the south, they found their route to Belmont blocked by approximately 2,000 troops under General Prinsloo. Methuen ordered his intelligence officer, Lt.-Colonel Verner, to survey the Belmont Hills and map the Boer positions. Verner did so under fire of Boer marksmen, though in doing so, he underestimated the distance to the Boer positions. The next day, on 22 November, British mounted troops and the Royal Engineers occupied the area, coming under fire from the Boer artillery on Gun Hill. British artillery returned fire. That same afternoon, the British infantry marched up from Witput 'to receive their dinner and a tot of rum.' Although Methuen planned to surprise the Boers with a dawn attack, with the infantry leaving their positions at 02h00 on the 23rd, Verner's map caused confusion and delay. As a result, the British lost 75 men killed and 220 wounded. The Boer losses were estimated at 26.

The Battle for Belmont was, however, considered to be a tactical victory for the British,

The Belmont Battlefield Vista, with Gun Hill to the centre.
(GM)

and the following day they left for Graspan, after which engagement (25 October) they would fight the next three battles on their inexorable march on Kimberley. Graspan was followed by Modder River (28 November), Magersfontein (11 December) and Koedoesberg Drift (5–8 February 1900). Kimberley was relieved on 15 February 1900. Two more battles were to follow, that of Paardeberg (17–27 February) and Boshof (5 April). The battle of Paardeberg was the largest and bloodiest single battle of the Anglo-Boer War, waged over ten days, with 350 Boer and 1,270 British casualties on 18 February alone. Despite his earlier declaration that 'I shall not surrender alive', General Piet Cronjé, in the face of continuous British artillery fire and desperate humanitarian circumstances, was forced to surrender, along with 4,069 burghers (including 50 women) on 27 February, on the day of the nineteenth anniversary of Majuba.

Yet of these battles, Magersfontein is considered to have been the main engagement of the Kimberley relief, and a key battle in what the British remembered as 'Black Week'.

After the battle of Modder River, the Boers withdrew to a tactical position under the Magersfontein ridge, 40km south of Kimberley, where, in his advance to relieve Kimberley, Methuen attacked them on 11 December 1899. The Boers were well dug in across a 19km front at the foot of the Magersfontein hills and ready to face the advance of 4,000 men of the Highland Division under Major-General A J Wauchope. At a 500m range, the Boers opened fire, causing 1,000 British casualties, including Wauchope who was killed.

The British Tommies were pinned down in the scorching mid-day sun – what they re-

Major-General Wauchope. (WF)

The Magersfontein battlesite viewed from the Boer positions on which Wauchope's Division advanced. (GM)

ferred to as 'old McCormick'.[22] As the British poem 'The Black Watch at Magersfontein' observes:

> Wire and the Mauser rifle, Thirst and the burning sun,
> Knocked us down by the hundred, Ere the long day was done . . .
> All day in the same position, Watching our own shells burst,
> Lying with our dead men and wounded, Lips swollen blue-black with thirst.

The outcome of Magersfontein has helped to reinforce certain mythologies about Boer military capabilities, including their extraordinary marksmanship. It is said that a Boer could shoot accurately up to the distance where he could no longer distinguish between the stripes on a springbok – around 400m. But in the days of open sights, this was unlikely. Today, using a magnification sight, accuracy at 300m qualifies a British soldier for a marksman's label.

On this topic, Pakenham observed about Colenso: 'There was no question of the Boers

'Last of the Gentleman's Wars'? Boers tend the British wounded at Magersfontein. (WF)

British soldiers cross Boer barbed-wire entanglements at Magersfontein several days after the battle. (*WF*)

being brilliant marksmen. Indeed, one of the things that struck some survivors most forcibly was how poor was Boer marksmanship, supposed to be one of their great points of superiority to the British. It was the sheer volume of rifle-fire – the emptying of a thousand Mauser magazines – that had the force of machine-guns and gave the British the impression that they were facing twenty thousand Boers.'[23]

After the British setback at Magersfontein,

Roberts obtained 12,000 horses from Argentina and Australia to aid mobility and, bypassing the Boer lines left of Magersfontein, General French relieved Kimberley on 15 February. This action was followed by the said successful British engagement with the Boers at Paardeberg under General Cronjé, who was withdrawing towards Bloemfontein. The fall of Bloemfontein occurred scarcely without a shot being fired on 13 March.

Thereupon, the British forces under Major-General John French advanced on Colesberg to prevent the Boers from moving deeper into the Cape Colony. This conventional phase of the war ended in Lord Roberts's march on Pretoria and Bloemfontein, having helped to relieve Kimberley and Mafikeng en route. But, as noted, the war then shifted from the conventional phase – arguably still a 'gentleman's war' – to the guerrilla and counter-insurgency phase in which civilians increasingly became embroiled in conflict, a foretaste of what was to happen in the 20th century.

Impact of the war

The 1899–1902 war became hugely expensive for the British and was not, from the outset, a popular war with the public. Indeed, the Colonial Secretary, Joseph Chamberlain, had difficulty in generating public interest, let alone support for his Africa policy. Instead this war served as a catalyst for anti-imperial sentiment world-wide, with republican-minded Europeans, including Russians, Germans, Scandinavians and Irish joining to fight for the Boer cause. In military terms, it was a harsh wake-up call for the British as to 'the realities of large-scale war'.[24] Until then, Britain's colonial wars had been fought against a poorly-armed if sometimes absurdly brave and brazen enemy where normally, after a massacre of a small garrison of British troops, a large British force would inflict a massive defeat on the natives. In these campaigns, strategy and tactics played second-fiddle to the critical issues of transport and logistical supply through desert and jungle.[25]

In the two Boer republics of the 1900s, however, the Boers, tough and ready frontiersmen that they were, quickly showed that they would not be defeated easily and certainly not by the customary knockout blow. Instead, the British soon learnt that, contrary to their hope to be 'home by Christmas' of 1899, they were up against a tough, resourceful, organised and extremely well-led adversary. (A similar false euphoria was expressed little more than a decade later at the start of the First World War, then ironically considered the 'war to end all wars'). The losses of 'Black Week' further confirmed the gravity of the situation in South Africa. It is said that the news of the defeat of the British at Colenso in December 1899 (on the day before the anniversary of the Battle of Blood River), along with the disasters of Stormberg and Magersfontein during that same 'Black Week', had stirred the British nation 'more deeply than at any period since Trafalgar', and alerted them to the plight of their soldiers. As Thomas Hardy wrote in 'Drummer Hodge':[26]

They throw in Drummer Hodge, to rest
Uncoffined – just as found:
His landmark is a kopje-crest
That breaks the veldt around;
And foreign constellations west
Each night above his mound.

Young Hodge the Drummer never knew –
Fresh from his Wessex home –
The meaning of the broad Karoo,
The Bush, the dusty loam,
And why uprose to nightly view
Strange stars amid the gloam.

Yet portion of that unknown plain
Will Hodge forever be;
His homely Northern breast and brain
Grow to some Southern tree,
And strange-eyed constellation reign
His stars eternally.

For the Boers, the Treaty of Vereeniging and the creation of the Union in 1910 restated those divisions within their own ranks which years before had seen splits leading to the Great Trek and were subsequently manifest in the debate around whether South Africa should enter into the First – and years later – the Second World Wars or remain neutral.

The Boers emerged from three years of bitter fighting with nothing to their name. Many no longer had families or homes to return to. The scorched earth tactics of the war had put an end to their previously pastoral and fiercely independent lifestyle and many were soon to migrate to the cities to live humble working-class lives. Despite generous British war compensation, some felt aggrieved that so much of it was channelled to the claims of *uitlanders* and *joiners* (Boers who fought on the British side). The stance of the *Bittereinders* (those who refused to surrender) was perhaps understandable in a people who felt that they had nothing left to lose.

The subsequent development of apartheid and the corresponding years of international isolation (in contrast to the international support received by the Boer movement during the Anglo-Boer War) in part had their origins in these political divisions, and in the perceived threat posed to this newly created urban Afrikaner underclass by black labour.

General Wauchope's Memorial, Matjiesfontein.

(*GM*)

CEMETERIES, MEMORIALS AND VISITOR CENTRES

The Anglo-Boer War routes are both well sign-posted and accessible today. A number of excellent guides exist, including:

- S B Bourquin and Gilbert Torlage's, *The Battle of Colenso* (Randburg: Ravan Press, 1999);
- Alan Chalmers's *Bombardment of Ladysmith Anticipated: Diary of a Siege* (Weltevreden Park: Covos Day, 2000);
- Michael Barthorp's *Slogging Over Africa: The Boer Wars 1815–1902* (Johannesburg: Jonathan Ball, 2002), and
- Ken Gillings's *Battles of KwaZulu-Natal* (Johannesburg: Art Publishers, 2004).

The resort village of **Matjiesfontein** is just three hours' drive from Cape Town on the N1 and 30km north of Laingsburg. It was developed as a refreshment stop for passing trains in the 1880s by Jimmy Logan, a Scots-born entrepreneur who had come out to South Africa at the age of 19. Logan started off as a porter on the infant Cape Colonial railways and quickly rose to the post of District Superintendent of the stretch of track between the Hex River and Prince Albert Road. Under his management Matjiesfontein soon developed into a Victorian health and holiday resort to which Cecil Rhodes, Olive Schreiner and other famous persons were frequent visitors. It became, too, the headquarters of Logan's refreshment empire (he held, at one stage, concessions to refreshment rooms from the Cape to Bulawayo).

During the Boer War, Matjiesfontein became the site of a vast remount camp, with 10,000 troops and 20,000 horses based on its outskirts. **The Lord Milner Hotel** served as a convalescent hospital for British officers. After Lo-

Matjiesfontein's Lord Milner Hotel. During the war, the hotel's turrets were used as British watchtowers. (*GM*)

gan's death at 63 in 1920, Matjiesfontein fell into quiet decline, bypassed by the National Road, until it was bought and restored by David Rawdon and reopened in 1970. Next to the Lord Milner is the Laird's Arms, an authentically furnished period pub well worth a visit if only to peruse the cricketing photographs.

Approximately 10km south towards Cape Town from Matjiesfontein (on the left hand side of the road travelling towards Cape Town) is the **Memorial to the Black Watch** and its commanding officer, General Andy Wauchope, who fell at Magersfontein but was buried here. Wauchope was brought to Matjiesfontein by train from Magersfontein. Also buried in the nearby cemetery is the founder of Matjiesfontein, James Logan.

The **Tourist Information Centre in Kimberley** (053) 832-7298 may assist with tour guides, places of historical interest and accommodation possibilities. It is also a good place to pick up pamphlets on the various battlesites of the Western-Central Front.

A visit to the **Magersfontein** battlesite (approximately 40km south of Kimberley, and clearly signposted from the N12) is recommended as it offers a very good vista from the Boer stronghold on the hill, which is now the site of the Highland Brigade Memorial.

Across the dirt road are the **Black Watch, Guards Brigade and Scandinavian Memorials,** and a variety of plaques informing the visitor of the relevance of particular points in the

Left: The Scandanavian Memorial, Magersfontein. (*GM*)
Right: Ladysmith Commonwealth Cemetery in the centre of the municipal cemetery, where
184 South African soldiers are buried. (*GM*)

battle. Access to the battle and camp-sites is just R5. Further down the road is the **memorial to the Boer burghers** who fell in the battle.

For those interested in battles that took place further afield in Mpumalanga and in Kwa-Zulu-Natal, **Majuba** is a worthwhile destination. The site of the Boer camp at the bottom of the Majuba mountain is just 25km from Volks-rust, off the N11 towards KwaZulu-Natal. The commemorative site has a Youth Centre with a museum and coffee-shop, and costs R20 per car to enter. O'Neill's Cottage is on the other side of the hill, up a rough path off the N11.

Don't miss the opportunity to visit the excellent siege museum in **Ladysmith** (entrance just R2,00 for adults; open weekdays 09h00–16h00, Sat. 09h00–13h00; tel.(036) 637-2992; email info@ladysmith.co.za), which has a number of interesting exhibits including one that focuses on the role of black South Africans in the conflict. The town was under siege for 118 days, during which time 600 inhabitants died, 510 from enteric or dysentery and 59 from wounds received. Outside the Siege Museum is a replica of the Boer Long Tom, and to its left the two British howitzers named 'Castor' and 'Pollux' (the same names as those of the figures that appear on Sir Herbert Baker's Delville Wood monument). Ladysmith was proclaimed a town in 1850, and is named after the Spanish wife of the later Governor of the Cape, Sir Harry Smith. Lady Juana Maria de los Dolores de Leon had been 'taken' as a wife at the age of 14 by the young English officer Harry Smith after the siege of the Spanish city of Badajoz was broken by Viscount Wellington's army in 1812.

Further down the main street in Ladysmith is the Anglican Church, where there is a complete record of the British troops who lost their lives in the siege.

In the centre of the town's gravesite are a number of **Anglo-Boer War graves,** including a **memorial to the Gordon Highlanders.**

The poorly-maintained if peaceful cemetery at Chieveley where Freddie Roberts is buried. (*GM*)

However, as in some of the sites elsewhere, these graves are sometimes in poor condition.

Also in the civilian cemetery is the comparatively well-tended Commonwealth War Graves Commission **gravesite for Native Military Corps and Coloured Corps soldiers.** The cemetery contains two Commonwealth burials of the First World War and 181 burials from the Second World War.[27] In addition there is the commemoration to a South African soldier who was killed when he fell down the Mont aux Sources escarpment in the Bergville District of Natal, and whose body could not be recovered. His name is recorded on a special memorial.

Around the towns of **Ladysmith** and **Colenso** are a number of sites including those at **Onderbroek Spruit** and **Hart's Hill** north of Colenso (where many of the dead from Buller's second Colenso attack were buried) and at **Ambleside** – in the hook of the bend of the Tugela at Colenso – where Hart's Irish Brigade was decimated on 15 December 1899 during the first battle of Colenso. A **memorial** now marks the site where the **Irish Regiments** in the Fifth Irish Brigade fell on that day.

HOW TO GET THERE AND WHERE TO STAY

From Cape Town to Matjiesfontein: Take the N1 along Du Toitskloof pass, Worcester, De Doorns and Laingsburg. The distance is 200km.

From Cape Town to Kimberley: Take the N1 to Beaufort West and onwards to Three Sisters. At Three Sisters, turn left on the N12 to Kimberley. The distance from Cape Town is 960km.

From Johannesburg to Kimberley: Take the N1 south out of Johannesburg and then turn west on to the N12. The distance is 467km.

From Johannesburg to Colenso: Take the Winterton/Colenso (R74) off-ramp from the N3. Turn left onto the R74 to Colenso.

From Durban to Colenso: Take the Winterton/Colenso (R74) off-ramp from the N3. Turn right onto the R74 to Colenso.

WHERE TO STAY:

To contact **Matjiesfontein**, phone (023) 561-3011 or email: Milner2@mweb.co.za. In 2006 rooms in the Lord Milner Hotel started at R260 per person, B&B.

There is a range of accommodation in and around **Kimberley** and **Magersfontein**. The tourism centre in Kimberley may assist with tour guides, places of historical interest and accommodation possibilities.
Kimberley Tourist Information Centre: (053) 832-7298.

Thomas's Farm, tel. 082 749 6685, in the **Belmont** district south of **Kimberley** is today both a commercial farm and a B&B-type resort, with accommodation costing around R250 per person per night. Its hosts, Lieb and Ella Liebenberg, will take you around the farm to visit the vantage from **Verner's Hill** and the **Guards Memorial** (both of which are a short distance away on the opposite side of the N12 highway), as well as the caves on the farm, which formed a rudimentary field-station during the **Battle for Belmont**. Don't miss the farm reservoir for an invigorating dip.

Apart from a range of accommodation in **Ladysmith**, there is also a number of luxury lodges in and around **Colenso**, from where the KwaZulu-Natal battlefields could be explored at leisure. **Spion Kop Lodge**, tel. (036) 488-1404; www.churchill.co.za, (R790 per night B&B), will arrange battlefield tours with your guide Raymond Heron, and is conveniently situated to explore Isandlwana, Rorke's Drift and Blood River.

Other nearby accommodation includes **Three Trees Lodge** (R995 full board/R795 low season per night, tours extra; tel. (036) 448-1171; www.threetreehill.co.za) or **Tugela River Lodge** (www.tugelariverlodge.co.za). Also, consult www.drakensberg.info or www.battlefields.kzn.org.za for further details on accommodation.

REFERENCES AND FURTHER READING

Michael Barthorp, *Slogging Over Africa: The Boer Wars 1815–1902*. Johannesburg: Jonathan Ball, 2002.

Nick Bleszynski, *Shoot Straight, You Bastards! The Truth Behind the Killing of 'Breaker Morant'*. London: Random House, 2002.

S B Bourquin and Gilbert Torlage, *The Battle of Colenso*. Randburg: Ravan Press, 1999.

Alan Chalmers, *Bombardment of Ladysmith Anticipated: Diary of a Siege*. Weltevreden Park: Covos Day, 2000.

Lewis Childs, *Ladysmith: The Siege*. Barnsley: Pen & Sword with Leo Cooper, 1999.

Winston Spencer Churchill, *London to Ladysmith via Pretoria*. London: Logmans, Green and Co, 1900.

Byron Farwell, *The Great Boer War*. London: Penguin, 1976.

Ken Gillings, *Battles of KwaZulu-Natal*. Johannesburg: Art Publishers, 2004.

Darrell Hall, *Halt! Action! Front! With Colonel Long at Colenso*. Weltevreden Park: Covos Day, 1999.

SA Museum of Military History, *Anglo-Boer War 1899–1902*. Johannesburg: SA Museum of Military History, 1999.

Thomas Pakenham, *The Boer War*. Johannesburg: Jonathan Ball, 1982.

H W Wilson, *With the Flag to Pretoria: A History of the Boer War of 1899–1900*. London: Harmsworth, 1900, Vols. I and II.

NOTES

* Rudyard Kipling's phrase to describe the war. This chapter is based partly on a research trip undertaken by Greg Mills to Kimberley, Magersfontein and Matjiesfontein in December 2004, Thomas's Farm in January 2005, and to Spion Kop, Chieveley, Colenso, Ladysmith and Majuba in March 2005.

1 Cited in S B Bourquin and Gilbert Torlage, *The Battle of Colenso*. Randburg: Ravan Press, 1999, p.30.

2 Thomas Pakenham, *The Boer War*. Johannesburg: Jonathan Ball, 1982, p.xvii.

3 Pakenham, *op cit*, pp.xvi–xvii.

4 Pakenham, *ibid*, p.39.

5 At *http://www.hants.gov.uk/museum/aldershot/biography/buller.html*.

6 Pakenham, *op cit*, p.234.

7 Pakenham, *ibid*, p.171.

8 At *http://louis-botha.biography.ms/*.

9 Ken Gillings, *Battles of KwaZulu-Natal*. Johannesburg: Art Publishers, 2004, p.40.

10 These were the terms used by Ben Viljoen, the member of the 'raad' for Johannesburg in which the Boers should put trust.

11 Pakenham, *op cit*, p.73.

12 Pakenham, *ibid*, p.151.

13 Lewis Childs, *Ladysmith: The Siege*. Barnsley: Pen & Sword with Leo Cooper, 1999, pp.29–31

14 *The Battle of Colenso: 15th December 1899*. Published by the Town Borough of Colenso, undated.

15 Town Borough of Colenso pamphlet, *op cit*.

16 Darrell Hall, *Halt! Action! Front! With Colonel Long at Colenso*. Weltevreden Park: Covos Day, 1999, p.106.

17 Bourquin and Torlage, *op cit*, p.35.

18 At *http://www.pinetreeweb.com/roberts-bio.htm*.

19 In W H Hannah, *Bobs, Kipling's General. The Life of Field Marshal Earl Roberts of Kandahar*, VC. London: 1972.

20 At *http://www.pinetreeweb.com/roberts-bio.htm*.

21 Pakenham, *op cit*, p.141.

22 Slang for the sun. Pakenham, *op cit*, p.233.

23 Pakenham, *ibid*, pp.230–231.

24 Pakenham, *ibid*, p.151.

25 Pakenham, *ibid*, p.151.

26 At *http://www.geocities.com/Athens/Acropolis/8141/boerwar.html*.

27 At *http://www.cwgc.org/cwgcinternet/cemetery_details.aspx?cemetery=12410&mode=1*.

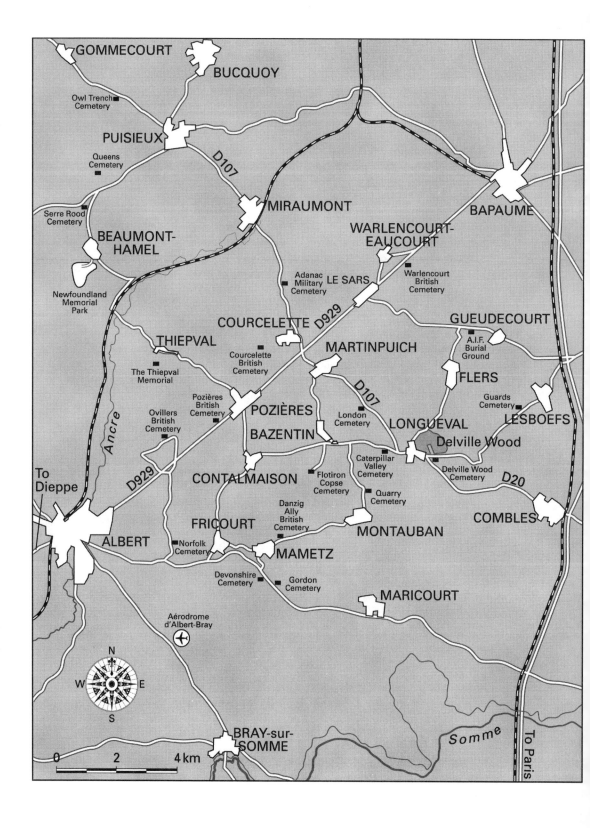

Delville Wood and the Somme. 1916

The young men of the world
Are condemned to death
They have been called up to die
For the crime of the fathers   *FS Flint*

Delville Wood is etched in South African history as a display of extraordinary valour in the face of unimaginable horror.

In the Battle of the Somme, the orders to the 1st South African Infantry Brigade were that the Wood had to be taken 'at all costs' as a means of breaking the impasse that had soon set in after the onset of battle on 1 July 1916. The South Africans, 3,153 strong, entered the Wood at 06h00 on 15 July 1916. When they were relieved six days later, only 143 men walked out unscathed. As General Sir Anthony Farrar-Hockley would later write:[1]

'At all costs' – the phrase came too readily to the lips of the higher commanders . . . The South Africans earned the ungrudging praise of their comrades and their enemies in holding and counter-attacking this awful corner of the ridge, in the crumbling Longue-val streets, in the ravaged orchards and wood whose defences drew in six divisions before acknowledging defeat.

Today single battlefield deaths are headline evening news. Yet it is less than 100 years since the first shots were fired signalling the start of the First World War – or the (perhaps inappropriately named) 'Great War' – a war of unprecedented human carnage. As the *ders des ders* – the 'last of the last' – who participated in this dreadful conflict, now aged over 105 and more, slip away (at the start of 2005 there were just 14 surviving veterans in France and 19 in Britain), it becomes all the more important to call to mind the battles of the Somme, Ypres, Verdun, Gallipolli, Mons, Neuve Chappelle, Cambrai, Vimy Ridge and others of 1914–18; to contemplate why they happened and should

109

There are 11,422 German soldiers buried in the Picardie Metz Cemetery. More than 80% of Germans killed on the Western Front have no known grave. (GM)

never happen again. The passing of the last of the veterans raises questions about how we should best remember them. To do so is to recall both the extraordinary folly and human cost of war, and the callousness and ineptness of political leadership.

Of the 1,1 million British Empire casualties in the Great War, nearly 750,000 soldiers, sailors and airmen died on the Western Front between 4 August 1914 and 11 November 1918, of which the majority died in France (500,000) and Belgium (200,000). These victims are commemorated in no fewer than 3,000 civil and military cemeteries or on the 20 memorials to the dead in France or on the 6 in Belgium, which carry the names of more than 300,000 with no known grave. This fact alone gives

some indication of the dreadful conditions under which the war was fought.

Russia, fighting on the Allied side, suffered two million dead; Germany 1,8 million; France 1,3 million (plus 250,000 civilians); and Austria-Hungary one million. Worldwide nearly ten million people died. The 1918 great 'flu accounted for a further 20 million, many of whom were weakened already by the four years of total war – a war involving nations and not just armies, the conditions and methods demanding the mobilising of entire societies. But worse was to follow. The blunder of the Versailles peace at the end of the war contributed to the rise of fascism and Nazism and laid the conditions for an even worse conflict to follow from 1939–45. This time another

The instantly recognisable Thiepval Memorial on the Somme. Designed by Sir Edward Lutyens, it is the largest British military memorial worldwide, carrying the names of 72,089 soldiers who disappeared, including 803 South Africans. The cemetery to the memorial's north contains the remains of 300 French and 300 Commonwealth soldiers resting 'side by side to remind the world of the common sacrifice of the two and half million dead of France and the British Empire during the Great War.' (GM)

55 million were killed, the majority of whom were civilians, and 35 million wounded.

Alliances, Treaties and Military Strategy

The 1914–18 war has become analogous with bloodletting by inept commanders unable to adapt their tactics to modern military technology. To understand why the casualties were so high and why so little appreciation was given to matching tactics with technology, it is necessary to understand the German strategy from the outset.

The war was triggered by a series of trea- ties and alliances, from which the military strategy followed. The German plan to conquer France and deal with the threat posed by the 1892 Franco-Russian Dual Alliance evolved in the early 1890s under the direction of the chief of staff, Field Marshal Count von Schlieffen. Under his plan, the Germans would defeat the French first, with the German army sweeping through France like a great military door hinged on Switzerland with the leading edge swinging through Belgium on to Paris. As Von Schlieffen had put it, the last soldier at the edge of the door should 'brush the Channel with his sleeve'. Once France had been defeated within six weeks, so the plan went, the

Germans would turn their attention on Russia where ten German divisions would keep them in check until the 62 other regiments had done their business on the Western Front.

The spark causing war was the assassination of the heir-apparent to the throne of the Austro-Hungarian Empire, Archduke Franz Ferdinand, by a Serb nationalist in Sarajevo in Bosnia on 28 June 1914. With Europe entangled in a series of alliances, Austria-Hungary's reaction to the death of its heir was to issue an ultimatum to Serbia to bring the assassins to justice in the expectation that Belgrade would reject the terms and Austria would have the pretext for launching war against Serbia. At the same time, Vienna had assurances that, should Serbia's ally Russia come to its aid, Germany would step in on Austria's side. France was bound by treaty to Russia while Britain, in turn, was obliged to come to the defence of both France (rather loosely under the terms of the 1904 Entente Cordiale) and neutral Belgium, the latter being the route for the German attack on the French.

A number of things happened, however, to slow the Germans when they invaded Belgium on 4 August 1914. First, the British Expeditionary Force was quick to deploy and engage around Mons, southwest of Brussels, thus slowing the German advance. Second, the Germans cautiously weakened the edge of their sweeping 1,5 million-strong 'door', concerned about the strength of the French around the contested area of Alsace-Lorraine. And third, the machine-gun and bolt-action rifle of the Allies were able to lay down previously unsurpassed firepower, with barbed-wire and the trench-based defensive system further slowing the advance, until the winter weather took over by November 1914, turning the frontline into an almost impassable bog of fortified trench-

lines. By this time, the Russians had mobilised and the Germans were fighting on two fronts simultaneously, exactly what Von Schlieffen's plan had intended to forestall. And fourth, the Germans failed to appreciate quickly enough the weakness of their lines of communication between the high command and the tactical units, and also failed to be flexible enough to respond to changing circumstances.

The war thus quickly became a stalemate of various strikes and counter-strikes, mostly centred on the Ypres salient near the Belgium border with France. The first and second Ypres offensives, Neuve Chappelle and Loos, all ended by October 1915 with little end in sight, and the armies bogged down by a combination of weather, casualties, and lack of mobility and imagination.

Slightly to the south, however, the Germans geared for a major offensive at the start of 1916 around the city of Verdun – the name of which was to enter French folklore. To understand the great battle of the Somme which followed six months later, one has to appreciate the scale of the carnage that became Verdun. It was less the Battle of Verdun than the Battle for France and the will of the French nation to continue to fight.

From Verdun to the Somme

On 21 February 1916, contrary to French intelligence, the German Fifth Army attacked the French in the fortified town of Verdun. *Operation Gericht* – referring to a 'place of execution' – lived up to its name: in a battle lasting for ten months, French casualties were some 540,000, German 430,000. Around three-quarters of the French army rotated through Verdun across a relatively small patch of territory with just a 15km front.

The idea behind the German onslaught was simple: it was to grind up the French army, killing so many soldiers that France would sue for peace. It was a concept of almost biblical foundations and proportions. More than 60 million shells were fired by more than 1,000 heavy guns over 300 days and nights in the *Trommelfeuer* (barrage) in the German effort to take a series of 39 forts atop the hilly ground around Verdun. At Fort Vaux, which finally fell in June after running out of water, the barrage peaked at more than 2,000 shells per hour including those from the 420mm 'Big Bertha' firing a one-ton projectile. Whole villages disappeared, including Fleury, today just marked by a small church amidst a moonscape of craters and trenches.

Instead Verdun became to the Germans what the Somme became to the British that same year. Indeed, one cannot understand the lessons from and impact of these two battles without looking at them together. Some of these lessons hold true today as then: that willpower cannot be broken and may, in fact, be strengthened in the face of military onslaught; that firepower alone cannot dictate the outcome of battle; and that mobility is key to victory. Some of these lessons took years to learn, and some are still being learnt today. The World War II Maginot line of defensive fortifications intended to prevent another German attack had their origins in the apparent successes of the fort concept at Verdun (even so the Maginot line was simply outflanked in 1940). The champion of the concept, Sergeant André Maginot, later the French Minister of Defence,

All that remains. The village of Fleury outside Verdun. (*GM*)

had served (and been wounded) as an infantryman at Verdun.

The Douaumont Ossuary is perhaps the most striking of the many French memorials on the battlesite. Through small apertures one can make out the bones of 130,000 French and German soldiers whose remains were collected from around the battlefield and placed in the vault. The building is surrounded by the graves of 15,000 identified French soldiers in the National Cemetery. No wonder Verdun has gone down in French mythology epitomised by the slogan: *'Ils ne passeront pas'* – 'they shall not pass'.

As Verdun ran its bloody course, the Allies prepared for the offensive, which they believed would offer them the breakthrough the politicians and high command craved for – what was to become known as the Battle of the Somme. Instead, the battle fought in this area of northeastern France from 1 July to November 1916 was to be the bloodiest in military history.

1 July 1916 – The First Day of the First Battle of the Somme

At 07h30 on 1 July 1916, 100,000 British and Commonwealth infantrymen attacked the German lines across the Somme valleys in the 'Big Push' that was supposed to break the back of the elaborate German defensive system. The build-up started with the digging of saps for 17 mines under the German trenches, such as those known as 'Hawthorn' in Beaumont-Hamel, 'Lochnagar' at La Boiselle, and 'The Tambour' at Fricourt. The Lochnagar Crater today measures 100m in diameter and is 30m deep.

For a week before the advent of battle, 1,500

Lochnagar Crater, Somme. (*GM*)

The Newfoundland Memorial, Somme. The park at Beaumont-Hamel covers 84 acres and was the scene of the attack by the 1st Battalion of the Royal Newfoundland Regiment on 1 July 1916. Every officer was either killed or wounded and of the 801 men only 68 were not wounded. (GM)

1 July 1916 was a day Siegfried Sassoon described as 'of breathtaking summer beauty', with a light mist creeping through the Ancre Valley. But by the time it ended, there were 57,940 British casualties, comprising 35,493 wounded and 19,240 dead. Half of the other ranks and three-quarters of British forces became casualties on that first day. Thirty-two battalions lost more than 500 men – out of their average strength of just 800. The Newfoundlanders lost 700 men in just thirty minutes, with only 68 men remaining unscathed and all officers either killed or wounded.

Today their valour is commemorated at Beaumont-Hamel where the trench layout and pockmarked land is still quite visible. There were more than 1,000 trenches crisscrossing the Somme in a series of web-like defences and jump-off points, with the German fortifications carefully staggered in three defensive lines effectively employing the gently rolling landscape to their tactical advantage, and with more than 1,000 machine guns able to deliver a deadly interlocking cross-fire, able to hit targets a mile away.

The vast majority of the carnage to the advancing Allied infantry was done by the enfilade of 100 German machine guns. As a German medical officer recalled:

> Machine-gunners and infantrymen crawled out of their holes with inflamed and sunken eyes, their faces blackened by fire and the uniforms splashed with the blood of their wounded comrades . . . they started firing furiously, and the British had frightful losses . . . The British and French generals had not yet learned that it was useless to let human beings run against machine-guns and intense infantry fire, even after 'softening up'.[2]

Allied guns bombarded German lines with 1,75 million rounds, a barrage the likes of which had never been seen before. As one German wrote:

> For seven days and seven nights, the ground shook under the constant impact of light and heavy shells . . . Down below, men became hysterical and their comrades had to knock them out so as to prevent them from running away. . . Even the rats panicked and sought refuge in our flimsy shelters; they ran up the walls and we had to kill them with our spades.

Despite the bombardment, the German forces had dug in well and, at the end of that week, met the advancing Allied infantry with a storm of machine-gun fire.

The still pock-marked Newfoundland Memorial Park at Beaumont-Hamel, Somme today. (*GM*)

Those wounded, lay out in the blistering summer sun. The German lines were only pierced in a few places by the British infantry (although the French were more successful in their sector to the south), and where they were, the advancing troops soon found themselves isolated.

By the time the first battle of the Somme was considered over in November 1916, another would follow to stem the final German offensive in 1918. The casualty toll on both sides was staggering: British and Empire (largely Australia, New Zealand, South Africa and imperial India), 419,654; French, 204,253; and German somewhere between 440,000 and 680,000. The gain for this cost: 45 villages, eight woods and 10km of territory. The original strategic aim of punching a hole right through the tiered German defences and lines of communication was not achieved. It may, however, have saved Verdun and France, though, by de-

flecting the attention of the Germans besieging the French defences at the border town 250km to the east.

Once it had dawned on the high command that bravery alone was not sufficient in the face of machine-guns and modern artillery, new military counter-measures were developed – including the use of more flexible and fluid formations, the 'creeping' artillery barrage, night attacks and, from September 1916, tanks. Total war was in. As a British veteran pointed out: 'Chivalry here took a final farewell. It had to yield to the heightened intensity of war, just as all fire and personal feeling has to yield when machinery gets the upper hand.'

The death toll at the Somme was both appalling and unique. It not only physically decimated a generation and shaped future military tactics, but arguably also fundamentally reversed the progressive pre-1914 world. After the horror of the Somme, there was a more open questioning of the role of the high command in planning the slaughter, where the basic infantry concept of surprise appeared to have been forgotten and intelligence non-existent. As one member of the 'Pals' regiments – so-named because they were recruited from among communities in Britain such as Accrington, Salford, Newcastle and Glasgow, a practice curtailed when the casualty lists came through – said: 'After July 1st, I hated the generals and the people who were running the country and the war. I felt we'd been sacrificed.'

At home, there was unprecedented public debate about the war and the tactics employed. While lacking the instant playback drama of television, first provided by Vietnam, this was inspired by the regular reportage from correspondents and the first use of the celluloid – one documentary being shown even while the Somme progressed. These battalions of Kitchener's 'New Army' to which friends, neighbours and workmates had so enthusiastically enlisted, had been all but wiped out. Certainly, the idea of building close-knit units from among towns and villages, was quickly abandoned.

But it is important not to overstate the failings of the generals – often dismissed as the 'donkeys' leading the ranks of British Tommy 'lions'. They were operating with the concepts, technology and knowledge available at the time, as inappropriate as these turned out. And the Somme did also have its military success. The deployment of the tank in September 1916 offered an unprecedented tactical advantage, while the gradual rolling-up of the German front until the onset of winter in November 1916 displayed the maturing of Kitchener's New Army – with the Germans withdrawing to behind the Hindenburg Line in adopting

the notion of 'defence in depth'. Overall, however, the major strategic achievement of the first Battle of the Somme was that it relieved the pressure on Verdun – without which the town and its forts may have fallen, France sued for peace and the war been lost.

Whatever these arguments, there are many reasons why one should remember the sacrifices made. This is not least for the sake of contemporary politics, which is still too often characterised by ethnic conflict. Given that the war was sparked in the Balkans, it is wise to remain wary of the old tribal divides that still permeate Europe and other areas of the globe. Consciously calling to mind the immense waste of war would, it is to be hoped, inspire better resolutions to political and ethnic differences.

The South African Contribution

In South Africa, the 1914–18 war has long been dismissed by some as an 'imperialist' conflict, reflecting perhaps a lack of understanding of the politics of the time, where, by the clear standards of the fight against Nazism (and that against apartheid), the morality of the struggle was more difficult to discern. The negative perception of the First World War has shifted lately, with greater acknowledgement being given to the role played by so-called 'non-white' troops in the world wars.

While the casualty rate among the Australians was the highest proportionately (with 215,000 casualties – or 65% – of the 417,000 recruits, including 59,000 dead), the South African commitment was very high as a percentage of its overall population. Over 146,000 white males and 382 nurses volunteered for service, plus 15,000 coloureds and nearly 83,000 of the Native Labour Contingent. Of the total of 265,775 volunteers, 12,452 were killed in action or died as a result of active service in this Great War.

Delville Wood

The initial Somme plan had envisaged the British Fourth Army under Sir Henry Rawlinson breaking the first and second German lines of fortifications, first from Serre to Montauban, and then through Thiepval, Guillemont and Pozieres, with the French army focusing on the southern sector around Peronne, from Maurepas to Flaucourt. It soon became clear that the 'Big Push' had met with only limited success especially in the southern sector, and the limited advances quickly came under determined German counter-attacks. It soon became a war of attrition. The attacks became concentrated after 1 July on the horseshoe of woods north of Montauban and after 14 July – Delville, High and Trônes Woods, and Waterlot Farm.

The South African contingent to the Western Front comprised:

- 1st SA Infantry Brigade, comprising the 1st, 2nd, 3rd and 4th SA Infantry Regiments and No. 1 SA Field Ambulance. This Brigade served from 1916 until the end of the war, and distinguished itself at Delville Wood in July 1916 and in holding up the German advance at Marrieres Wood in 1918.
- The 71st, 72nd, 73rd, 74th, 75th and 125th South African Siege Batteries, Royal Garrison Artillery.
- No.1 General Hospital.
- XV South African Signal Company.
- No. 7 and No. 8 South African Light Operating Railway Companies.
- The 84th South African Miscellaneous Trades Company, Royal Engineers.
- Nos. 22, 5, 2, 8, 10 and 11 Horse Transport Companies, Army Service Corps.
- 43 battalions of the South African Native Labour Corps. The responsibilities of this group included the movement of large quantities of supplies for the Allied effort, the laying and repairing of roads and railways, tree felling and timber cutting, and battlefield clearance.

Delville Wood, 2005. The inscription reads:
'Here in a shallow trench stood the battle headquarters of the South African Infantry Brigade during fighting in Delville Wood.' (GM)

On 15 July, the 1st South African Regiment and 27 Brigade were ordered to capture the town of Longueval near Delville Wood, but were unable to do so. The remainder of the South African Brigade under the command of Lt.-Colonel W E C Tanner was ordered into the fray to capture the Wood, and did so by the morning of 15 July, apart from strong German positions on the western corner. Although several attempts were made to unseat the Germans, these failed, and the attacking troops had to endure considerable shelling and counter-attacks. On 18 July, the German 76 Brigade launched a major counter-attack resulting in the recapture of much of the town of Longueval, with the South Africans only holding onto a small corner of the Wood on its southeastern edge. By this time Tanner, who had been wounded, had handed over command to Lt.-Colonel E F Thackeray. On 20 July, the 9th Division, of which the South Africans formed part, was relieved by soldiers of the 3rd Division following a desperate note from Thackeray to Brig.-General Henry T Lukin, the commanding officer of the SA Brigade:

> Urgent. My men are on their last legs. I cannot keep some of them awake. They drop with their rifles in their hands and sleep in spite of heavy shelling. We are expecting an attack. Even that cannot keep some of them from dropping down. Food and water has not reached us for two days . . . I am alone with Phillips, who is wounded, and only a couple of Sgts. Please relieve these men today without fail, as I fear they have come to the end of their endurance.[3]

The South Africans had hung on in the face of the German attacks, but at a tremendous cost.

Delville Wood eluded capture until 27 August, but not until it had been a killing field for both the Allies and Germans. It was only secured from German counter-attacks and shelling by 3 September. The 9th (Scottish) Division (part of XIII Corps, commanded by Lt.-General Walter Congreve VC[4] suffered 314

officer and 7,203 other rank casualties in the first three weeks of July. The remaining German 76 Regiment numbered just 10 officers and 250 other ranks from 2,700 all ranks.[5]

When the South Africans were relieved at Delville Wood at 16h15 on 20 July, they had suffered over 2,000 casualties. Of these, 662 men had been killed and 104 more were to die of their wounds. Thackeray led just 140 men and two remaining officers, Lt. Edward Phillips and Second-Lt. Garnet Green, out of 'Devil's Wood', both of whom, like him, had been wounded. The South African Brigade had entered the Wood with 121 officers and 3,032 other ranks. Just 29 officers and 751 other ranks answered the roll call on 21 July.

On that day, the survivors paraded before Brig.-General Lukin, a tough veteran of the Anglo-Zulu War of 1879, who was moved to tears at the presence of the 29 officers and the 751 men.[6] Enemy artillery fire, which had reached rates exceeding 400 shells per minute, coupled with incessant rain had reduced the landscape to mud, water, shell holes and broken tree stumps. The remains of 538 South Africans lie in unmarked graves in the wood and are commemorated along with 72,089 others on the Thiepval Memorial to the Missing.

The Somme is thus inextricably linked emotionally with South Africa. As one British writer has noted:

> There are three places . . . which should be marked by us. One is the slope of the Hawthorn Ridge, looking down on the Y Ravine, where the Newfoundland men attacked. Another is that slope in Delville Wood where the South Africans attacked. The third is all that great expanse from Sausage Valley to the windmill which the Australians won and held. Our own men lie as it was written for them. But over the graves on these places it should be graven, that these men came from

many thousands of miles away to help their fellow-men in trouble, and that here they lie in the mud, as they choose.[7]

The South African Infantry Brigade continued to serve on the Western Front, suffering more than 4,000 fatal casualties and winning two Victoria Crosses: those by Private W F Faulds at Delville Wood, and, later, the second by Lance-Corporal W H Hewitt at Ypres.

Second Battle of the Somme

In the second battle of the Somme, the South Africans again distinguished themselves, this time in defending Marrieres Wood in the face of the final German offensive in March 1918, ironically only a few kilometres from Longueval. The 1918 offensive – Operation Michael – was the final, desperate throw of the dice for the Kaiser's army. But their advance – preceded by a barrage of 6,000 guns, a larger number than that used by the British offensive on the Somme in July 1916, the British offensive at El Alamein in October 1942, and the Allies against Saddam Hussein's Iraqi Army in 1991 added together – ran out of steam after initially taking back all and more of the ground won by the Allies in the 1916 offensive. The German offensive ground to a halt east of the cathedral town of Amiens, with the British

Four South Africans earned citations for the VC at Delville Wood: Lt.-Colonel Thackeray, Lieutenant Walter Hill, Sergeant John Naisby, and Private William Frederick Faulds. All of these, apart from Faulds, were turned down, Thackeray receiving the Distinguished Service Order (DSO), Hill a 'Mentioned in Dispatches', and Naisby the Distinguished Conduct Medal (DCM).

The citation for Faulds reads: 'For most conspicuous bravery and devotion to duty. A bombing party under Lieut. Craig attempted to rush over 40 yards of ground which lay between the British and enemy trenches. Coming under very heavy rifle- and machine-gun fire the officer and the majority of the party were killed or wounded. Unable to move, Lieut. Craig lay midway between the two lines of trench, the ground being quite open. In full daylight Private Faulds, accompanied by two other men, climbed over the parapet, ran out, picked up the officer, and carried him back, one man being severely wounded in so doing. Two days later Private Faulds again showed most conspicuous bravery in going out alone to bring in a wounded man, and carried him nearly half a mile to a dressing station, subsequently rejoining his platoon. The artillery fire was at the time so intense that stretcher bearers and others considered that any attempt to bring in the wounded man meant certain death. This risk Private Faulds faced unflinchingly, and his bravery was crowned with success. The VC was gazetted on 9 September 1916. Faulds, who was promoted to Lieutenant in May 1917, was taken prisoner in the battle for Marrieres Wood in March 1918. After the war he returned to Kimberley but later moved to Bulawayo. He served in Abyssinia in World War II with the rank of Captain, and died in Salisbury, Rhodesia in August 1950.[15]

Bill Hewitt, who fought at Delville Wood, was wounded later at Warlencourt and at Ypres where, on 20 September 1917, he earned the VC. He returned to Africa to farm in Natal and Kenya, and served as a Major in the Second World War.

Delville Wood today. (*GM*)

Army and dominion forces now functioning effectively across all arms and nations, stopping the Germans outside Amiens in what became known as the 'black day of the German Army' on 8 August 1918, and pushing them back through France and Belgium. Once the main Hindenburg line was broken in September 1918, Germany, facing offensives on four different fronts and coupled with the crippling effects of the naval blockade, was convinced to sue for peace. The Great War was over.

The battlefields of the Somme were once a sight of terrible carnage, with corpses and the bloated carcasses of horses strewn everywhere, the ground thick with gorged flies. Today those fields, once swept by artillery and rifle-fire, are a model of tranquillity and rural life.

Remembering the Somme and the Fallen

Writing on the 50th anniversary of the Somme, one veteran said that 'When it comes up to 75 years, we'll all be dead . . . and the Somme will seem as abstract as Waterloo'.[8] Yet this and other battle sites are frequently visited. The Commonwealth War Graves Commission maintains immaculately some 240 cemeteries and memorial sites around the Somme alone. Each of these cemeteries has its own story to tell – of their location relative to the battlefield, and of the men who lie there. Many of them are adjacent to the battlefield where the men fought, or are the site of casualty-clearing stations or field hospitals were men died of their wounds. But their constant feature is the distinctive simplicity of their design,

121

and the stone of remembrance (designed by Sir Edward Luytens) and cross of sacrifice (the work of Sir Reginald Bloomfield).

A number, too, of French and German cemeteries dot the landscape, even though 80% of the half a million Germans who fell have no known resting place.

Delville Wood – or 'Devil's Wood' as it became known to the troops – is today a 63-hectare site of an SA National Memorial and Museum inaugurated in 1926 and 1986 respectively. The Herbert Baker-designed memorial stands at the end of an oak-lined avenue grown from South African trees.

The statue on the arch of the monument represents unity between Afrikaans and English South Africans, with Castor and Pollux set with a single-steed between them. This was deemed an important symbol in a war fought just over a decade after the Anglo-Boer War and against which there was considerable (and understandable) Afrikaner resistance.

In the politics of the time, this memorial perhaps expectedly overlooked the contribution of the SA Native Labour Corps (SANLC) to the conflict. Yet the South African bond with the tragedy of 1914–18 was strengthened with the loss of 607 men of this contingent when the troopship *SS Mendi* taking them to France was sunk after a collision with the *SS Darro* in the English Channel off the Isle of Wight. They are commemorated today on the Hollybrook Memorial at Southampton in the United Kingdom 'for those who have no grave but the sea'.

The number of brown and black soldiers who volunteered for military service in both world wars, Ian Gleeson notes, 'accounted for a sizeable percentage of the South African military effort.'[9] Of the 266,000 South Africans who served in the 1914–18 war, 84,000 were

Castor and Pollux atop the SA Memorial at Delville Wood, with the Museum in the background. (*GM*)

'non-white' soldiers. The percentage was even higher in the Second World War – 123,000 of a total of 335,000 men and women. The fatalities suffered by Indian, coloured and black units in World War I was 3,901 (including 938 of the SANLC and including the 607 of the *Mendi* disaster) of the total number of 12,452 South African servicemen who were killed in action or died as a result of active service; and in the 1939–45 war, 2,300 of the 9,500 killed in action or who died on duty were 'non-white'.

The policy in both wars was that 'non-white' soldiers would serve in non-combatant functions – stretcher-bearers, orderlies, drivers, labourers – but by the Second World War, 'practical exigencies made it imperative to arm those soldiers deployed in combat areas.'[10] But, Gleeson notes, 'Smuts and Botha got round this by putting them in Imperial Units, where the British footed the bill, which enabled the coloured units to be armed in Palestine where the Cape Corps fought with valour at the Battle of Square Hill.' In the Second World War, non-white units were armed as part of other units simply by dint of geographic distance from Pretoria.[11]

The Native Labour Corps came to France in early 1917. Some 25,000 men of the SA Native Labour Corps volunteered for overseas service, carrying out mainly transport and supply work in France around the ports and lines of communication and sometimes in the forward areas. King George V recognised their contribution, on inspecting the contingent at Abbeville in 1917, as 'part of my great armies which are fighting for the liberty and freedom of my subjects of all races and creeds throughout Europe.'[12]

Most of the burials in the Arques-la-Bataille Cemetery are of men of this contingent, many of whom died at No 1 General Labour Hospital established at the SANLC camp southeast of Dieppe, mainly of tuberculosis and acute bronchitis as a result of the severe winters. The cemetery also contains a memorial, erected by their comrades, to all men of the Corps who died in France. The inscription on the Memorial reads:

To the memory of those natives of the South African Native Labour Corps who crossed the seas in response to the call of their great chief, King George V, and laid down their lives in France for the British Empire 1914–18. This memorial is erected by their comrades.

One can only speculate why men such as Private Shadrack Funyufunyu, Corporal Lonegone Bapadene or Private Tati might have an-

General Smuts inspects SA Native Corps troops, France, 1917. (*IWM Q5105*)

swered the call to go to France: adventure, money, a job, a higher calling for King and Country? Whatever the case, their sacrifice was crucial to the war effort. As Gleeson, the author of the excellent *The Unknown Force – Black, Indian and Coloured Soldiers through Two World Wars*, remarked:

> Black soldiers were, in many respects, an afterthought and a convenient reserve in the minds of those who ran the country and its armed forces at the outbreak of hostilities in both world conflicts. Because of the existing politics and prejudices they could not be used in a combatant capacity and were relegated to the more menial tasks and unimposing functions. Simply because they were black or brown, they were told they could not fight.

They were then, Gleeson observes, treated as second-class citizens in their own country and were thus considered second-class soldiers, though their record of gallantry contradicts this impression.[13] As Gleeson notes:

> In the end the high hopes of the returning soldiers soon turned to disappointment and finally bitterness, as they went home with a cash payment of a few pounds, some with a bicycle; others with a new set of carpenter's tools; and all with a simple khaki suit. Their white colleagues at least had the media, their business connections, their political representatives and, finally, the ballot box in 1948, through which they could vent their anger.[14]

Across the road from the Museum and Memorial in Longueval is the Delville Wood Cemetery. Of the 5,439 soldiers buried here, two-thirds are unknown, grim testimony to the epic struggle in the wood opposite. Here 152 South Africans have their final resting place.

It is said that a trench could, on the one hand be a (relatively) safe and dry place to be, but also one that was a target for the enemy and his artillery, or a place where men waited before intense action and feared death 'not so much for themselves, but the future of their families, their sweethearts and friends.' The sometimes forgotten aspect of the loss of life in war is the experience of the 'other victims', those who were left behind by the physical casualties, whose lives were forever altered and who, more than likely, never had a chance to say goodbye or even partake in a burial ceremony.

The Somme was the bloodiest day in the British Army's long history. It was undoubtedly a battle less of tactical brilliance than simple attrition. Was it futile? Perhaps. Was it necessary and inevitable? Probably. Was it a victory? Maybe. Was it a waste? Undoubtedly. Today its many memorials are a brooding presence to the profound sense of loss, grief and waste of the Battle of the Somme, particularly when one considers that the average age of those killed was under 26 years. Indeed, those who experienced the 1914–18 conflict said that it was the 'war to end all wars'. It is scripture to humankind's failing that it was not. As one captain noted then: 'Those who talk of the next war are people who never suffered in a front line trench; for never again will those who have come back, advocate another war'. Now, nearly 90 years on, with the passing of the last of the generation of veterans, it will in the future be not so much a case of 'do you remember?' but of 'lest we forget'. Not to do so would undermine the foundations of the peace that Europe has enjoyed since 1945 – based, no doubt, on their justified hatred of war and their profound understanding of the costs of war.

CEMETERIES, MEMORIALS AND VISITOR CENTRES

Belgium

Nearly 205,000 Commonwealth war dead of the two world wars and over 3,900 of other nationalities are buried or commemorated in the Kingdom of Belgium in 210 **Commonwealth war cemeteries** and more than 400 other sites. Of the war dead, over 102,000 who have no known graves are commemorated on memorials. The most notable is the **Menin Gate Memorial at Ypres**, commemorating the names of 55,000 soldiers who fell in the Ypres salient from the start of the war until 15 August 1917 or who simply disappeared.

The Sir Herbert Baker-designed **Tyne Cot Memorial in Tyne Cot Cemetery** at Passchendaele, is in the largest of all Commonwealth war cemeteries with 12,000 gravesites and a memorial wall commemorating almost 35,000 soldiers who died after 15 August 1917 and who are not listed on the Menin Gate. No wonder Sir Winston Churchill said of Ypres: 'A more sacred place for the British race does not exist in the world.' The Menin Gate bears 560 South African commemorations.

France

Nearly 575,000 Commonwealth war dead of the two world wars and over 12,700 of other nationalities are buried or commemorated in France in 818 **Commission war cemeteries**, 496 non-constructed plots and more than 1,600 small plots or single graves in communal cemeteries. Of the war dead, nearly 218,000 who have no known grave are commemorated on memorials; the largest being the **Thiepval Memorial on the Somme** which carries the names

Ancre Cemetery, the Somme. (*GM*)

of over 73,000 British and South African men (the other Empire forces are commemorated on their own memorials or elsewhere) who have no known grave and who fell on the Somme between July 1915 and 20 March 1918. The work of architect Sir Edward Luytens (who, with Sir Herbert Baker, designed, too, the Union Buildings in Pretoria and Delhi's Parliament), it is the largest British war memorial in the world.

The village of **Combles** was entered in the early morning of 26 August 1916 by units of the 56th (London) Division and of the French Army; and it remained in Allied occupation until 24 March 1918 when it was captured after a stubborn stand by the South African Brigade at Marrieres Wood. It was retaken on the 29th of August 1918 by the 18th Division. The cemetery was first used in October 1916 by French troops, but the 94 French graves made in 1916 have been removed to another cemetery. The first British burials took place in December 1916. In June, July and August, 194 German soldiers were buried in what was afterwards called Plot I, but these graves, too, have been removed. There are now over 1,500 1914–18 war casualties commemorated on this site. Of these, over half are unidentified. Special memorials were erected for nine soldiers from the United Kingdom and one from South Africa known or believed to be buried among them.

Arques-la-Bataille is a small town six kilometres south-east of Dieppe on the Dieppe-Neufchatel-en-Bray Road. **Arques-la-Bataille Cemetery** is reached by taking the road from Martin Eglise to St Aubin le Cauf on the D51, or by taking the D54 from Dieppe. The cemetery is to be found at the end of a winding country track indicated by a CWGC sign. There are now 381 burials of the 1914–18 war in the cemetery, 270 of which are of the SA Native Labour Corps, the remainder being Indian and Chinese labourers, who were with the British Army.

Around 50,000 visitors call on the **museum and cemetery at Delville Wood** annually in the town of **Longueval**.

The museum, inaugurated in an overtly political move by P W Botha in 1984 (in an effort to improve South Africa's international reputation in the apartheid years), is a replica of the Cape Town Castle and is dedicated to the South African contribution to the two world wars and the war in Korea. The interior includes a series of bas-reliefs depicting South African soldiers in action in these three wars. There is also an excellent bookshop. Tel: +33(03) 22 85 02 17; fax: +33(03) 22 85 79 99. The museum is open from February to November, except on Mondays and public holidays.

Other significant cemeteries and memorials for South Africans in France are at **Thiepval** (830 commemorations), **Pozieres** (321 commemorations), **Brown's Copse Cemetery** (130 SA graves), **Warlencourt British Cemetery** (128 graves) and **Ors British Cemetery.**

The **Thiepval Memorial** (about 10km from Delville Wood) has an excellent museum and information centre recently opened about 50 metres from the memorial to the east. It has a well-stocked and competitively priced bookshop and a very informative series of displays. It is open all year around and entrance is free. Similarly, the **Museum to the Great War** in nearby Peronne (Tel: +33(03) 22 83 14 18; www.historial.org) is well worth a visit.

The town of **Albert** is a good base for exploring this region and is itself worth a few hours.

Albert and its Golden Virgin by night. (*GM*)

It was a centrepiece of action on the Somme, with 7,343 inhabitants in 1914 and just 120 in January 1919. It was occupied by the Germans from 29 August to 14 September 1914, evacuated after the Battle of the Marne, and then subject to 'ceaseless bombardment' thereafter. Its basilica housing the statue of the Golden Virgin was hit by a German shell and toppled over to the horizontal. Known as the 'Leaning Virgin', it 'gave rise to a belief among the troops that its fall would mean the end of the war.' After the British relieved the French units in the town in July 1915, it became a centre for their operations on the Somme. It was recaptured by the Germans in their final offensive in March 1918 and, when finally recovered by the British in August 1918, little remained of the town.

Websites

The website link to the Commonwealth War Graves Commission (CWGC) South African Member Government leaflet, which is available in PDF format, has some useful information and may help you to identify a number of cemeteries and memorials that you will want to visit. It can be downloaded from:

www.cwgc.org/cwgcinternet/CWGCLit/WG%20South%20Africa8pp.pdf

Also go to www.cwgc.org/cwgcinternet/search.aspx for general CWGC information.

HOW TO GET THERE AND WHERE TO STAY

From Paris to the Somme: Regular trains travel to the area from the Gare du Nord in Paris, and via the TGV from Roissy, Lille or Brussels. However, the best (and only practical) way to tour the battlefields is by car, as public transport in the area is limited, and caters for the locals moving between towns. To reach the Somme from Paris, the most practical route is via the A1 toll motorway entering from the 'Porte de la Chapelle' from the north circular road ('Boulevard périphérique') around the city. Exit at Roye for direct access to Amiens, or at Assevillers for access to Péronne, or at Bapaume to reach Pozières (follow the signs to Albert) or Bullecourt (follow the signs to Douai). The Paris-Amiens route is about 150km.

From Paris to Longueval: Longueval is reached on the D20 via the D929 and then D104 from Albert. To get to Delville Wood, continue through Longueval village and follow the signs to the South African Memorial.

The battlesites in the Somme are extraordinarily well sign-posted, perfect for the tourist and explorer. It is recommended, however, that one purchases a **battle-guide** such as the outstanding Holt's series, which can be easily obtained at most museums and information centres, including the comprehensive new facility at the Thiepval Memorial.

Personal guides can be hired at virtually every town, though these can vary greatly in quality and cost.

Search 'Somme' on the **Internet** and a vast range of travelling possibilities exist. Some options are **self-drive** (which is a highly recommended and inexpensive way), others **package tours**, including: Salient Tours, Bartlett's Battlefield Journeys, Milestone Tours, Holt's Battlefield Tours, Battlefield Tours Limited, and the War Research Society Battlefield Memorial and Pilgrimage Tours. See for example:
www.somme-normandy-tours.com
www.battlefieldtours.co.uk

Outside the village of Longueval, Somme.
(ME)

WHERE TO STAY

A good place to start any tour from is the **town of Albert**, just 8km west from the Thiepval Memorial. As with most French battlefield towns, there is a very helpful tourist information office with details of accommodation and places to see. Expect to pay around 40–50 Euro per night for a bed in a two-star hotel, and perhaps half that for a B&B *Chambres d' Hôtes*. (Remember that hotels get more expensive the closer one gets to Paris.)

Recommended in Albert is the Hotel de la Paix +33 (0)3 22 75 01 64 and the Hotel de la Basilique +33 (0)3 22 75 04 71, email: hotel-de-la-basilique@wanadoo.fr

The Somme Tourist Board (*Comité du Tourisme de La Somme*) is the official regional tourist body, which can be contacted at: 21 rue Ernest Cauvin, Amiens (phone: +33 (0)3 22 71 22 71; fax: +33 (0)3 22 71 22 69; email: accueil@somme-tourisme.com; internet: http://www.somme-tourisme.com). It is open Mondays to Fridays from 09h00-12h30 and 13h30-17h30 (16h30 on Fridays).

For those wishing to visit **Verdun** and the **Maginot line** to the north, there is an informative tourist office in Verdun, which will also assist with suitable accommodation in the area. Also go to: www.ligne-maginot-fort-de-fermont.asso.fr for tours of the remaining Maginot defences at Fermont. Please note that many of the Verdun forts and sights are closed during January, though this should not deter the self-drive tourist.

Although he was not present at Delville Wood, Jan Smuts's contribution to the Empire cause in both world wars was immense, and the more unusual given his background as a Boer commander in the war against the British only 15 years before Delville Wood.

Not only was Smuts a political giant in South Africa, prominent or dominant in its politics for 50 years, but his counsel was also sought in Britain, Europe and the United States. The only other modern politicians whose longevity can be compared with that of Smuts are Winston Churchill and Fidel Castro. When Smuts lost his parliamentary seat of Standerton in the 1948 general election for whites (no other South Africans had the vote), the shock was tremendous. For the tens of thousands of 'Springbok' servicemen who volunteered to fight on Britain's side in two world wars, his stature was comparable to that of Churchill. Even his enemies would acknowledge his massive contribution to South Africa, and in his spartan personal tastes and selfless dedication to service, he was comparable to the greatest South African of them all, Nelson Mandela. No other statesman of the century could offer Smuts' intellectual brilliance; few apart from Mandela can have matched his dedication, in principle at any rate, to reconciliation as the greatest political virtue.

It was the British politician Enoch Powell who pointed out that all political careers end in death or failure, and there were many who felt that Smuts had failed to address himself effectively to the issue of political rights for blacks. But in this he was a man of his time, and it is often forgotten that he was already in his fourth decade at the time of the Second Anglo-Boer War. One of his biographers, Kenneth Ingham, summed up his political position after his 1948 defeat in words that might have been appropriate in describing much of his career: 'Smuts, though a hero to many, seemed aloof and unsympathetic to many others. For the latter his ideas were too rigid or too unconcerned with popular feeling. When he remained steadfast, his critics condemned him as obdurate. When his pronouncements showed greater flexibility, they said he was still the old "slim Jannie" whose word could not be trusted. Louis Botha might have broken through that wall of hostility. Smuts had not the warmth of character to do it.'

Field Marshal JAN CHRISTIAAN SMUTS was born on the farm Boplaas in Riebeeck-West in the Cape on 24 May 1870. Smuts enrolled at Stellenbosch University where he quickly distinguished himself before graduating in 1891, winning the Ebden Scholarship for overseas study. From 1892–1894, he attended Cambridge University where he gained a Double First with distinction in the Law Tripos, whereafter he practised as a lawyer in Cape Town and Johannesburg. In April 1897, he married Sybella Margaretha (Isie) Krige (later better known as 'Ouma Smuts'), and the next year he was appointed as State Attorney in the Transvaal, where he soon drew the attention of Kruger and his cabinet.

During the Second Anglo-Boer war he served with distinction, first under General Koos de la Rey and later as Commandant-General of the Republican Forces in the Cape. After the war he practised as a lawyer in Pretoria. In 1907, when he was only 37 years old, he was appointed as Minister of Interior and Minister of Education in the Transvaal government. From 1909–10, he served as a delegate to the National Convention, which drafted the Constitution of the Union of South Africa. In the years 1910–15, he served as Minister of Defence, Minister of Interior and Minister of Mines, and from 1915–19 as Minister of Defence and Minister of Finance.

With the advent of the First World War in 1914 he was appointed Major-General and in 1915 was placed in command of the Southern Force during the German South West African campaign. He was soon promoted to Lieutenant-General and from 1916–17 served as General Officer Commanding of all forces in German East Africa. In the period 1917–18 he was also a member of the Imperial War Cabinet (the only person to have served in this capacity in both wars). In 1919, he was the representative for South Africa at the signing of the Peace of Versailles and was viewed as instrumental in the creation of the League of Nations.

In the next five years he became Prime Minister, Minister of Defence and Minister of Native Affairs, and from 1924–33 Leader of the Opposition. Thereafter he served as Deputy Prime Minister and Minister of Justice, and in the critical period 1939-48, after he led South Africa into the war against Nazi Germany, as Prime Minister, Minister of Defence and Minister of External (Foreign) Affairs. Promoted to Field Marshal by King George VI in 1941, he acted as Commander-in-Chief of the Union Defence Forces and Rhodesian Forces during the Second World War.

At the end of the war, he was again instrumental in the creation of a world body, this time the United Nations. Smuts proposed the insertion of a Preamble to the Charter of the United Nations, which would contain 'a declaration of human rights and of the common faith'. The Preamble adopted by the UN at the San Francisco Conference in 1945 contained most of the elements of Smuts's original draft. His reference to the use of legal sanctions to safeguard human rights was, however, omitted, but his vision of a world government dedicated to the preservation of world peace, the maintenance of human rights and the eradication of the root causes of political strife were adopted. The Preamble ironically reinforced those values inimical to apartheid in South Africa, and Smuts soon came under attack at the UN for his government's racial policies.

Having lost the 1948 election (and his own Standerton seat) to the National Party in 1948, he died on 11 September 1950 on his farm Doornkloof at Irene near Pretoria. The Field Marshal's many international honours include his chancellorship of the Universities of Cambridge and Cape Town, and his appointment as a Privy Councillor.

Various war veteran-oriented societies, including the General Smuts Foundation, have promoted Smuts's home at Doornkloof as a national site. The Smuts House Museum can be contacted at (012) 667-1176 or at smutshouse@worldonline.co.za. In the last ten years, the house has come into its own as a 'House Museum' after the return of General Smuts's study from the SA Institute of International Affairs (SAIIA) at Smuts House on the Wits campus, and after the restoration of Doornkloof.

REFERENCES AND FURTHER READING

Malcolm Brown, *Somme*. London: Pan with the Imperial War Museum, 1996.

Nigel Cave, *Delville Wood: Somme*. Barnsley: Leo Cooper, Pen and Sword Books, 2003.

Barry Cuttell, *148 days on the Somme*. Peterborough: GMS Enterprises, 2000.

Martin Marix Evans, *Battlefields of World War 1*. Wiltshire: Airlife, 2004.

Toni and Valmai Holt, *Battlefields of the First World War*. London: Parkgate, 1995.

Alistair Horne, *The Price of Glory: Verdun 1916*. London: Penguin, 1993.

Jean-Pascal Soudagne, *La Ligne Maginot*. ECPAD, 2004.

Hew Strachan, *The First World War*. London: Simon and Schuster, 2003.

Ian Uys, *Rollcall*. Germiston/Gibraltar: Ashanti/Uys Publishers, 1991.

Verdun: The Battlefield and its Surroundings. Verdun Tourist Office.

NOTES

1   General Sir Anthony Farrar-Hockley, *The Somme*. London: Pan Books, 1966.

2   German medical officer Stephen Westman cited in Malcolm Brown, *Somme*. London: Pan with the Imperial War Museum, 1996.

3   Cited in Ian Uys, *Rollcall. The Delville Wood Story*. Johannesburg: Uys Publishers in association with Ashanti Publishing, 1991, p.113.

4   Congreve won his VC at Colenso in the South African War in 1899 for his part in the attempt to save the life of Lieutenant Freddie Roberts. His son, Major Billy Congreve, was killed while reconnoitring the situation near Delville Wood on 20 July. For his conspicuous bravery he, too, was awarded the VC. This is one of only three cases where father and son have won the VC.

5   See Nigel Cave, *Delville Wood: Somme*. Barnsley: Leo Cooper, Pen and Sword Books, 2003, pp. 25–27.

6   Uys, *op cit*, p.117.

7   John Masefield, *The Battle of the Somme*. London: Heinemann, 1919, cited in Brown, *ibid*.

8   Lance-Corporal Sydney Appleyard cited in Brown, *ibid*, p.341.

9   Ian Gleeson, *The Unknown Force: Black, Indian and Coloured Soldiers Through Two World Wars*. Rivonia: Ashanti, 1994, p.x.

10 *Ibid*.

11 Telephonic interview with Ian Gleeson, 24 November 2005.

12 At *http://www.cwgc.org/cwgcinternet/CWGCLit/CWG%20South%20Africa8pp.pdf*.

13 In the First World War, four white and six black NCOs of the SANLC were awarded the Meritorious Service Medal. In the same war, members of the Cape Corps earned 11 Distinguished Conduct Medals (DCM), seven Military Medals and two Belgian decorations for deeds of bravery. During the Second World War, 39 medals for gallantry and distinguished conduct were awarded to the men of the 'Non-European Army Services' (including one DCM, 29 Military Medals, and nine British Empire Medals), plus seventy 'Mentions in Dispatches', fifteen King's Commendations, one award of the King's Medal for Bravery, and over a hundred Chief of the General Staff's Commendations.

14 *Ibid*, p.265.

15 Uys, *op cit*, p.173.

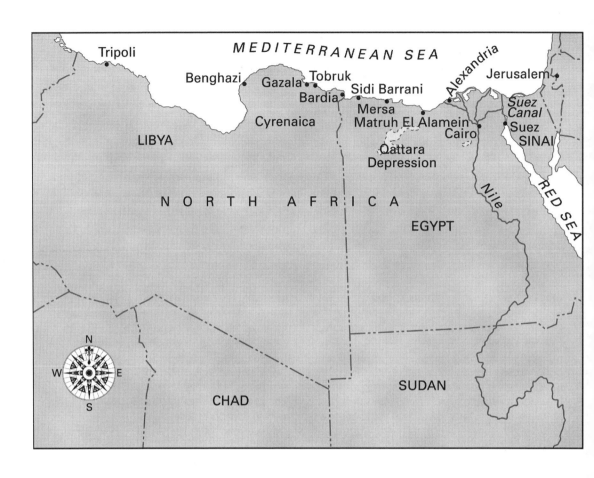

The Western Desert: El Alamein
1942–1943

The battle which is now about to begin will be one of the
decisive battles of history. It will be the turning point of the war.
Lt.-General Bernard Montgomery,
Personal Message to the Troops, 23 October 1942.

At exactly 21h40 on 23 October 1942, a thousand-gun barrage, the largest since the First World War, signalled the start of the final Battle of Alamein. It was the culmination of a series of engagements that had seen the initiative in the desert swung back and forth for nearly three years from late 1940 to early 1943.

The North African desert itself was not worth fighting for, of course, but command of it held the key to the defence of Egypt and perhaps the war itself. The British-led presence in the Middle East was 'the connecting cog round which revolved the great wheels of the Allied coalition'. Aside from its strategic presence in Cairo and Alexandria, it was not only the obstacle to German control of the oilfields in Iraq and Persia (now Iran), but also 'the moral and physical prop' that kept Turkey out of the Axis. It also offered protection to a struggling Soviet Union's southern underbelly, and kept the hope of a British victory alive, with implications for the nature and scope of the United States' participation. If the Middle East Command had folded at Alamein, the outcome of the war could have been different – if not a German victory,

133

then a conditional peace and an even more devastating nuclear conclusion.

South Africans volunteered in their tens of thousands in World War II, joining British and other Commonwealth forces to fight the scourge of Nazism. South Africa was the only country that participated in that war whose forces consisted entirely of volunteers. Many of the Springboks, as they called themselves, played an important role 'Up North' in the Western Desert. The Eighth Army contained South Africans in just about every arm of service: artillery, engineers, armoured cars, signals, quartermaster and medical services. There were pilots, ground crew and drivers; nurses, railwaymen, water surveyors and camouflage specialists. And there were the infantry brigades of the 1st and 2nd SA Divisions. Among the famous units involved were the Rand Light Infantry, the Royal Natal Carbineers, the Transvaal Scottish and the Cape Town Highlanders. By mid-1942 nearly 75,000 South Africans were serving in the Middle East.

The British and their allies, mainly from Australia, New Zealand, South Africa and India, were supplied from the eastern end of the vast battlefield, from their great bases centred on the ancient Egyptian cities of Cairo and Alexandria. The Germans and Italians – two of the Axis powers – were sustained from the west through the Libyan ports of Tripoli and Benghazi, which in turn were fed by naval convoys coming south across the Mediterranean from Italy.

The Western Desert, said one of the German commanders, 'is very wide in area, but very limited in the number of soldiers,' allow-

The grave of Private R S Hancock, age 20, Rand Light Infantry, El Alamein Cemetery, Egypt. (GM)

ing the Generalfeldmarschall to 'apply practically naval tactics.'[1] Operations traversed a battlefield some 3,000km long and several hundred kilometres deep. Then as now, it was a brutally hard, hot, and dusty environment, varying in shades from incandescent white to light brown. Dust and the hot desert wind – the vicious *khamseen* – together were capable of stopping operations entirely, clogging up tank tracks and carburettors, and infiltrating into fuel, food and the soldiers themselves.

In many ways it was the simplest of battlefields: no civilians, few animals, no buildings beyond the few settlements that hugged the coastline. There was almost no water, no food and virtually no landmarks or proper roads, and just a single-line coastal railway of limited reach. Men spoke of navigating through the desert as if they were at sea. Any occasional piece of high ground, usually almost imperceptible in the surrounding flatness, was fought over bitterly. Success in the desert required lorries, tanks and artillery, as well as air superiority and engineers capable of sowing and lifting mines; and, in the end, the infantry had to take and secure the ground.

Nothing was possible without constant renewal of supplies: the desert was aptly described as a tactician's paradise and a quartermaster's nightmare. Every litre of water and petrol had to be transported to the battlefield, often over hundreds of kilometres. More fuel was consumed by the lorries carrying petrol for the tanks than by the tanks themselves in action. This emphasis on logistics created a paradox: the more rapidly and successfully a general advanced, the greater the problems he created for himself. It was as if each army was tied to a gigantic elastic band – the further it moved away from its source of supply, the more resistance there was to further advance.

While coastal resorts have sprung up since 1942 scarring the white beaches, the hinterland is still inhabited by few people, apart from the occasional passing Bedouin 'going from nowhere to nowhere', and with little sign of animal and plant life except the occasional horned viper and scorpion, ubiquitous flies and fleas, and the *jerboa* – the 'desert rat'. As Jocelyn Brooke wrote in 'Landscape from Tobruk':

This land was made for War. As glass
Resists the bite of vitriol, so this hard
And calcined earth rejects
The battle's hot, corrosive hand, no green
And virginal countryside for War
To violate. This land is hard,
Inviolable; the battle's aftermath
Presents no ravaged and emotive scene,
No landscape á la Goya. Here are no trees.
Uprooted, gutted farms; the unsalvaged scrap –
The scattered petrol-cans, the upturned
And abandoned truck, the fallen Heinkel; all
The rusted and angular detritus
Of war, seems scarcely to impinge
Upon the hard, resistant surface of
This lunar land . . .*

It is a tough, unyielding earth made for war and not for easy living. The men who served here were often at risk as much from disease as they were from the enemy – although there was a certain spartan cleanliness to life out in the desert itself. In Egypt, 'disease had a medieval virulence, and a friend with whom one drank at supper time might be dead and buried before the next day's breakfast.'[2]

As the ranks of the generation of soldiers who participated in the desert campaign over seventy years ago start thinning and memories falter, the great offensives, operations, bat-

* From John Lehmann (Ed.), The Penguin New Writing, No. 21. London/New York: Penguin Books, 1944, p149.

tles, missions and skirmishes that drew them to this part of the African continent should be recalled and remembered, just as the sacrifice and the reasons for which this war was fought should not be forgotten. The obscure railway halt 130km west of Alexandria, Tel al Alamein – pronounced 'Alameen' and meaning 'the hill of twin cairns' – has become synonymous with the desert war, but it is only part of a series of battles crisscrossing the desert and ranging the coastline from Tripoli to Alexandria. And although many Commonwealth soldiers participated in the final Battle of El Alamein in October 1942 (220,000 men, including around 15,000 South Africans) – as Thucydides reminds us, those that take part in a campaign often know least about it.

The desert war may be portrayed as the last of the conflicts in which chivalry and comradeship between enemies played a part, due mainly to the mutual struggle of the two sides against the elements, the swarming flies and pervasive, invasive dust. It was as much at times a 'private war' as one between foes. But it was nevertheless brutal and costly. Some 100,000 men lost their lives over the three years of fighting.

Even the tanks offered little protection: 'The demented ricochet within the steel trap, the spattered brains, the torn entrails of a gunner impossible to extricate, the charred skulls and calcinated bodies of boys who seconds before were alive and beautiful.' Or as Captain James Graham wrote of the fate of tank crews: 'A tank cannot readily be fought with corpses or bits of them in it, but one hesitates to tip a friend out into the unfeeling sand for the jackals to vandalise, and it was not uncommon for me to have to hold a grave-digging session after food and before sleep.'[3] Aside from the tension as to their fate, the discomfort of the

tank crews was considerable, inside a bucking, noisy machine, hot enough literally to fry an egg on the outside. Daylight hours were sometimes spent entirely inside a tank, with much of the night spent replenishing and maintaining the vehicle, or serving on 'stag' (guard) duty or radio watch.

The desert war was never part of Hitler's strategy. It had its source in Mussolini's declaration of war against the Allies on 10 June 1940. Italian forces invaded British-held Egypt that September, advancing just 100km inside the territory to build a series of fortified camps around Sidi Barani. In December 1940, the 30,000-strong Commonwealth army (without South African units at that stage) under the command of Major-General Richard O'Connor 'cut the wire' between Egypt and Libya, in what was supposed to be just a five-day operation. O'Connor advanced so rapidly that he captured 110,000 of Mussolini's troops in just two months. As Anthony Eden told Churchill: 'If I may debase a golden phrase, never before has so much been surrendered by so many to so few.'

Although there has long been a prevailing contempt for the capability of Italian troops, they often fought as bravely as any, but were let down by 'the [poor] Italian record in adapting operational concepts to technology'. Training was inadequate, communications neglected, equipment almost 'universally poor', doctrine inept, and the officer corps elitist and interested more in its own comforts than those of its troops.[4] And to add to their troubles, as their German allies were to discover three years later, in the desert the likely alternative to capture was death by thirst.

O'Connor's early successes were reversed, however, following the arrival of the German general Erwin Rommel's Deutsche Afrika Korps

ERWIN JOHANNES EUGEN ROMMEL – the 'Desert Fox' – is considered one of the most distinguished German soldiers of World War II.[5] Winston Churchill paid a remarkable tribute to him in 1942: 'We have a very daring and skilful opponent against us, and, may I say across the havoc of war, a great general.' One of his opponents in that desert war, General Sir Claude Auchinleck, was later to say that 'Germany produces many efficient generals: Rommel stood out amongst them because he had overcome the innate rigidity of the German military mind and was a master of improvisation.' In a general order in 1942, Auchinleck noted that 'there exists a real danger that our friend Rommel is becoming a kind of magician or bogeyman to our troops, who are talking far too much about him.'

Erwin Rommel was born in 1891, the son of a schoolmaster mathematician. He wanted to be an engineer, but his father opposed this, and instead he went into the army and was commissioned into the infantry in 1912. As a result of his record in the 1914-18 war, his biographer Desmond Young described Rommel as 'the perfect fighting animal, cold, cunning, ruthless, untiring, quick of decision, incredibly brave.' He received both the Iron Cross and Prussia's highest medal, the Pour le Mérite.

After the war Rommel's diaries, *Infanterie Greift An* (*Infantry Attacks*), were published and became a standard textbook, reportedly attracting Hitler's attention. He was placed in command of Hitler's personal protection battalion. In 1940, he was given command of the 7th Panzer Division, nicknamed the 'Ghost Division' for its speed and surprise. His success in the invasion of France was rewarded with his appointment as commander of the German troops sent to Libya in early 1941 to aid the Italian Army, thus forming the *Deutsche Afrika Korps*. Following Auchinleck's successful offensive to relieve Tobruk in 1941, Rommel counter-attacked, outmaneuvering, outwitting and outfighting British forces.

It has been suggested that Rommel's withdrawal of his army back to Tunisia following the defeat at El Alamein was a greater success than his capture of Tobruk – in contrast to the fate of the German Sixth Army at the Battle of Stalingrad under the command of Field Marshal Friedrich Paulus.

Antony Beevor compared the performance of the young Rommel and Paulus in World War I in *Stalingrad*.[6] 'Unlike Rommel, a robust leader prepared to ignore his superiors, Paulus possessed an exaggerated respect for the chain of command.' This empathy with his troops rather than blind obedience was to gain Rommel the ongoing loyalty of the Afrika Korps – despite the suffocating heat, biting cold, flies, poor diet and dust of the desert.

When Rommel was sent to command the Axis in North Africa, he was unknown to the Allies and simply one of many German tank commanders who had taken part in the Blitzkrieg that saw most of western Europe overrun by the Nazis in 1940. Within months of arriving in the Western Desert he had become a legend among the men of the Deutsche Afrika Korps. They regarded him with affectionate awe for his daring and his instinctive talent for handling armour in the vast space of the desert.

Rommel was the epitome of the battlefield commander rather than the staff officer. He personified the tactical virtues of mobility, surprise and relentless attack. His bravery bordered on recklessness. He insisted on sharing the arduous desert conditionswith his men, and was contemptuous of the way Italian officers ensured that they had better food than the men they commanded.

Rommel's repeated humiliation of the British armoured forces meant that he also achieved an iconic, almost mythical status among the soldiers of Eighth Army. They compared him favourably with their own generals, and there arose a powerful image - which endures to this day – of Rommel as 'the good German.' It would be argued that he was not a Nazi at all, merely a professional soldier carrying out orders. There was the story of how the Afrika Korps overran a New Zealand field hospital, and Rommel walked among the beds, chatting to patients as one soldier to another.

It was Rommel's fate to have his genius negated by Hitler's obsession with the invasion of the Soviet Union. For the general staff in Berlin, the African desert was usually seen as little more than a side-show, and Rommel as an irritation. He was always starved of supplies, and after the first Battle of Alamein in July 1941 the steadily increasing British weight of men and material meant that retreat and defeat for the Axis became inevitable.

Rommel was generous to his opponents. He was to say that Wavell was the only British commander who showed a touch of genius, and acknowledged Auchinleck's tactical skill in fighting him to a standstill at Alamein.

Rommel's last major command was over the German defences for the expected Allied invasion of Europe in 1944. Then he was suspected (probably wrongly) of involvement in the plot to kill Hitler in July of that year, and was given a choice by the Führer: take poison and receive a state funeral, or face public humiliation and execution. Rommel chose the poison, which he took in the back of a car in the woods.

(DAK) in February 1941, which had been sent to bail out Hitler's southern ally.

Rommel's mobile tactics and superior German equipment, especially the tanks and the Krupp 88mm gun (an anti-aircraft weapon that proved devastating when lowered for use against British tanks), were together perfectly suited to the desert war. But the mythology of Rommel does not match, at times, the reality of his successes and failures, his stubbornness, egocentrism and recklessness. He took risks, and sometimes got away with them. He was revered among his own troops because of his willingness to lead from the front; while Tommy Atkins admired Rommel precisely because he appeared to have everything the British commanders lacked – daring, genius, guts, luck and success. Rommel was also fortunate in that the British got distracted: the Greek campaign denuded O'Connor of forces just as he was poised to take Tripoli, while the Far East crisis and the entry of the Japanese into the war did much the same to Auchinleck's offensive in late 1941. Political pressure also played its part: Churchill was desperate for a victory, and pressured the Eighth Army to undertake a series of pointless offensives in 1941 before it was ready to do so.

But if Rommel was a tactical genius, he was not alone in seeing which way warfare was going. The desert bred its own style of warfare, the lessons which are still with us today. It saw the development of 'special forces' in guerrilla, insurgency-type formations – and the British were in the vanguard of their formation.

O'Connor's superior, Lt.-General Sir Archibald Wavell, was the overall Middle East commander in 1940 and early 1941. Nearly 25 years before, in 1917, Wavell had entered Jerusalem with General Allenby and T E Lawrence (Lawrence of Arabia). In 1935 he wrote, in reply to an enquiring subaltern in the Durham Light Infantry: 'A problem I have often considered is the motor guerrilla, who may be a prominent feature of the next war. This country (Egypt) is unlikely to be invaded; but if it was, consider what effect a corps of young men in motors or on motor bikes with a uniform coat and a rifle automatic might have on the enemy's communications.' The young subaltern, Lt. Fox Davies, had written originally suggesting that 'far more attention should be paid from the outset towards destroying the 'brains', that is the commanders and headquarters, from within, rather than on wasting time, men and ammunition on a formal attack on their external lines.'[7] Fox Davies later commanded a Long Range Desert Patrol, essentially the forerunner for David Stirling's Special Air Service brigade, well known for their clandestine operations behind enemy lines.

These lessons of guerrilla warfare had been learnt in the Boer War – and largely forgotten in the quagmire of the trenches of 1914–18. (In 2005 they were being relearned in Iraq by the US-led coalition, as it grappled with the transition from an anti-Saddam 'democratic revolution' to a counter-insurgency campaign.)

The South Africans had been deployed in the desert in June 1941, following their successful campaigns in East Africa, Abyssinia, Somalia and the Sudan as part of the British-led effort in driving the Italians out. From the first engagement on 16 December 1940 at El Wak in Italian Somaliland, through British Somaliland and the fall of Addis Ababa, until the final surrender of the Italian forces in May 1940, the South Africans notched up success after success against little opposition. The total South African casualties were 270 men including 73 killed in evicting 300,000 Italian forces from the two Somalilands, and what are now Eritrea and Ethiopia.

By mid-1941, Lt.-General Sir Claude Auchinleck had replaced Wavell as Commander-in-Chief Middle East. Auchinleck's first major offensive was Operation Crusader, which ran from November 1941 to January 1942.

Going into Crusader, the South African strength had been boosted to two divisions: 1st SA Division under the command of Major-General George Brink, and 2nd SA Division under Major-General I P de Villiers. The former was based at the port of Mersa Matruh, halfway between Alexandria and the border with Libya, the latter at Mareopolis near Alexandria.

On 21 November 1941, five days after the Crusader offensive started, the 5th SA Brigade (part of the 1st SA Division) was hammered

5th SA Brigade Gunners, Sidi Rezegh.

(*SR*)

The aftermath, Sidi Rezegh. (*SR*)

at Sidi Rezegh on the Libyan side of the border by more than 100 of Rommel's Panzers and mobile infantry, with the loss of 3,394 men killed, wounded and taken prisoner. However, the 1st SA Infantry Brigade distinguished itself at Taib el Essem on the western flank of the offensive, beating off an attack of Panzers with artillery fire. On the coast, the 2nd SA Division took the 8,000-strong Axis garrison at Bardia in December 1941, and in January Sollum and Halfaya Pass both fell to the South Africans – their major achievement before they were to be sucked into the defence of the Gazala line and Tobruk.

Rommel soon regained the initiative after Crusader, and his unexpected headlong charge into Libya culminated in the fall of Tobruk, leading to the capture of 13,400 South Afri-

cans and a sense of national military humiliation back home.

The Libyan port of Tobruk is blessed with an excellent deep-water harbour. During the war it was important to Allied and Axis forces alike, for the reception of supplies and reinforcements from Mediterranean shipping. In January 1941 it had been taken from the Italians by O'Connor's forces, and after the clearance of the demolitions in the harbour the port was usable and proved invaluable.

When Rommel commenced his first drive across the vast Cyrenaica region of eastern Libya towards Cairo and the Suez Canal, the Allies deemed it essential that Tobruk be held, and the resulting siege lasted from 11 April to 10 December 1941, when the Axis forces were driven back. They recovered far more quickly

The Gazala line. (*SR*)

than was expected and by early February 1942, it was the Allies' turn to fall back towards a line running southwards from Gazala to Bir Hakeim. Again orders were given to hold Tobruk, but it fell to Rommel on 21 June. It was only retaken five months later by the Eighth Army in their final sweep along the North African coast into Tunisia.

Major-General Hendrik Klopper, the South African commander of the Tobruk garrison, had sealed the fate of Tobruk with his final, confused message: 'Am sending mobile troops out tonight. Not possible to hold tomorrow. Mobile troops nearly nought. Enemy captured vehicles. Will resist to last man and round.' Klopper is remembered, more than a little unfairly, as 'Klop, Klop Klopper' – Rommel only had to knock at his door and he capitulated.

141

The collapse of Tobruk, a symbol of Allied resistance, was not only a blow to the troops and their leadership, but its repercussions were felt further afield. But this, some argue, is neither a correct nor a fair portrayal. The formal court of inquiry exonerated Klopper, finding that 'in view of the difficulties involved, it is questionable whether even the most experienced commander with a highly trained staff could have grappled with the problems in the time available.' Klopper's wartime colleague, Brigadier E P Hartshorn, restated in the book *Avenge Tobruk* Churchill's conclusion that 'the burden of blame falls upon the High Command rather than on General Klopper and still less on his troops.'[8] Ironically, it was Churchill who had placed great pressure on Auchinleck to invest in the holding of Tobruk.

David Chandler notes of Tobruk: 'Long sectors of the defences – including the anti-tank ditch – were in a state of ill-repair, and several large gaps existed in the minefields. Secondly, the prospects of any air support rapidly faded as the Desert Air Force hastily evacuated its forward bases . . . Thirdly, the Royal Navy could offer little hope of positive assistance. Finally, General Klopper was short of one vital piece of equipment which might have redressed some of these deficiencies – the anti-tank gun.'[9]

In a more recent assessment, Jon Latimer asserts: 'The second siege of the fortress could never be a repeat of the first, however brave the defenders. Furthermore, 2nd SA Division had never been issued with desert-worthy transport by the Eighth Army, so the South Africans were unable to manoeuvre even within their own brigade sectors except on foot.'[10]

But such analysis obviously was not available to the troops at the time, fed up with what they saw as bad leadership – which they compared unfavourably with Rommel's. 'Every-one believed he [Klopper] had sold out to the enemy,' said one soldier. Permitted by Rommel to address his fellow POWs at a temporary 'cage' at Derna, Klopper was heckled and booed and had to give up trying to deliver his message.[11] Paradoxically, the focus on Klopper's leadership (or lack of it) also does a disservice to Rommel's tactical brilliance. Instead of attacking Tobruk on its western defences, he swung round to cut in from the southeast, thereby also severing the line of retreat.

Klopper escaped as a POW from Sulmona after the capitulation of Italy in September 1943, and reached Allied lines 15 days later. Upon his return to South Africa he served as Chief of the General Staff before retiring to farm outside Pretoria.

Some good came from this humiliation, though. Churchill was in the presence of US president Franklin D Roosevelt when the latter was handed a telegram informing him of the fall of Tobruk. After the British prime minister growled; 'Defeat is one thing, disgrace is another,' Roosevelt responded by asking: 'How can we help?' and offered to supply 300 of the new Sherman tanks and 100 self-propelled 105mm howitzers under the US/UK lend-lease arrangement. These items would later help tip the balance in the Allies' favour at El Alamein.[12]

Nonetheless, Tobruk's collapse was seen as a slur on South African fighting abilities and their honour, which they were keen to defend. Upon entering a bar in Cairo, a group of South Africans were approached by Australians. 'Sit down, cobber, and take a drink' said one to the leading South African. 'You look all in. What's the matter – just run all the way from Tobruk?' As Jon Latimer observes: 'What followed was one of the most spectacular bar brawls the Middle East has seen, even taking into account the destruction of Shepheard's during the First World War.'[13]

Although Klopper picked up much of the blame for the fall of Tobruk, this conveniently obscures the responsibility (and failings) of the senior British leadership in this debacle and the fact that the majority of the troops present were British. Of the 35,000 Allied prisoners taken, 19,000 were British and 2,500 Indian.

Rommel's success had been stunning and he hungered for more, looking further east. By June 1942 there was panic in Cairo and Alexandria. The future of the Nile Delta itself and the vital oil fields seemed to hang in the balance; indeed, to the more pessimistic, was already as good as lost to the Axis. Women and children were evacuated; the Middle East fleet sailed from Alex. If the Germans broke through, the entire strategic balance of the war might be altered – and both sides knew that. The Allied cause might not recover from such a blow.

But the man in charge of Eighth Army, Auchinleck, decided calmly to make his stand near a nondescript railway station called El Alamein, just 95km from Alexandria. His army was bewildered but not demoralised, and he knew Rommel's troops were almost exhausted. The Allies' defensive tactical position was strong. Instead of having to defend a front stretching hundreds of kilometres to the south, and risk being outflanked yet again by Rommel, Auchinleck now had a front of only about 65km long. It stretched between the sea in the north, and the great Qattara Depression in the south – a swampy, muddy salt-flat that was impassable to vehicles. The line was narrow, but only relatively. It was the equivalent of the distance between Johannesburg and Pretoria and would have to be defended stoutly – and it was, with the Springboks playing a key role.

Having escaped from Tobruk, the 1st South African Division under Dan Pienaar reached Alamein on 25 June and, with the remainder of the Eighth Army, immediately set about preparation of the defences. The 3rd SA Brigade occupied the El Alamein 'box', a fortified semi-circle of pill-boxes and trenches that had been prepared in 1941 but was never used. The 1st and 2nd SA Brigades were inserted between the box and Ruweisat Ridge.

The Order of Battle for 1st SA Division at the First Battle of El Alamein, a 'forward effective strength' of some 17,000 men:

1. 1st SA Infantry Brigade (commanded by Brigadier E P Hartshorn): Royal Natal Carbineers, Duke of Edinburgh's Own Rifles, Transvaal Scottish.
2. 2nd SA Infantry Brigade (Brigadier Evered Poole): Field Force Battalion, Natal Mounted Rifles, Cape Town Highlanders.
3. 3rd SA Infantry Brigade (Brigadier Bobby Palmer): Imperial Light Horse, Durban Light Infantry, Rand Light Infantry.
4. In Support: Regiment Botha and Regiment Steyn (machine guns), 3rd SA Armoured Car Regiment, 8th Royal Tank Regiment, South African Artillery (anti-tank, anti-aircraft, field regiments), engineers, signals, quartermaster services, field ambulances, brigade workshops and military police.
5. SAAF: Three squadrons of fighters, two squadrons of bombers, and one squadron of reconnaissance aircraft.

Rommel attacked and attacked again, but could not break through. Low on supplies, Rommel had been hoping for a quick, decisive breakthrough. His first move was on 1 July, a combined thrust involving the German 90th Light

MAJOR-GENERAL DAN PIENAAR CB, DSO and Bar, was killed with eleven others in an aircrash at Lake Victoria on 19 December 1942. At the time of his death, Pienaar was at the zenith of his military powers in a career that had begun in 1911 when he joined the Natal Police as a Trooper Second Class, aged 18.

Pienaar served with the South African Mounted Riflemen in the German South West African campaign (1914–15), and with the South African Field Artillery Brigade in German East Africa (1916–17), Egypt, Palestine and Syria. In 1918 he was commissioned into the Royal Artillery. In 1940, Pienaar, now a Colonel, was appointed as commander of the 1st South African Infantry Brigade. Promoted to the rank of Brigadier in October, he served with distinction in East Africa during the raid on El Wak (16 December 1940) for which he was awarded the DSO; the Battle of Combolcia (17–22 April 1941); the capture of Dessie (26 April 1941); and the attack on Amba Alagi (15 May 1941). In June 1941, Pienaar and his brigade were transferred to North Africa, again distinguishing themselves during the 'Crusader' offensive during the Battle of Taib el Essem (25 November 1941). Soon after that, Pienaar was promoted to Major-General and took over from Major-General George E Brink DSO as commander of the 1st South African Division, commanding the Division during the Battle of Gazala (26 May–14 June 1942), the defence of the Alamein line (1–9 July 1942) and in the Battle of El Alamein itself (23 October–4 November 1942).

Pienaar was not without his own personal demons and critics. His was known to have a weakness for drink, a habit he managed to cure only when deployed outside of South Africa in 1940. As Smuts put it in Pienaar's funeral oration: 'He first conquered himself and his own weakness and from that victory passed on to the greater victories for which he will remain famous.'[14]

A religious man, he was not enamoured with his British colleagues, and had numerous run-ins with his senior officers in Abyssinia, notably his Divisional Commander Major-General H E de R Wetherall, and those in the Western Desert. His sensitivity to British leadership was heightened by events at Tobruk, and even more so by Auchinleck's comment when giving him his orders about where to stand in the Alamein box: '. . . and, Pienaar, if you run away from here, you will have the honour of knowing you have lost the war for the British Empire.'

Pienaar was reportedly left speechless. Thus it is not surprising that he was apparently most taken with Montgomery: 'Man, . . . there's a General for us. We've never had anyone like this before – I'll follow that man – I'll follow him anywhere.'[15]

This may have had a bearing on his comment to an American war correspondent: 'Rommel will not get the Alexandria naval base; he will not get the Suez Canal; he will never dine in Cairo unless as a tourist after the war.'[16]

The 'Gun Park' at the SA Museum of Military History in Saxonwold is named after General Pienaar, while the adjoining hangar containing museum aircraft is named after General Brink.

Infantry Division and the 15th and 21st Panzer Divisions of the Afrika Korps. But the 90th Division were thrown off course by a sandstorm, making them easy targets for the South African guns. The 18th Indian Brigade at Deir el Shein mounted a heroic defence, repelling the advance of the Axis armour but being destroyed in the process. The remainder of July saw offensive and counter-offensive, with Auchinleck mounting no fewer than five major attempts to destroy Rommel's forces, costing 12,700 Allied casualties in the process. This phase concluded with both sides preparing their defences based on a series of elaborate minefields and tactical 'boxes' on the Allied side.

In those first two weeks of July, Egypt was saved. Rommel was not yet defeated, only thwarted; he would still provide tenacious and bloody opposition to the Allies. But in July 1942 he had his last chance to take Egypt before the British could build up their strength and supplies. That battle has became known to some military historians as the First Battle of Alamein.

The battle was a reminder, if one were needed, that a modern army required a considerable and complex logistical tail. By January 1941 it was calculated that a British division in the Middle East (some 18,000 men) required another 41,000 to maintain it in the field. Rommel had completely outrun his supply abilities in getting to Alamein, a situation worsened by the fact that just one in every four of his supply ships was reaching Tripoli and Tobruk; the rest were intercepted by the Royal Navy and Royal Air Force, operating out of Malta. By 2 September, Rommel wrote, 'Out of 5,000 tons of petrol which had been due to arrive by the 3rd, 2,600 tons had already been sunk and 1,500 tons were still in Italy.'[17] Many of the supplies which did make it to

North Africa 'consumed themselves' in their delivery to the front. Nonetheless, 'modern warfare is a matter of administration . . . the art of the possible'[18] – a key factor that Rommel failed to heed as he overextended his beloved DAK and its logistical backup in his race for Alexandria.

The Second Battle of Alamein followed 'the Auk's' dismissal as Commander-in-Chief of the Middle East (and Acting Commander of the Eighth Army) and his replacement in the field by Lt.-General Bernard Law Montgomery. It is also known as the Battle of Alam Halfa and lasted from 30 August to 9 September, with probing attacks from Rommel repulsed by the well-organised British defences and masterly defensive tactics by Montgomery.

That set the stage for the final and decisive battle, the Third Battle of Alamein – and the one that is generally associated with the name.

Montgomery built up his forces to outnumber the opposing German and Italian units. He left nothing to chance. The Allied army had 220,000 men to the Axis' 96,000; 800 aircraft to 300; 1,100 tanks including 270 heavy Shermans and 210 Grants, against 500 tanks comprising 200 German panzers with just 30 heavy Mark IVs. The Eighth Army was also supported by more than 1,000 artillery pieces, 800 anti-tank guns and 100 self-propelled guns. The Germans had only 24 of the legendary 88mm anti-tank and anti-aircraft weapons, and a number of short-range Italian field guns.

Monty's approach involved more than just technical and logistical support. He built his defences and battle-plans on those established by Auchinleck, with extensive use of minefields. It was based on an elaborate deception plan, reputedly hatched by British military intelligence at the Cecil Hotel in Alexandria. Instead of swinging south to attack the weaker Italian units, Montgomery concentrated his main strike on the central front, obliging Rommel to move his mobile units northwards.

It was a bloody, terrible battle that sometimes had to be waged hand-to-hand. The intensity was a shock to those in combat. As Private John Bain of the Gordon Highlanders (who achieved later literary fame as Vernon Scannell) remembered: 'All of that shrieking, whining venom is directed at you and at no one else. You hunch in your hole in the ground, reduce yourself to as small a thing as you can become, and you harden your muscles in a pitiful attempt at defying the jagged, burning teeth of the shrapnel. Involuntarily, you curl up into the foetal position except that your hands go down to protect your genitalia. Montgomery doesn't protect his privates, but Christ, I protect mine.'[19]

The perversely named Operation Lightfoot involved the clearances of two corridors through the enemy's minefield through which the armour would pass. For Rommel, who had returned from leave only on 25 October and whose stand-in commander, General Stumme, had died of a heart attack the previous day, it was a 'battle without hope'. During the period between 23 October and 1 November both sides consolidated their positions, with the Afrika Korps occupying an area known as 'Kidney Ridge,' a strategically important site 25km southwest of Alamein. The apparently flat desert yielded innumerable folds, ridges and depressions that were of incalculable tactical importance. At Alamein, as at Alam Halfa, names such as Kidney Ridge, Miteirya Ridge, Ruweisat Ridge and El Taqa Plateau were key areas of control and contest.

At Alamein, the 1st SA Division fought in the tactical 'box' alongside the Indian Division (an ironic partnership perhaps, given the years of political estrangement that followed between the two nations over racial discrimination), moving northwards to Miteirya Ridge in forming the southern flank. The battle honours list reads like a 'Who's Who' of South African regimental history. The three South African brigades comprised Royal Natal Carbineers, Duke of Edinburgh Own Rifles, Transvaal Scottish, Field Force Battalion, Natal Mounted Rifles, Cape Town Highlanders, Imperial Light Horse, Royal Durban Light Infantry and Rand Light Infantry.

After a week of bitter fighting, the next phase of the Allied offensive – Operation Supercharge – began, concentrating on the sector south of the Australian Division, intent on breaking the Axis resolve. The Afrika Korps defended for three days, but on the night of 3 November Rommel ordered his army to conduct a fighting withdrawal, accepting that Alamein was a lost cause, only for Hitler to overrule him and order the troops to carry on the defence. On 4 November, the Allies broke through the Korps's lines and forced them into a full-scale retreat, capturing scores of Italian and German troops. By 6 November, Rommel's Afrika Korps had arrived in the town of Sollum on the Egyptian-Libyan border with only 20 tanks remaining out of the 900 they had started with nine months earlier. The result was inevitable: lacking supplies and heavily outnumbered, the Afrika Korps fell back rapidly, with Tobruk being recaptured by 12 November and the fall of Tripoli on 23 January 1943. Tunis fell on 7 May that year, and the remaining 250,415 German and Italian troops surrendered five days later.

Churchill said of the victory at Alamein

The 4/6 SA Armoured Car Regiment distinguished itself at the Battle of Alamein, being the first unit to relieve Tobruk on 12 November 1942. It was a 'fashionable' outfit, which included among its officers Harry Oppenheimer. (SR)

that it was 'not the end. It is not even the beginning of the end. But it is, perhaps, the end of the beginning'. Victory in the Middle East was crucial to Britain, bolstering morale at a difficult time when victories were few and American materiel support limited.

As Montgomery's words to his officers and men on 23 October 1942 suggest, the Battle of El Alamein may have changed the course of the Second World War and global history, elevating a little-known railway station to the level of Waterloo, Balaclava, Isandlwana, the Somme and Stalingrad. On this dusty, heat-soaked plain – not unlike the Karoo in many respects – 20,000 soldiers lost their lives in a series of battles from July to November 1942. If the British and Commonwealth armies had failed at Alamein and Rommel's Korps had

smashed through to Alexandria and Cairo, not only Egypt and the Middle East, but also the survival of the Soviet Union and the future of Europe could have been dramatically affected.

It has been disparagingly said that 'if Rommel was an artist, Montgomery was an artisan'.[20] The mythology around Rommel is that of a superior general beaten only by a massively superior force at Alamein. General Siegfried Westphal, Rommel's Chief of Staff, observed: 'What really defeated Rommel in the end was a lack of supplies'.[21] Certainly the need to stop Rommel at Alamein was key in a wider concern about supply routes and lines of communication in the Mediterranean, centred around the British-held island of Malta – which was 'essential to success at Alamein, and victory at Alamein would be essential to relieving Malta'.[22]

The Military Career of Harry Oppenheimer*

HARRY OPPENHEIMER (28 October 1908–19 August 2000) is best known for his role as chairman of the Anglo American Corporation (1957–82) and De Beers Consolidated Mines, Ltd. (1957–84).

Yet the 1939–1945 war interrupted the careers of millions of people, including Oppenheimer's. On 26 January 1940 he applied for inclusion in the reserve of officers for the Union Defence Force (UDF), and a few days later was appointed to the rank of temporary Second Lieutenant. Within two months he had been called up for service with the intelligence section in the UDF.

After completing a number of courses and while based at the Chief of General Staff in Pretoria, he applied for a transfer to Number 5 Armoured Car Company of the South African Tank Corps in order to go 'up north' to see action. Accepted into the re-designated 4th South African Armoured Car Regiment, Lieutenant Oppenheimer sailed for North Africa and into the war against Germany and Italy.

In Alexandria German bombing raids were ongoing affairs, and on one occasion during training a German bomber crashed, nearly hitting the unit. Mr Oppenheimer recalled that while his men were cradling the dying German airmen it gave him the idea that 'war was rather silly.'

It was Oppenheimer's job to collate all the information gathered by the four sections of armoured cars, and to pass it on to divisional HQ. In mid-September 1941, when Rommel's Afrika Korps launched a major offensive, the HQ was attacked in the regiment's baptism of fire, forcing a withdrawal. Oppenheimer escaped capture thanks to a passing 25-pounder field-gun of the Royal Horse Artillery. On 21 November 1941, the HQ was attacked by Stuka dive-bombers. The Colonel of the Armoured Car regiment, after he had been awarded the DSO, wrote that the award was '. . . earned by the Regiment as a whole and not least by Harry [Oppenheimer] who has done his job with outstanding courage and good humour under very trying circumstances.'

By July 1942 Harry was back in South Africa and had taken up a new position at Coastal Command in Cape Town. He would remain in Cape Town until 1943 when he would be transferred back to Johannesburg with the rank of Captain.

* This is sourced from *http://www.bdb.co.za/kimberley/kimpub/on_track_17.htm*.

Should Auchinleck or Montgomery be given the credit for the victory at Alamein? It's a debate in part fuelled by the latter's personal antipathy towards his predecessor as well as his egotism, unedifying vanity and media savvy. The controversy was fuelled when Montgomery denigrated the generalship of Auchinleck in comments made to troops. Monty claimed that he had torn up Auchinleck's (non-existent) plans for withdrawal – an unnecessary slight perhaps, but arguably required to build up the morale of the Eighth Army so corroded by the helter-skelter retreat from Rommel.

Montgomery and Auchinleck did have in common a disdain for the life of what was known in the desert slang as the 'Gaberdine swine' – as the staff officers in Cairo were derogatorily known – referring to the material of their uniforms. 'Monty' and 'the Auk' preferred to slog it out with their men in the field. This attribute, along with his abrasive yet straightforward personality was arguably Montgomery's greatest strength. Yet it is sometimes forgotten that the future Viscount Montgomery of Alamein took over from Auchinleck only because of the death in an air crash of General 'Strafer' Gott, the Eighth Army Commander-designate.

Whatever the arguments about his abilities, his undoubted vanity and public relations touch, Montgomery was an inspiration to his men, particularly when measured against Auchinleck, who had taken the brunt of failure over the previous year. Egocentric to a fault, Montgomery, in the words of one of the soldiers who served under him, 'wasn't a nice man – but nice men don't win wars'. Churchill said of him: 'In defeat, unbeatable: in victory unbearable.' Yet Monty's three rules for commanding an army – good equipment, training and trust in leadership – were the necessary tonic for the time.

Doubts about British generalship were evident from the estimated 25,000 desertions during the retreat following Tobruk, and reflected the unreal atmosphere pervading in Cairo at the time. The Egyptian capital was from various accounts less of an efficient logistical and administrative centre than a hedonistic, gossip-fuelled escape between embassy parties, dinner and dancing at the Shepheard's Hotel, tea at Groppi's and various high-society trysts. The troops based in the Delta were dis-

Groppi's today. (*GM*)

missively referred to as 'Groppi's Light Horse' or 'Groppi's Hussars,' after the famous confectioner in Cairo.

Cairo was also a place, however, where the troops went to let their hair down, drown their sorrows, and relieve their frustrations in the seedier districts. Olivia Manning recalls: 'At Shepheard's . . . in surroundings as ponderous as a Pall Mall club . . . one night the vestibule was invaded by two Australian privates wearing potted palms on their heads. The civilians watched with delight as the Australians weaved about, stumbling against chairs and tripping over feet in suede desert boots, but the owners of the feet saw, heard and felt nothing. They stared at each other or at newspapers, knowing that no British officer in his senses would try and discipline an Australian drunk.'[23]

When Rommel's 1942 advance was not stopped at Tobruk, Sollum or even Mersa Matruh, Cairo's expatriate community was caught in a panic – known as 'The Flap' – when secret papers were burnt (Wednesday 1 July 1942 was known as 'Ash Wednesday' due to the falling soot from the burning documents) and the city paralysed with rumour and intrigue. But normality – if Cairo was 'normal' compared to the deprivations of the frontline – soon returned with the stabilisation of the Alamein Line.

While the levels of anxiety in the capital may have related to events at the front, their different worlds were reflected in the attitude of the commanders. General Neil Ritchie, for example, continued to have his shirts laundered in Cairo.[24] At the time of the opening salvo of the third battle of Alamein, the air commander Arthur Tedder was dining in Cairo with his wife. The demoralised state of the army was complicated by Egypt's reluctant

support for the Allied cause. A number of Egyptian military officers, including future president Anwar el Sadat, actively plotted against the British government. As Egypt's King Farouk put it, after being told in September 1939 of the need to strengthen British control over his country: 'Oh, all right. But when it's all over, for God's sake lay down the white man's burden, and go!'[25]

This may explain why Egyptians, despite having granted the land on which the various World War II cemeteries and memorials reside, seem to have little connection today with the war. In those war years, the Europeans were regarded as standing between Egypt and its independence. There was also an unbridgeable social divide. Inasmuch as there is sentiment today in Egypt towards the war, this revolves around the tourism potential and, more perniciously, the legacy of the millions of landmines laid in great swathes across the desert by German, Italian and British forces alike, and which continue to maim and claim the lives of Bedouin. Today there is little evidence of the detritus of war, apart from the odd memorial and local attempt at a museum, such as the 'Romel [sic] Cave' at Mersa Matruh (where the 1st SA Division was for a time headquartered). But a walk into the desert at Alamein still reveals the odd button or comb – and the mines are still out there.

When viewed over the longer term horizon of history, the outcome of Alamein contributed to the character of Western involvement in the Middle East and shaped relationships with regimes and institutions that perhaps understandably continue to bedevil international relations today.

Despite tense relationships among senior generals of the 'mother' country, the South Africans were respected soldiers, especially the

Then. Mersa Matruh, 1st SA Division HQ. (*SR*)

Now. Mersa Matruh today. (*GM*)

armoured car and artillery formations, and their leadership was sought at both the strategic and operational level. Churchill valued the advice of Prime Minister Jan Smuts, while commanders such as Generals Dan Pienaar, Commander of the 1st SA Division, his predecessor 'Uncle' George E Brink, and W H Evered Poole, commander of the 6th SA Division in Italy, were highly regarded.

But this was not just a land battle. The SA Air Force made an invaluable and occasionally overlooked contribution to the struggle on the ground. They had fought with considerable success in East Africa, despite their outdated and outnumbered machines, which initially included Hawker Fury, Gloster Gladiator and Hartbeest biplanes, and converted Junkers 86 and Fairey Battle bombers. By the time of Alamein, however, the SAAF formed a key component of the Desert Air Force (DAF), with 14 squadrons operating more than 200 modern aircraft, including Hawker Hurricane and Kittyhawk fighters, and Blenheim, Maryland, Boston and Baltimore light bombers.

The Battles of El Alamein – the battle for Egypt – were arguably the pinnacle of South African achievement and involvement in the Second World War. Their success not only stopped Rommel and the rot of British defeats, but helped to restore South African military pride after the Tobruk debacle. The all-volunteer nature of South African forces cemented, too, a longstanding national military tradition of a citizen-based army.

El Alamein is possibly the best remembered battle of Commonwealth forces in the Second World War, not least because it turned the seemingly unstoppable Nazi tide, but also in that it was the last battle of the war where Commonwealth forces achieved success under their own overall command. As Winston Churchill noted: 'Before Alamein we never had a victory. After Alamein we never had a defeat.'

A number of South Africans were decorated for their role in the desert battles, including Quentin Smythe VC and Gerard Norton VC, MM.

South African casualties at El Alamein were 734 out of a total for the Western Desert campaigns of 23,625, comprising 2,104 dead, 3,928 wounded and 14,247 POWs. No less than 227,281 South African white men and women volunteered for service in World War II. A further 123,088 'non-whites' also joined up. Of the total of 12,080 South African dead in the Second World War, the bulk (5,626) were from the 'white' land forces, 2,060 'white' airforce, 456 'white' naval, 1,584 'coloured', and 1,690 'natives'. A total of 2,473 were killed in action, while 6,160 died in service, including 34 members of the merchant navy.[26]

Most Africans served as medical aids, stretcher-bearers and in other non-combatant roles. But they were highly praised for their bravery. During the battle for El Alamein, Corporal Lucas Majozi was awarded the Distinguished Conduct Medal (DCM) for bringing in a wounded man through a minefield under heavy fire. Lance Corporal Job Maseko was awarded the Military Medal (MM) for single-handedly sinking an enemy steamer in Tobruk harbour while a prisoner of war.

Today, a total of 11,914 South African dead from the 1939–45 war are commemorated by the Commonwealth War Graves Commission (CWGC). South African casualties were relatively heavy at Alamein. Of the 7,970 buried at the Commonwealth cemetery in El Alamein, 495 are South Africans. Another 1,255 South Africans are commemorated on the memorial. South Africans who died in the West-

CAPTAIN QUENTIN SMYTHE VC, died in South Africa in October 1997, aged 81.

Smythe won a VC at Alem Hamza, Libya, on 5 June 1942, where he, although seriously wounded and losing much blood, managed single-handedly to obliterate a machine gun post, taking all the surviving crew prisoner. Then, again single-handedly and armed only with rifle and bayonet, he promptly did the same with an enemy anti-tank gun crew, after which he consolidated the position. However, because of the deterioration of the situation elsewhere, Smythe found himself ordered to withdraw. In spite of a vigorous attempt by the enemy to cut him off, he managed to lead his men back to their lines.

The Victoria Cross awarded Smythe for this action was the first VC won by a South African in the Second World War.

GERARD NORTON VC, MM, died on 29 October 2004, aged 89, leaving just 14 survivors of the Victoria Cross.

Norton won the Victoria Cross while seconded to the Ist/4th Battalion of The Royal Hampshire Regiment during the breaching of the Gothic Line in Italy in 1944. The regiment's task was to take the Monte Gridolfo feature, one of the key positions in the line and defended by a series of concrete strong-points with interlocking zones of fire.

The leading platoon of Norton's company was pinned down by flanking fire almost as soon as it had crossed the start line. Entirely on his own initiative and with complete disregard for his personal safety, Norton began to attack the enemy strong-points in turn. He silenced the first with a grenade. Then, alone and armed with his Thompson sub-machine-gun, he took on the crew of a second strongpoint from which the enemy were holding up the advance with their Spandaus. A ten-minute fire-fight ensued, at the end of which Norton had killed all but a handful of the enemy who surrendered.

Bringing his platoon forward to maintain the forward momentum, Norton cleared the cellar and upper rooms of a fortified house and took several more prisoners. Finally, although weak from loss of blood due to a head wound that had severed a vein, he led his platoon up the valley to capture the remaining enemy positions on his company objective. He was also wounded in the thigh during the course of the action.

Lucas Majozi, DCM, who single-handedly sunk
a steamer, while a prisoner of war. (*SR*)

ern Desert are also buried in a number of cemeteries elsewhere, notably in Knightsbridge War Cemetery in Acroma (where there are more than 420 SA dead), Tobruk (161) and Heliopolis in Cairo (226) where many of the wounded and sick of various battles were taken. The two cemeteries in Alexandria (Hadra and Chatby) house both WWI and WWII dead. The large number of so-called 'Cape Corps' and 'Native Military' contingent troops buried at Heliopolis, Hadra and El Alamein testifies to their considerable role in the South African effort.

Back in South Africa, there was a political impact from the involvement in the war. General Smuts had won a narrow 13-vote major-

ity in Parliament to bring South Africa into the war on the side of Britain, against General J B M Hertzog and the Nationalists who favoured neutrality. Entry by the Union into the war closely linked the fortunes of white South Africa and Smuts with the interests of the West and the British Empire. Yet this involvement arguably foreshortened Smuts's tenure as Prime Minister. He was voted out of office by the National Party in 1948. His and the ruling United Party's departure may have been hastened by the limited value of South Africa's war commitment to safeguarding white interests in the changing post-1945 environment. At the same time Smuts came under pressure at the United Nations – the very world body he helped to create – for the Union's racial policies. Sadly, for the next four decades the majority of white South Africans were to see a more radical form of these very policies as the 'solution' to securing white rule in South Africa.

With the National Party victory in 1948, there was soon a significant political cost to the senior officers who had participated in the war. The new Minister of Defence, F C Erasmus, purged the officer corps, including the Chief of Defence Staff-designate General Evered Poole, who was 'bowler-hatted' and sent off to become the South African representative on the Allied Military Control Council and, later, ambassador to Rome, Athens and Argentina. The sidelining of experienced officers, including Brigadier Jimmy Durrant CBE, DFC and Brigadier Peter Hingston, was followed by the so-called 'Midnight Ride' on 30 November 1953, when 14 selected senior officers received letters of dismissal. All had volunteered for war service. The new government turned its attention on citizen force units, focusing on standardising 'foreign' uniforms with the intention of subverting regimental traditions, and with the aim of reducing the number of 'English-speaking' units.

The unhappiness over South Africa's participation in the war, and the involvement of key Nationalists in anti-war, anti-government subversive organisations like the Ossewabrandwag (whose interned members included future SA prime minister B J Vorster), meant that South Africa's post-war military reorganisation was characterised by unfinished political business. The rapid disintegration of military capabilities repeated the post-1918 experience and, as in 1939, led to a sudden surge in military expenditure in the 1970s, as the change in regional and domestic political and security circumstances caught the National Party government by surprise.

For more than a generation after the war, South Africa's participation was a matter of pride or resentment, depending on where you stood. These standpoints also served to hobble and divert white politics from the real issues that demanded attention in the country's politic. Either way, South African soldiers played an important role at a vital stage of the war, and for many it would be the defining experience of their lives.

The 1992 Memorial Service

In October 1992, 50 years to the month after the Third Battle of Alamein, about 130 South African veterans returned to the desert. Following the release of Nelson Mandela and the unbanning of the ANC, the country's political isolation had crumbled just in time.

The pilgrimage centred on the 50th anniversary service at the British Commonwealth cemetery, out on the edge of the desert near the Alamein battleground. In 1967, at the 25th anniversary of the battle, there had been less than a dozen people present; this time there were nearly 5,000. All that Sunday morning before the service they moved down the dusty path, thousands of medals glinting in the hot desert sun. A few moved slowly – the very frail and disabled. But the vast majority of veterans had clearly made the arduous trip precisely because they were tough and in reasonably good health. Very few were under 70; some were touching 90.

The Commonwealth cemetery is open to the sky and wind. The more than 10,000 graves are laid out symmetrically, each with its simple headstone, and the men of different nationalities and ranks are placed at random. A South African sergeant's grave, with its Springbok head, might lie between those of a Black Watch officer and an Australian infantryman. From anywhere in the cemetery, bleak but well kept, you can look up and see the desert.

Peter Bunton, a veterinarian and farmer from Addo in the Eastern Cape, fought with the South African artillery at Alamein. His brother fell at his side in that battle; 50 years later, Peter came with his sister, Pauline McLachlan of Knysna, to lay a wreath. It was made of flowers from Peter's own garden, specially dried by a friend. He transported it carefully from his farm, guarding it constantly on his lap against the hazards of plane and bus travel.

Anne Kresfelder of Stellenbosch came to see the grave of the father she never knew; she was too young to remember him when he went Up North.

Govindsamy Naicker of Durban had joined up when he was 19, mainly in search of adventure; he became a driver and in the desert was attached to the Cameron Highlanders when he was captured.

Audrey Robinson of Namibia had been a nurse in the combat zone, at a casualty clearing station.

Dudley de Vaux, a Rand Light Infantry veteran, was pleased to have brought with him both his son Dudley and his grandson Gareth, aged 10.

Bertie Simpkins, another RLI member and later the commanding officer of his regiment, wore for the Sunday service the uniform that he had put on for the battle 50 years before. This excited much discreet interest – and respect.

At that memorial service the South Africans mingled with the veterans of other allied countries, all together for the first time in 50 years. The proceedings began with the marched entrance of a small guard of honour, found from soldiers of the present armed forces of Britain, Australia and New Zealand. Most unusually, the guard members carried no weapons, due to Egyptian sensitivities about foreign soldiers bearing arms on their territory. A few South African veterans noted resignedly that they were not represented in the guard – but then, nor were the Indian forces, whose veterans were, for whatever reason, not in evidence at all.

The guard was marched onto parade by the fiercely impressive Sergeant-Major Jackson of the Scots Guards. His clipped tones and air of iron discipline were remarked on approvingly by the old soldiers. In fact, the characteristic British sense of occasion and attention to detail – a simple service, but properly conducted – were both comforting and respectful towards the thousands of veterans.

Martial music was provided by the Band of the First Battalion, Worcestershire and Sherwood Foresters Regiment. The ushers, in dazzling white, were sailors from *HMS Argonaut*. The flag escort was provided by the Royal Marines, the Grenadier Guards and the Royal Air Force. There were pipers from the Queen's Own Highlanders and the Royal Irish Regiment. The Act of Remembrance was read by the Duke of Kent, representing the Queen:

> *They shall not grow old, as we who are left grow old;*
> *Age shall not weary them, nor the years condemn,*
> *At the going down of the sun and in the morning,*
> *We will remember them.*

And then the congregation responded, muttering in the gusty desert air: 'We will remember them . . .'

Wreaths were then laid at the Stone of Remembrance, after a procession of the standard-bearers (including those representing South Africa's veterans). The wrenching *'Lament'* was played by one of the pipers – and then the almost unbearable poignancy of *'The Last Post'*, sounded to perfection by Corporal Nelson McLeod of the Royal Green Jackets. After that, the minute's silence, disturbed only by the tugging of the desert breeze. Then, as if to summon back the living from their contemplation of the dead, the bugler sounded *'Reveille'*.

The then British Prime Minister, John Major, read from John, Chapter 15, verses 11–13: 'This is my commandment, that ye love one another as I have loved you. Greater love hath no man than this, that a man lay down his life for his friends.'

CEMETERIES, MEMORIALS AND VISITOR CENTRES

It is now more than sixty years since the final Battle of Alamein commenced. While there is little evidence of the war in North Africa today, what does serve as a reminder is the considerable number of Commonwealth, Italian and German cemeteries and memorials around El Alamein, and the cemeteries in Alexandria and Cairo, and further afield in Libya.

In Egypt, over 52,000 Commonwealth war dead of the two world wars and over 1,600 of other nationalities are buried or commemorated in 24 sites. Of the war dead, nearly 28,000 who have no known graves are commemorated on eight memorials.

Alexandria

The ancient port of Alexandria, once a centre of learning and high point of civilisation, lies 230km (approximately 4 hours by bus) from Cairo in the northeasterly direction.

The writer Lawrence Durrell, a British press officer in Egypt during the war, observed about the modern version of the city: 'Alexandria, princess and whore. The royal city and the *anus mundi*.' While its grand facades hint at the erstwhile status of its 100,000-strong European population (forced to leave by Nasser after the 1956 Suez crisis), the rest of the city remains a smaller version of Cairo with its whirling, snarling traffic and vitality.

As a rather exotic war-time destination, the city became the setting for the movie classic, *'Ice Cold in Alex'*, set in 1942, in which a British ambulance officer (played by John Mills) escapes from the siege in Tobruk and tries to get his passengers to safety in Alexandria, where he dreams of having an ice-cold glass of beer. His passengers include two nurses (the heroine played by Sylvia Syms), a Sergeant-Major, and a South African officer (Anthony Quayle). Despite the fact that the South African has apparently saved the group from the Germans, it turns out he is a German spy. Yet the camaraderie forged in the heat of the desert sees Quayle being handed over as a German after they have enjoyed their joined beers together, rather than letting him be shot as a spy.

Alexandria (Hadra) War Memorial Cemetery is on the eastern side of Alexandria, south of the main carriageway to Aboukir, known as Al Horaya, near the University of Alexandria. The cemetery is on the road to Sharia Manara.

In March 1915, the base of the Mediterranean Expeditionary Force was transferred to Alexandria from Mudros and the city became a camp and hospital centre for Empire and French troops. Among the medical units established there were the 17th, 19th, 21st, 78th and 87th General Hospitals and No 5 Indian Hospital. After the Gallipoli campaign of 1915, Alexandria remained an important hospital centre during later operations in Egypt and Palestine. The port was much used by hospital ships and troop transports bringing

Hadra Cemetery, Alexandria. (*GM*)

reinforcements and carrying the sick and wounded out of the theatres of war.

This cemetery was begun in April 1916 when it was realised that the cemetery at Chatby would not be large enough. Most of the burials were made from the Alexandria hospitals, but a number of graves from December 1917 were due to the loss of the troop transports 'Aragon' and 'Osmanieh', sunk by torpedo and mine as they entered the port. The cemetery continued in use until December 1919 but later some graves were brought in from small burial grounds in the Western Desert, Maadia and Rosetta.

During the Second World War, Alexandria was again an important hospital centre, taking casualties from campaigns in the Western Desert, Greece, Crete, the Aegean Islands and the Mediterranean. Rest camps and hostels were also established there together with a powerful anti-aircraft base. Alexandria was also the communications centre for the Middle and Near East and became the headquarters of the Military Police. The cemetery at Hadra was extended for Second World War burials and was used from 1941. There are now 1,700 First World War burials in the cemetery and 1,305 from the Second World War. The cemetery also contains war graves of other nationalities and some non-war burials.

Alexandria (Chatby) Military and War Memorial Cemetery is located close to Hadra, within the main Alexandria Cemetery complex, which is bordered by Al Horaya on the south and the electric tramway parallel with Sharia Champollion on the north. The cemetery has a central front entrance building with an archway secured by a metal gate, leading into it from two small, grassed areas which form part of the roadside in front of the cemetery.

The Chatby Cemetery (originally the Garrison Cemetery) was used for burials until April 1916, when a new cemetery was opened at Hadra. Thereafter, burials at Chatby were infrequent, although some graves were brought into the cemetery after the war from other burial grounds in the area. There are 2,259 First World War burials in the cemetery and 503 from the Second World War. The cemetery also contains war graves of other nationalities and many non-war and military graves, some of which date from 1882. **The Chatby Memorial** stands at the eastern end of the cemetery and commemorates almost 1,000 Commonwealth servicemen who died during the First World War and have no other grave but the sea. Many of them were lost when hospital ships or transports were sunk in the Mediterranean, sailing to or from Alexandria. Others died of wounds or sickness while aboard such vessels and were buried at sea.

As an agency service on behalf of the United Kingdom Ministry of Defence, the Commonwealth War Graves Commission maintains 4,550 non-world-war graves in Egypt. The Commission also cares for the civilian graves in the Tel el Kebir 1882 Plot and Cairo and Port Said British Protestant Cemeteries, the latter using funds derived from the former cemetery committees, and the South African Memorial in El Alamein War Cemetery, on behalf of the South African government.

As there were few operations in Egypt during the 1914–18 War, the graves from that war are mainly those of sailors who died off the coast of Egypt, and of other servicemen who died of disease or accident or who were casualties from the Gallipoli and Palestine campaigns.

The graves of the 1939–45 War are of servicemen who died in action in the Western Desert or while stationed in the Suez Canal

Zone and Lower Egypt. Almost all the battle casualties are buried in El Alamein and Halfaya Sollum War Cemeteries; sailors buried at sea with no known graves are commemorated on their manning port memorials at Chatham, Plymouth and Portsmouth. Some 3,200 Commonwealth airmen who died in the Egyptian theatre of operations, and who have no known graves, are included among those commemorated on the Alamein Memorial.

Alamein

Alamein is a 5,000-strong coastal village, bypassed by the main coast road and approximately 130km west of Alexandria, on the road to Mersa Matruh.

The **El Alamein War Cemetery** lies off the road, slightly beyond a ridge, and is indicated by road direction signs approximately 25m before the low metal gates and stone wing walls. These are situated centrally at the road edge at the head of the access path into the cemetery. The Cross of Sacrifice feature may be seen from the road.

This cemetery contains the graves of men who died at all stages of the Western Desert campaigns, brought in from a wide area, but especially those who died in the Battle of El Alamein at the end of October 1942 and in the period immediately before that. The cemetery and memorial were designed by Sir Hubert Worthington, and the memorial was unveiled by Field Marshal Montgomery in 1951.

The El Alamein Cemetery and Memorial Cloisters. The inscription above the arches reads: 'Within this cloister are inscribed the names of the soldiers and airmen of the British Commonwealth and Empire who died fighting on land or in the air where two continents meet and to whom the fortune of war denied a known and honoured grave. With their fellows who rest in this cemetery, with their comrades in arms of the Royal Navy and with the seamen of the Merchant Navy they preserved for the West the link with the East and turned the tide of the war.' (GM)

The cemetery now contains 7,240 Commonwealth burials of the Second World War, of which 815 are unidentified. There are also 102 war graves of other nationalities. **The Alamein Cremation Memorial**, which stands in the southeastern part of El Alamein War Cemetery, commemorates more than 600 men whose remains were cremated in Egypt and Libya during the war, in accordance with their faith. The entrance to the cemetery is formed by the **Alamein Memorial**.

The Land Forces panels on this memorial commemorate more than 8,500 soldiers of the Commonwealth who died in the campaigns in Egypt and Libya, and in the operations of the Eighth Army in Tunisia up to 19 February 1943, and who have no known grave. It also commemorates those who served and died in Syria, Lebanon, Iraq and Persia. The Air Forces panels commemorate more than 3,000 airmen of the Commonwealth who died in the campaigns in Egypt, Libya, Syria, Lebanon, Iraq, Greece, Crete and the Aegean, Ethiopia, Eritrea and the Somalilands, the Sudan, East Africa, Aden and Madagascar, and who have no known grave. Those who served with the Rhodesian and South African Air Training Scheme and have no known grave are also commemorated here.

In 1987 the Commission agreed to the construction of an Australian memorial at El Alamein. The CWGC maintains on repayment, the **Australian Memorial at Tobruk** and the **South African Memorial at Knightsbridge** on behalf of their respective governments.

The German Memorial – *Deutsche Kriegsgraberstatte* – about five kilometres west of the Commonwealth Cemetery was commemorated on 28 October 1959. The octagonal, slab-sided ossuary contains the remains of 4,313 soldiers brought together from various burial sites. The stone for the building was sourced in Mersa Matruh; the vaults containing the soldiers' remains are detailed with regions in Germany. Thirty-one soldiers of various nationalities are commemorated in a mosaic in the centre of the building.

The Italian Memorial is the most ostentatious of all at El Alamein, situated 3km to the west of the German Memorial.

En route you will pass a plaque marking the furthest point of the Axis advance with the inscription: *Manco la Fortuna, Non Il Valore, 1.7.1942, Alessandria 111km* (Lacking Fortune, Not Valour).

The dedication at the site reads: 'To 4,800 soldiers, sailors and airmen. The desert and sea did not give back 38,000 who are missing.' Completed in 1960, it comprises an avenue dotted with the names of various Italian fighting units leading to a marble ossuary containing the remains of 4,634 soldiers, 2,447 of whom are identified and 2,187 'ignoti'.

The War Museum (entrance E£10,00; camera E£5,00; video/camcorder E£20,00) 600m from the Commonwealth Cemetery and Memorial offers a good overview of the battle, complete with electronic map boards and all sorts of exhibits.

Some 150km west of El Alamein lies the port of **Mersa Matruh**. There is little to recommend it, including the 'Romel [sic] Cave' museum which takes all of an unhurried five minutes to stroll through. (Entrance is E£5, cameras another E£10 or E£15 for video recorders). The beaches are, like most spots on the coast, strikingly white and the sea deep blue, but you

Above: Italian plaque marking the furthest point of the Axis advance. (*GM*)

Right: The Rommel Museum at Mersa Matruh is hardly worth a visit, though its signs are quaintly intriguing. Egypt takes little interest in maintaining any of the battle sites or, for that matter, using them as tourist attractions. (*GM*)

will have to pay to swim and women are required to cover up.

Cairo, its surrounds and further afield

General Headquarters, Middle East Command, set up in Cairo shortly before the 1939–1945 War, and remained there all through the war years. In January 1941, the Royal Air Force Sector Headquarters for Fighter Defence Canal Zone was established. The same war period also saw Cairo utilised again as a hospital centre. The command included labour units recruited in the countries in which British forces were operating – notably Palestine, Syria, Iraq and Persia (now Iran) and also from colonies such as Mauritius and the Seychelles; from Malta and Cyprus, from Basutoland (now Lesotho) and Bechuanaland (Botswana); and from East and West Africa. Troops from the Dominions and India, and those of the Allies – Poles, Free French, Czechs and others – all had to be

provided for separately. Cairo was also a place where soldiers went when they were on leave, and many facilities sprung up as a result.

Heliopolis War Cemetery is situated opposite El Banat College in Nabil el Wakkard Street, and access to the cemetery is from this street. Heliopolis is a major suburb of Cairo, ten kilometres to the northeast of the main city centre and approximately six kilometres from the airport.

The cemetery was opened in October 1941, and took casualties from the many hospitals established during the Western Desert campaigns. On the rear boundary of the Heliopolis Cemetery is the **Heliopolis (Aden) Memorial**, commemorating the Aden Field Force and sailors and soldiers who fell in the defence of Aden in the 1914–1918 War, and who have no known grave.

Also within Heliopolis, on panels erected in the entrance pavilion, is the **Heliopolis (Port Tew-**

fik) **Memorial** commemorating the Indian dead of the Great War in Egypt and Palestine. When the First World War broke out, Cairo became the headquarters of the British garrison in Egypt, and the principal military hospital was in the citadel. The city became a main hospital centre for Gallipoli in 1915. During the war it dealt with the sick and wounded from the army in Egypt and Palestine.

Libya

Libya proved impossibly difficult to get to for the purposes of researching this chapter. Despite numerous overtures to the Libyan Embassy in Pretoria, no assistance was forthcoming. It would appear, however, that the best means to travel there is either on an organised tour (only one, *Midas Tours,* based in the UK, would appear to run tours to Tobruk: email info@midastours.co.uk) or by road through Egypt. It is advised that visas be acquired before you leave South Africa, while the CWGC advises that 'Visitors to Libya need to obtain approval from the People's Tourism Committee in Batnan.'

The war burials in Libya resulted from the advance and subsequent withdrawal in 1940–41, the siege of Tobruk in 1941 and the final campaign through North Africa in 1942–43. The graves contained in **Tripoli Military and Benghazi British Military Cemeteries** are of British servicemen, their dependants and service employees who died in Libya between the end of the Second World War and the departure of British servicemen in 1972.

In Libya, over 8,500 Commonwealth war dead from the Second World War and 235 of other nationalities are buried in four sites. Soldiers who died in Libya, and airmen who died while based there, and who have no known graves

are commemorated on the Alamein Memorial in El Alamein War Cemetery, Egypt. The Commission also cares for 588 non-world-war graves on behalf of the United Kingdom Ministry of Defence as an agency service.

Tobruk

Tobruk is on the Mediterranean coast in Libya, about 600km west from Alexandria. Leaving the port of Tobruk on the main road east to Alexandria, one travels about seven kilometres inland to reach **Tobruk War Cemetery**, set back about 100m along a clearly visible access track branching from the left side of the road.

The Libyan port of Tobruk today.

The cemetery incorporates the burial ground used during the siege. The memorial erected there at the time by the Australians has been replaced by a permanent memorial of similar design. Many battlefield graves in the desert have been brought into this cemetery. There are now 2,282 Commonwealth servicemen from 1939–45 buried or commemorated in the cemetery, including 1,200 British, 560 Australian and 160 South Africans. Of the burials, 171 are unidentified but special memorials commemorate a number of casualties known or believed to be buried among them. The cemetery also contains 171 war graves of other nationalities, most of them Polish.

HOW TO GET THERE AND WHERE TO STAY

From Cairo to Alexandria (230km): Alexandria can be reached by plane, train or bus from Cairo. There are two classes of trains (the faster Turbini trains; and the slower French variety). The air-conditioned Superjet buses do the 230km journey in quick time along the two main roads – the scenic Delta via the town of Tanta, or the desert road which passes through Giza. There are regular petrol stops and restaurants en route for the 4–5hr journey.

From Cairo to El Alamein (300km): El Alamein is best reached by bus or taxi from Cairo or Alexandria on the Mersa Matruh road. A taxi will cost around E£100 from Alexandria in a round trip. Expect to pay around one-tenth of this amount for a bus or minibus from Alex.

Taxis from Cairo to El Alamein (which can be managed in a single day in a round trip of 300km) will cost US$150–200. Public transport does do the route, but bank on it taking several days to get to your destination and back.

El Alamein, railway station, 2005. (*GM*)

WHERE TO STAY:

Alexandria is a natural jumping-off point for Alamein, which is about 130km further west. There are a variety of cheap places to stay in Alexandria. The beer, however, contrary to the legend of the film, is not cheap – deference to Egypt's Islamic status, no doubt. Hotels range from the **Sofitel Cecil** (where Churchill, Durrell, Noel Coward and Somerset Maugham all stayed) at around US$120 per night, to lower-end bargains at less than 10% of this amount.

Tourist Information Office: (+2046) 484-3380. This helpful **tourist office** is just round the corner from the Sofitel Cecil Hotel, on Sa'ad Zaghloul Square.

Alamein offers a number of places to stay, the most luxurious being the recently-opened **Movenpick Resort** (in July 2004), about 20km from the Commonwealth Cemetery in the direction of Libya. Rooms (in the off-season) were US$75 B&B per night. Contact: elalamein@movenpick.com; fax. (+2046) 419-0069.

Also recommended is the **El-Alamein Hotel** at Sidi Abd El-Rahman (US$49,00 for a single, US$81,00 for a double room, breakfast extra). Note that there are usually different rates for foreigners and Egyptians. Contact: elalamein@egoth.com.eg; fax. (+2046) 468-0341.

There is reputed to be a dead-Panzer park about ten kilometres towards the desert from the road at Sidi Abd El-Rahman, but numerous enquiries were met with only blank stares.

REFERENCES AND FURTHER READING

J A I Agar-Hamilton and L C F Turner, *The Sidi Rezegh Battles 1941*. Cape Town: Oxford University Press, 1957.

J A I Agar-Hamilton and L C F Turner, *Crisis in the Desert*. Cape Town: Oxford University Press, 1958.

Vic Alhadeff, *South Africa in Two World Wars: A Newspaper History*. Cape Town: Don Nelson, 1979.

Corelli Barnett, *The Desert Generals*. London: Pan, 1983.

John Bierman and Colin Smith, *The Battle of Alamein: Turning Point, World War II*. London: Viking, 2002.

James Ambrose Brown, *A Gathering of Eagles*. Cape Town: Purnell, 1970.

James Ambrose Brown, *Retreat to Victory*. Gibraltar: Ashanti, 1990.

Artemis Cooper, *Cairo in the War, 1939–45*. London: Penguin, 1995.

Nigel Hamilton, *Master of the Battlefield: Monty's War Years 1942–1944*. New York: McGraw-Hill, 1983.

Frank Harrison, *Tobruk: The Great Siege Reassessed*. London: Brockhampton Press, 1999.

E P Hartshorn, *Avenge Tobruk*. Cape Town: Purnell, 1960.

John Keene (ed), *South Africa in World War 2*. Johannesburg, Human & Rouseau, 1995.

Jon Latimer, *Alamein*. London: John Murray, 2002.

James Lucas, *Rommel's Year of Victory: The Wartime Illustrations of the Afrika Korps by Kurt Caesar*. Stackpole Books: Pennsylvania, 1998.

Field Marshal Viscount Montgomery of Alamein et al, *Alamein and the Desert War*. London: Sunday Times, 1967.

Neil Orpen, *War in the Desert: SA Forces in World War II*. Cape Town: Purnell, 1971.

Barrie Pitt (series editor), *The History of the Second World War*. London: Purnell, 1972, especially 'Alamein' (No.39) and 'Tobruk' (No.34).

Barrie Pitt, *The Crucible of War*, Volumes II (Auchinleck) and III (Montgomery). London: Macmillan, 1987.

A M Pollock, *Pienaar of Alamein*. Cape Town: Cape Times, 1942.

Reader's Digest, *Illustrated Story of World War II*. Cape Town: Reader's Digest, 1980.

Springbok Record, South African Legion of the British Empire Service League, 1945.

NOTES

* This chapter is partly based on research trips undertaken by Greg Mills to Egypt in October 2002 and January 2005. Grateful appreciation is expressed to Michael and Franszica Lange for their hospitality and assistance with logistics.

1 'Desert – The War in North Africa', 1940-1943, *The World at War*, Thames TV.

2 Field Marshal Viscount Montgomery of Alamein *et al*, *Alamein and the Desert War*. London: Sunday Times, 1967, p.168.

3 Cited Jon Latimer, *Alamein*. London: John Murray, 2002, p.68.

4 Latimer, *ibid*, pp.14-15.

5 At *http://erwin-rommel.biography.ms* and *http://riri. essortment.com/erwinrommelde_rnqi.htm*

6 Anthony Beevor, *Stalingrad*. London: Penguin, 1998, p.53.

7 Montgomery et al, *op cit*, pp.130-1.

8 See E P Hartshorn, *Avenge Tobruk*. Cape Town: Purnell, 1960.

9 'Tobruk', Barrie Pitt (series editor), *The History of the Second World War*. London: Purnell, 1972, p.945.

10 Latimer, *op cit*, p.22.

11 John Bierman and Colin Smith, *The Battle of Alamein: Turning Point, World War II*. London: Viking, 2002, p.184.

12 Latimer, *op cit*, p.51.

13 Latimer, *ibid*, p.146.

14 Hartshorn, *op cit*, p.33.

15 Hartshorn, *ibid*, p.167.

16 A M Pollock, *Plenaar of Alamein*. Cape Town: Cape Times, 1942, p.142.

17 Cited in Montgomery et al, *op cit*, p.41.

18 Latimer, *op cit*, p.318.

19 Cited in John Bierman and Colin Smith, *The Battle of Alamein: Turning Point, World War II*. London: Viking, 2002.

20 Latimer, *op cit*, p.96.

21 Montgomery et al, *op cit*, p.127.

22 Latimer, *op cit*, p.7.

23 Montgomery et al, *ibid*, p.167.

24 Artemis Cooper, *Cairo in the War, 1939-45*. London: Penguin, 1995, p.182.

25 Montgomery et al, *op cit*, p.13.

26 This information was generously supplied by Professor Deon Fourie.

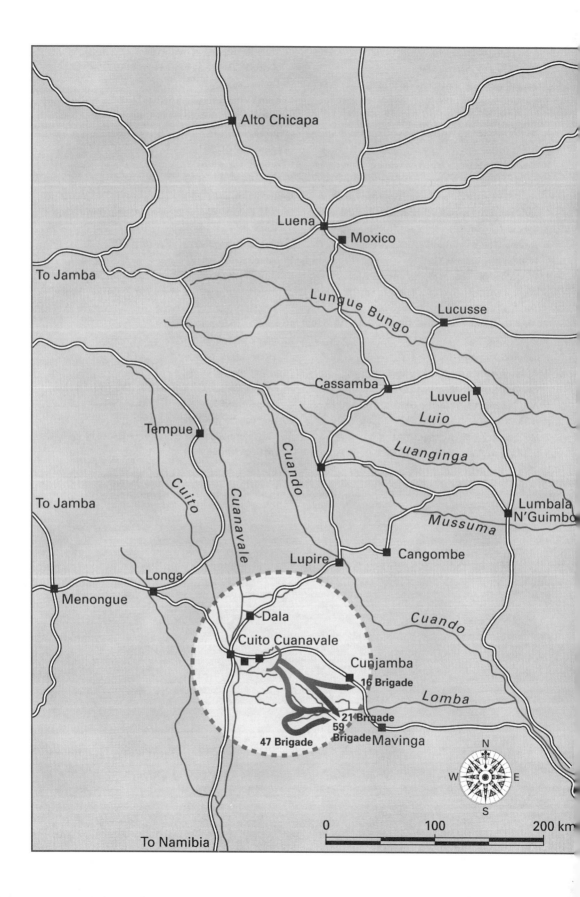

Alto Chicapa

Luena
Moxico

To Jamba

Lungue Bungo

Lucusse

Cassamba
Luvuel
Luio

Tempue

Cuito

Cuando

Luanginga

To Jamba

Cuanavale

Lumbala
N'Guimbo

Mussuma

Longa
Lupire
Cangombe

Menongue

Dala

Cuando

Cuito Cuanavale

Cunjamba

16 Brigade

Lomba

21 Brigade

**59
Brigade** Mavinga

47 Brigade

N

W   E

S

To Namibia

0   100   200 km

Every cause needs a victory

Cuito Cuanavale
1987–88

'On the Border' – that was the informal term used by tens of thousands of white South Africans to refer to the low-intensity war fought in northern Namibia (then known officially as South West Africa) and in Angola. It began when the South African Defence Force (SADF) took over border patrol duties from the police in the early 1970s, and ended with the series of major battles around the Angolan town of Cuito Cuanavale in 1987 and 1988.

Cuito Cuanavale stimulated in South Africa a later 'battle for history' as conflicting assessments of this war emerged among writers and historians. Some, like the English journalist Fred Bridgland believed that the events in Angola in 1987–88 were important enough to be described as 'the war for Africa', as the title of his book denoted. Others, such as the historians of the political and diplomatic history of the 1980s ignored it. Depending on where you stood, Cuito Cuanavale was described as a defeat or a victory for the SADF, or a stalemate. What is certain is that the stakes were high for both sides; that the engagements represented the biggest conventional operations involving South African forces since World War II; that the South African public knew very little at the time about what was happening and that this information was, in fact, actively and deliberately withheld from them by their government.

The vagueness of the term 'border war' reflected the ambivalent, shadowy nature of the Pretoria government's involvement through nearly two decades. On the one hand, details of operations were seldom released. If there were casualties, only the names of servicemen killed were announced, with no mention or confirmation of the battle or skirmish in which

South African tanks leaving Mavinga with the commencement of the Cuito Cuanavale front in December 1988, F Squadron, School of Armour. Note the additional tracks attached to the armour plate, enabling quick repairs in the veld. *(HRH)*

they had been involved. On the other hand, the activities of the SADF could hardly be kept completely secret, because there was, after all, conscription for all white men from 1967 to 1990. Generally they would serve full time for up to two years, followed for at least another ten years by annual 'camps' of between 30 and 90 days.

South Africa's forces, made up of full-time and part-time conscripts with a small core of regulars and part-time volunteers, were acknowledged as easily the most formidable in Africa, and there was pride in this capability – but at no point did the number of men on operations in Angola exceed 3,000. At the time South Africa was isolated politically because of its apartheid policies and it was anxious not to be seen as an aggressor. And support for the

border war was by no means unqualified in the white population, which meant that the SADF was extremely reluctant to accept casualties in what was essentially a citizen army. They were operating within a peculiar mixture of confidence and insecurity.

South Africa's strategy in fighting this border war had its origins in a much earlier conflict. At the outbreak of World War I in August 1914, Britain requested the Union government under Prime Minister General Louis Botha to render 'urgent imperial service' and seize control of German South West Africa, thereby denying Germany access to the colony's harbours. This was achieved in a remarkable campaign in hostile terrain by Botha, a most skilful soldier/politician, who at the same time also had to put down a rebellion by bitter men who had

168

been his Boer comrades just a dozen years before in the 1899–1902 war against the British Empire.

Botha's campaign was also the first fought by the newly created SADF; it saw the first use of military aircraft in Africa and the genesis of the SA Air Force, the second-oldest in the world; the first use of armoured vehicles in Africa; and one of the last cavalry operations (using horses and camels) before the introduction of motor vehicles. The effect of the campaign on South African politics was also profound, preserving the emotional fault line within Afrikaner politics that eventually led to the accession of the anti-British 'purified' National Party in 1948.

The success of Botha's military campaign led to South Africa being mandated by the League of Nations after the war to administer this territory of some 815,000km^2 (larger than the UK, Italy and Germany combined) once it had been taken from Germany in 1919. South Africa did so for the next 70 years, with major strategic and military implications that dominated the thinking of the Nationalist government in Pretoria until the fall of apartheid. But the authority over Namibia was increasingly contested after South Africa refused to recognise the United Nations' claim to inherit the League trusteeship. In turn, the UN revoked the mandate and South Africa's occupation was declared illegal.

By the mid-1970s, Namibia's transition to independence – accepted in principle by Pretoria – had reached a virtual impasse. South Africa's policies had become hostage to wider domestic, political, economic and security considerations. These factors largely explain South African efforts in the 1970s and 1980s to attempt an 'internal' SWA (South West Africa) solution by installing a moderate government and moving the territory towards independence on Pretoria's terms.

South Africa's occupation of that country was supported by Namibia's estimated 110,000 white population of ex-German settlers and Afrikaners, which constituted about 10% of the total. Fearing charges of 'selling out' Namibia's whites, it was deemed crucial – especially in the light of its own racial politics – for Pretoria to adopt a firm stand over the independence issue.

Since the late 1960s, South Africa had been confronted by Swapo (South West African People's Organisation) guerrillas. These operated mostly from bases in neighbouring Angola. Virtually guaranteed strong support because of their powerbase among the majority Ovambo tribe in the north and their wide recognition as the only Namibian organisation to have actively fought for the departure of the South Africans, Swapo was by contrast portrayed by Pretoria as a communist organisation and a tool of the Soviet Union.

After the collapse of the Portuguese empire and the granting of Angola's independence in 1975, the threat posed by Swapo became considerably more effective and demanded the use of SADF troops to counter it. A large South African military presence was maintained in Namibia (which stimulated the economy in the north), and in addition to intensive counter-insurgency patrolling, numerous raids were made against Swapo camps in Angola. The SADF also co-operated for the entire period between 1975 and 1989 with Jonas Savimbi's Unita (Uniäo Nacional para a Independência Total de Angola) rebels, who were engaged in a civil war against Angola's self-proclaimed Marxist MPLA (Movimento Popular para a Libertaçao de Angola) government.

A crucial factor was the support provided to

the Angolan government by communist Cuba, which first became involved in 1975 and by the late 1980s had an estimated 60,000 troops in Angola – more than ten times the number ever deployed there by the SADF. Pretoria portrayed this foreign communist presence as the main stumbling block to a peaceful resolution of the Namibian conflict. The US government shared this view, as shown both by its military support for Unita and its insistence that South African participation was a condition for a Namibian settlement. Until the end of the 1980s, the Angolan and Namibian issues thus remained as inseparable as ever for South Africa's domestic and foreign policy-makers.[1]

Nearly 400,000 Cuban soldiers rotated through Angola in 15 years. This massive involvement has to be understood in the context of Cuba's overall supportive relationship with African liberation movements, having started with assistance in the form of medical teams sent to Algeria in 1963. This was done partly in the zeal of socialist brotherhood, given Cuba's ancestral connections through its African diaspora. But such assistance was not without cost. Overall, from 1975 until their disengagement in 1991, 2,700 Cubans lost their lives in Angola in an operation that was principally paid for by the Soviets and the Cubans themselves.[2]

Understanding Cuba's Motivation

In 1975, with the collapse of Portuguese colonial authority, and encouraged by the promise of American aid in addition to assistance from a number of moderate black African states, South African Prime Minister John Vorster eventually committed an estimated 3,000 SADF troops to the support of the pro-Western FNLA (Frente Naçional de Libertacao de Angola) and Unita guerrillas in Angola. However, the SADF was forced to withdraw quite close to the capital of Luanda, after US support failed to materialise. By then, Cuba had also rushed in around 15,000 troops to help the MPLA launch a counter-offensive. On 19 December 1975, the US Senate voted in favour of the Clark Amendment which effectively prevented further US aid to Unita, prompting then South African Defence Minister P W Botha to comment: 'If the West does not want to contribute its share for the sake of itself and the free world, it cannot expect South Africa to do it ... South Africa is not prepared to fight the West's battle against Communist penetration on its own.' The South African military, too, found itself dissatisfied with the politicians' handling of the war, their frustration being reflected in the official SADF account of the war, entitled 'We could have gone all the way'.[3] But the war had also exposed certain technical military vulnerabilities on the South African side, with regard to trucks, machine-guns, tanks and armoured cars, and, critically, long-range artillery.

The National Party government found itself by the mid-1970s faced with a worsening international, regional and domestic security situation. The fall of the Portuguese empire in Angola and Mozambique and the advent of Marxist governments in both countries; the tightening noose on the embattled Smith regime in neighbouring Rhodesia; the 1976 Soweto uprising and the 1977 UN arms embargo – all this prompted in South Africa a process of internal militarisation, including a massive arms build-up, and a more aggressive regional military response characterised by the term 'destabilisation'.

As Piero Gleinjeses has documented in his *Conflicting Missions: Havana, Washington and Africa, 1959–1976*, the intent of Cuba's missions to African countries such as Algeria, Congo/Zaire, Guinea-Bissau as well as Angola, reflected two basic drivers in Cuban foreign policy: 'self-preservation and revolutionary zeal'.[4] Cuban leaders 'were convinced that their country has a special empathy for the Third World and a special role to play on its behalf'. While 'history, geography, culture and language made Latin America the Cubans' natural habitat', it was also the place 'where their freedom of movement was most circumscribed'. In Africa, by comparison, 'Castro incurred fewer risks'. In Africa, Havana was only operating against a colonial (and therefore illegitimate) power or 'defending established states' and not flouting international law in acting against legal governments. As Castro told the East German leader Erich Honecker in 1977: 'In Africa . . . we can inflict a heavy defeat to the entire policy of the imperialists . . . We can free Africa from the influence of the US and the Chinese'.[5] In Angola in 1975 – as in 1988 – Cuba faced a stark choice as a result of the South African intervention: 'intervene or seal the fate of the MPLA'.[6]

By 1987, things were going badly for the joint Angolan, Cuban and Soviet force. Several Soviet-led dry-season attempts to advance via Mavinga on the capital of Dr Jonas Savimbi's Unita movement, Jamba, in southeastern Angola had been successfully and bloodily forestalled by Unita troops, bolstered by South African special forces, artillery and air-strikes. These advances were deemed necessary since, by the mid-1980s, with substan-

A Unita parade at Jamba in 1986 in front of a portrait of the late Unita commander
Brigadier Kafandanga Chendovana. (*JS*)

tial South African backing, Unita's operations had grown to the point where they posed a considerable threat to the security of the MPLA government. For its part, Pretoria saw Unita as key to the creation of a *cordon sanitaire* between Luanda and Namibia without which the struggle for independence in Namibia and for majority rule in South Africa would dramatically escalate.

In August 1987 South Africa decided to insert a relatively small force to help Unita defend its southern bases against an expected large-scale offensive by Angolan forces. The importance of the small town of Cuito Cuanavale lay in its air strip, its location as a supply base, and in its control of the major bridge over the Lomba River. Without air support based at Cuito, Fapla would find it very difficult to advance further against Unita and get closer to Savimbi's stronghold at Jamba.

The SADF planners knew their objective: to block the imminent offensive. But they had a range of options on the method to be used, ranging from limited secret support for Unita (as had often been provided in the past) to all-out SADF air attacks on Angolan bases, with substantial ground forces attacking and taking Cuito Cuanavale. The latter course was rejected, because once occupied, Cuito would be difficult to supply and defend, quite apart from causing diplomatic tension and possibly scuppering the delicate peace process that was proceeding glacially alongside the fighting. As General Kat Liebenberg, the Chief of the South African Army, expressed it, if Cuito had been taken, 'we would then be in the position of the dog that caught the bus.'

Instead plans were drawn up for Operation Modular, the objectives of which were not to occupy ground but to stop the advance by Fapla, and to destroy its forces. At first, SADF support to Unita was confined to rocket-launchers and mortars, with a company of infantry as protection. It was soon clear that this would not be enough, and it was decided to commit the large conventional formation known as 61 Mechanised Battalion, or '61 Mech', as well as a battery of G5 guns, the pride of South Africa's artillery arsenal. Then came further reinforcements in the form of 4 SA Infantry Battalion, or '4 SAI' (pronounced 'four-sigh'); a troop of G6 guns (as powerful as the G5s, but self-propelled); and a squadron of Olifant tanks – the first time tanks had been deployed by the SADF in battle since World War II.

It was at the hands of this small but well-trained SADF force that, on 3 October 1987, the numerically superior Angolan army suffered a devastating defeat at Cuito Cuanavale. It resulted in the virtual destruction of Fapla's 47 Brigade, along with the loss of considerable quantities of material and valuable technology including, famously, a complete Soviet SAM 8 missile-system (see below). This operation was superbly run by the SADF and a tactical victory in military terms, yet one rendered infamous and virtually unmentionable today – as then – given the political regime represented. The guns and the fighters of the SAAF (South African Air Force) kept the Angolans pinned down, and from 9 October the G6s 'pounded Cuito Cuanavale base into uselessness', as the military journalist Willem Steenkamp put it.

More importantly, this was an 'open' South African military intervention, unlike previous years when this was done under the guise of Unita, and very different to Operation Savannah in 1975–76, when the troops were actually kitted out in different uniforms with the cover that they were white mercenaries. In 1987, the SADF went in not only to stop the enemy column, but also to destroy it. More-

P W Botha and Jonas Savimbi in Jamba, 1984. *(JS)*

over, P W Botha openly visited the troops in Angola. This was all of great concern to the Cubans who 'came to the conclusion that if we helped, we needed a big effort as it was a dangerous operation, since we needed to weaken our forces at home [in Cuba] with the enemy [the US] 90 miles away, to get the South Africans out of Angola, otherwise we would be there for 100 years'.

But the South Africans had already upped the ante some time earlier, in May 1985 with the abortive Special Forces mission that led to the capture of Captain Wynand du Toit in Angola. Most of the details of this operation have never before been published.

Upping the Ante, Lowering the Periscope

The South African submarine, SAS Johanna van der Merwe, was tasked with dropping off the nine-man Special Forces team at Cabinda

in the extreme north of Angola with the express purpose of blowing up the Malongo oil terminal. Wynand du Toit was the operational commander of the Special Forces unit for this operation (Operation Argon), and Hannes Venter, the Officer Commanding 4 Recce Regiment based at Langebaan, the mission commander.

The plan was for the Recce team – comprising seven white South Africans and two ex-

The Daphne-class Johanna van der Merwe on its arrival voyage from France, pictured at Simonstown and escorted by the anti-submarine Type-12 class frigate SAS President Steyn and a patrol aircraft. *(CT)*

173

Angolans – to blow up the oil storage tanks and set fire to the oil that leaked out. The submarine journey from Simonstown to Cabinda via Langebaan took 12 days, using the anti-satellite detection techniques of running at night on the surface and recharging the batteries, and moving underwater during the day.

Until that time there had been only two previous Special Forces operations by submarine attacking Angolan targets, both of which were successful: Operation Nobilis to attack ships in Luanda harbour; and Operation Bougainvillea to destroy railway rolling stock in the port of Lobito.

The mission was complicated by the absence of charts for the area. The crew therefore had to use Gulf Oil drilling charts which comprised an unfamiliar grid reference system. The submarine also had to make its way in and out of the oil rigs in the area, both an advantage in that the ambient noise of the rigs made detection less likely, but a disadvantage in that the South Africans had to cope with a lot of light and activity in the surrounding oilfield. The water close in was also fairly shallow (just 20m deep some 2,4km offshore, while the Daphne-class submarine measured 10m from the top of the fin to the keel).

The plan was for the submarine to make a run into the area, lie on the bottom until nightfall, and then move closer to the beach to drop off the Special Forces team using inflatables. After an initial recce, a decision was made to go in the following night. However, the team was delayed moving away from the beach by the presence of Angolan troops, which had not been the case in the two previous onshore reconnaissance sorties (June 1979 and November 1983). Because of the delays on the beach, the team never made it to the oil terminal to set the explosives before first light.

Instead, their tracks were detected and they came under fire. The group split into two, with Du Toit and two other men (Liebenberg and Van Breda) drawing the fire. Du Toit was captured and the other two killed. The other group, including the two Angolans and Krubert Nel, the second-in-command, were also hit, but managed to evade their pursuers and make it back to the beach under fire.

Meanwhile, they had failed to make the rendezvous with the submarine, which had to move in closer to the beach in the early hours of the morning to pick them up, again using the inflatables. Contact was made between the inflatables and the six-man team, three of whom were badly wounded. This was complicated by the depth of the water, the fixed nets of local fishermen and the lack of navigational information and bearings. Also, the vessel's radar warning receiver had gone down during the mission.

At some stage the surfaced sub was detected by two Russian-built patrol vessels (OSA and SHERSHEN class), using surface radar and searchlights. These patrol vessels were sent to the area in reaction to the contact made with the team in the vicinity of the oil storage tanks. The men were rapidly embarked, the inflatables dumped and the submarine immediately dived. However, the water was very shallow and the boat badly trimmed with the newcomers on board and it hit the bottom, sandpapering the keel for a third of its length. Even so, the sub managed to evade the enemy and run out to sea as fast as possible.

So, were the Angolans tipped off? This certainly seems to be the case, since the previous reconnaissance ops had proceeded without incident. The submariners point to a probable leak in Defence Head Quarters, which could have alerted Washington. While the Americans might have been supporting Unita at the time, safeguarding their oil supplies remained a key national interest – as it does today. What about a satellite tip-off? This is unlikely given the modus operandi of the submarine, and the fact that only the actual operation was intercepted, not the (dummy) recce ops.

Progress in the submarine was slow due to the fact that the propellers and rudder had also been damaged during the emergency dive. Eventually it rendezvoused with the two strike-craft about 100 nautical miles away from the coast and transferred the team. From there the strike-craft conducted a high- speed run south-

Wynand du Toit at the press conference after his release in 1987. His capture in 1985, after an abortive Special Forces mission, made world news headlines. (R)

wards to the mouth of the Cunene River where the badly wounded men were transferred to the SAS Protea for medical treatment.

The Johanna van der Merwe eventually made it back to Simonstown, 35 days after starting out – not bad for a vessel designed to go to sea for 28 days. The crew by this stage was presumably on emergency rations and drinking water out of the torpedo tubes. Even so, they were ordered to stay to seaward of the shipping lanes and to sail past Simonstown and divert to Port Elizabeth to avoid the press, and with the cover story that they had been out on exercises. The orders were 'not to be identified for what you are', though the world was soon to know otherwise as the capture of Du Toit was splashed across the world's media. Wynand du Toit was eventually released in October 1987.

SAM 8s and Campaign Tipping Points

Campaigns can reach, in modern social science parlance, a 'tipping point'. If such a critical point was reached in the battles for Cuito Cuanavale and, more importantly, for peace in Angola and Namibia, it was on 4 October 1987, after the destruction of Fapla's 47 Brigade, when a forward element of South Africa's 32 Battalion along with a military intelligence liaison team (one of three such advisory groups with Unita) discovered and managed to remove intact a complete Soviet-built SAM 8 missile-system from the banks of the Lomba River. This group had spent much of August and September that year trying to 'marry up' the Unita-operated, US-supplied Stinger mobile missile-systems with South African G5 artillery. The SAM 8 was therefore an important find in terms of the new technology it contained but more seriously it proved beyond doubt the extent of the Soviet/Cuban stake in this war.

Major Johan Lehman had been given the responsibility, along with Captain Piet 'Boer' van Zyl, a 32 Battalion reservist, of blending the use of Stingers and G5s in the eastern sector. Lehman had also assisted in designing the UNITA air-defence and command-and-control systems in 1984. With that done, the two were 'floating around, looking for fun' and ended up at a forward 32 Battalion command post under Jan Hougaard. Van Zyl and Lehman were asked by Hougaard to go forward to assess the situation around the Angolan Army bridgehead that had been occupied by Fapla's 47 Brigade on the southern bank of the Lomba River.

The South Africans' vantage point overlooked a large floodplain – or *anhara* – typical of the Angolan landscape. What they saw were

Top: Destroyed SAM 8 missile carrying vehicle, 1987. (JS)

Bottom: Soldiers relaxing, 1987, with Johan Lehman in the foreground. He was the one who saw the abandoned SAM 8 through his binoculars, walked onto the deserted battlefield and, with Piet van Zyl, towed it out.

the remnants of 47 Brigade, which had crossed the river at its source in the attempt to advance on the Mavinga airfield prior to moving onto Savimbi's headquarters at Jamba. In Lehman's words: 'It looked like those photographs of Delville Wood. There were body parts everywhere. Not a branch was left on a tree. It was how I imagine Armageddon would look'.

The Angolans had laid a road of logs to the river to escape the shellfire, but only their PT76 amphibious tanks were able to cross. Around 150 vehicles remained intact on the south bank; the rest had been destroyed.

Looking through binoculars from 1,500m away, Lehman noticed a number of apparently abandoned and intact air defence vehicles. 'I said to Piet that we should get down there,' he recalled. 'HQ, of course, would not believe that these were SAM 8s, and the forward command post was around 30–40km back.'

The radar-guided SAM 8 is a mobile system comprising three separate vehicles: a six-wheeled launcher with radar carrying six launcher tubes, a logistics vehicle with up to 36 additional missiles, and a fire control vehicle in the form of a modified BTR-60 armoured personnel carrier.

The team knew from intercepts that the commanding officer of Angola's 47 and 59 Brigades had been instructed to 'take all measures' to prevent the SAM 8s from falling into South African hands.

Lehman and Van Zyl walked in across the floodplain with around 20 UNITA soldiers. 'The latter were intent only on raiding things from the lorries, grabbing food and clothing and "gapping it"'. When the two South Africans came across a SAM 8 missile launcher vehicle, they knew they had hit the jackpot. But the vehicle was stuck up to its belly in the mud and its engine appeared to be damaged.

Lehman recalls: 'Piet was a boer [farmer]. He spotted a T54 tank nearby and still idling. He reckoned that he could drive the thing as he had driven bulldozers on the farm. He got in and drove it around, erratically at first, to the two SAM vehicles. We then towed them out, the missile-carrying vehicle first. He was driving the truck and I was trying to steer the "8", clinging to the wheel. We managed to get this lot to the tree-line, unhitched and camouflaged them, and then went back for more. But by this time, the other side [headquarters] had woken up as to what was happening. They threw everything at us [made resources available]. At about 10 or 11 in the morning, we successfully made the second trip in the tank with the missile system in tow'.

This was followed by a further 'five or so' trips. 'We radioed back and told HQ that we had got the "8". They told us to go and find out what was in the trucks. We found a command vehicle with lots of documents. We also took a BMP with Saggers [missiles] and were "gapping in" that towards the tree-line when I flicked a switch that threw oil onto the exhaust. Just at that time, enemy MiGs arrived and started bombing us. That's when I decided to bail out and run back to the tree-line.'

They waited at the tree-line until last light, under continuous enemy bombardment. 'They were looking for those two SAM 8 vehicles', said Lehman. The following morning HQ sent a recovery team from Hougaard's position. They hooked the weapons' system up and towed it out, with Van Zyl driving and Lehman sitting behind on the missile carrier. On their arrival at Hougaard's forward command position, they were greeted by the arrival of choppers carrying SA Air Force electronics specialists to examine the booty.

The SAM 8 system came with 'quite a few

missiles' and relevant operating documentation – all of which was in Spanish. It was shipped to Israel and fired there, and also fired in South Africa to assess its operational parameters and frequencies. The information gained was reputedly supplied to the US in time for the Gulf War, even though the US had also gained some knowledge from the pieces of the four smashed systems recovered by Unita from down the river.

Was the capture of the SAM 8 a tipping point? Certainly it confirmed the stakes of the Cubans and Angolans, and the existence of the captured SAM system is reputed to have encouraged the Americans to go all out in their diplomatic efforts to end the conflict, putting pressure on the Russians to pressurise their Cuban allies for the final settlement. If so, the impact of one soldier's lucky sighting across the floodplain in October 1987 helped to change the face of Africa. Both Lehman and Van Zyl received the Honoris Crux (South Africa's equivalent of the Victoria Cross or Medal of Honour, awarded between 1975–93) for their actions.

Castro Rolls the Dice

In response to the deteriorating situation, following a top-level meeting in Havana on 15 November 1987, Fidel Castro gambled on turning the military tide to prevent a 'political and military catastrophe'. The Cubans had not favoured the Soviet military plan to attack Savimbi all along, because 'if you went to Jamba, Savimbi would just move, as the guerrilla is not fixed. There were no guarantees that South Africa would not interfere'.

According to Jorge Risquet, then Castro's top Africa hand in the Central Committee of the Cuban Communist Party, the situation was complicated by two issues: first, attempting to intervene might well weaken the Cubans' defensive position. Second, the relationship between the Soviets and Americans was improving and thus a Cuban intervention 'could have provoked an interruption in this process'.

Castro decided to take direct control, sending Cuban forces from their defensive positions on the Lubango-Menogue line to the northwest of the fighting, to stiffen the defences of Cuito Cuanavale to where the Angolans had retreated and regrouped.

The town was held, though skirmishing continued between Angolan/Cuban and SA/Unita forces until March of the next year. While the joint Angolan-Cuban force manned the defences, the South Africans engaged in operations initially intended to push the Angolan-Cuban force from their bridgehead on the east bank of the Cuito River. When this proved unsuccessful, they later began a tactical disengagement that involved laying a substantial minefield in the area. The SADF's small force was close to exhaustion and they were experiencing increasing difficulties with supplies and spare parts.

Jorge Risquet, African expert in the Cuban Communist Party in the 1980s, photographed in Havana in 2004.

Unita crossing the Cuito River, 1987. (JS)

Castro dispatched an extra 25,000 troops, including elements of the crack Cuban 50th Division from his island, along with additional aircraft and top pilots. He even removed key elements of the air defence systems from Havana and transported them to Angola to successfully, as it turned out, up the stakes for the SA Air Force. More than 1,000 extra anti-aircraft weapons – comprising missiles, guns and radar systems – were sent as part of the force.

Castro also sent a major combat force southwards in a dramatic surge towards the Namibian border into Cunene Province, numbering 11,000–12,000 troops by May 1988. The Cubans had by then established a southern front of more than 350km, parallel with and close to the Namibian border, equipped with MiG-23s (which were disassembled on the ships over), helicopter gunships, a complex SAM network of at least five different missile and gun types, and an estimated 200 tanks. A new airstrip was constructed at Khama close to the border within two months, and the strip at Changombo was enlarged to function 'as a combat airport' for the MiGs.

For the Cubans, this was a game of machismo, of old-fashioned chicken, dramatically raising the stakes. Castro's escalation was a dangerous roll of the dice. If the South Africans had responded in force, this could have spiralled into all-out conventional war. Although the Chief of the SADF had described the support for Unita by that November as 'limited military action against surrogate forces,'[7] this sustenance was, in fact, far from limited: at least two mechanised infantry battalions and supporting artillery were committed, being supplemented by 32 Battalion. And al-

179

ready SADF tanks had been deployed around Cuito Cuanavale. The Cubans also feared the deployment of Pretoria's six nuclear weapons. Some signalling of this degree of escalation had become evident with the readying of the Kalahari nuclear test facility at about that time.

Yet fortunately, instead of leading to bigger clashes, this change in tactics coincided with the start of tripartite Angolan-SA-Cuban peace talks. The SADF commitment which had steadily increased from Operation Modular (1 July–15 December 1987), to Operation Hooper (15 December 1987–March 1988) was gradually wound down through tactical disengagements in Operations Packer. All the while the broader, strategic landscape shifted with the application of political and diplomatic resources. This was acknowledged by P W Botha in an address to the Democratic Turnhalle Alliance and other non-Swapo party leaders in Windhoek at the Administrator-General's residence in April 1988, in which the SA State President reportedly said that South Africa was going to get out of Namibia and 'the Namibians would have to get used to it.' As he put it, things were happening at the time that were 'bigger than them [the Namibians] and bigger than South Africa.' The diplomatic stage had been set by a meeting in Geneva between South African Foreign Minister Pik Botha and US Assistant Secretary of State for Africa Dr Chester Crocker at which the steps necessary to implement the plan for UN independence, UN435, were discussed.

Thus while Castro's military gamble could have sparked a cycle of escalating violence, it instead helped to set the conditions for an 'honourable exit' for both his forces and the South Africans from Angola. Much of this was due to the extraordinary diplomacy pursued across a variety of venues from Havana to New York and Moscow, to London, Cairo, Geneva and Brazzaville.

At the Coffee Station: The Diplomacy of Peace-Making

At the start of May 1988, the negotiators met for the first time in London. This was followed in the same month by meetings in Congo-Brazzaville and the groundbreaking Cairo summit, a process that ended in Namibia's independence in March 1990. But what were the obstacles that had to be overcome in making peace? And what were the wider lessons that could be taken away from this process and employed in the subsequent negotiations towards majority rule in South Africa?

The diplomatic process involved strange locations and many anecdotal experiences.

Neil van Heerden, who as Director-General of Foreign Affairs, led the department's negotiating input and whose leadership had to keep all the South Africans including the SADF – to use Lyndon Johnson's phrase – 'inside the tent aiming out', recalls two anecdotes in particular about the negotiations. The first concerned the regular meeting place of the negotiators around the 'inevitable, inimitable' coffee station in various venues, where many of the seemingly more intractable problems were resolved over a warm beverage rather than around the negotiating table.

'The London meeting, which had been deliberately hosted by the US in a tucked-away venue out of the mainstream, started off with Chet Crocker cracking a joke that went down like a lead balloon. The talks were very stiff and formal, with Jorge Risquet in particular wild and full of machismo. Halfway through that painful event, Chet suggested that we take a break. I got up to get a cup of coffee and was joined there by one of the Cubans who then introduced me to the leader of his delegation. It reinforced that we were all human beings thrust into particular roles. We had frequent breaks thereafter.'

Another attendee recalls that the gatherings at the coffee station at Brown's Hotel in London at the first meeting were instructive. He noted the three generals – Jannie Geldenhuys (South Africa), Rosales del Toro (Cuba) and Antonio Dos Santos Franca 'Ndalu' (Angola) – 'huddled in a corner of the room, having coffee during the first break. The three were clearly bonding long ahead of the others.'

The second Van Heerden anecdote relates to President Fidel Castro's personal interpreter. 'Castro had a very, very attractive Cuban interpreter with an olive skin and an excellent grasp of both English and Spanish. I had never met an interpreter quite as good as her. Accuracy is one thing, but keeping pace in a way that doesn't interrupt the discussion is another and is the ultimate test for any interpreter. When Castro spoke, she sat on the armrest of his chair and spoke in lockstep with him – and used the same physical expressions including the use of her hands, as he did. These dinners and meetings were mostly attended by just Jannie Geldenhuys and myself, and it was much nicer to focus on her than on the grisly if kindly and courteous Fidel. He was a typical old man in these exchanges, with more memories than future prospects. But scratch him and he would go into his vision of agriculture or his vision of the cultural aspect of Latin life. Our interpreter was a great relief to these four-hour or longer monologues of Fidelio.' At one meeting late in the process attended by Van Heerden and several South African diplomats and military, one recalled that 'Whenever Neil asked a question that Castro needed to think about, the sexy interpreter sitting on the arm of Castro's chair would slowly uncross and cross her legs which succeeded rather well in diverting our attention.'

Many lessons of process and methodology were learned by the negotiators. The first lesson made this much clear: one, that there is always a solution; two, that it will be found if you look hard enough; and three, that if you don't look hard enough, you actually sabotage yourself.

Second, the importance of negotiating at the right level became evident. Delegations headed by bureaucrats had to be convened with clear mandates, allowing for reflection and consultation when difficulties arose. It also encouraged the delegations to co-operate in selling agreed positions to their governments.

Third, an inclusive process and methodology are key. It was imperative to make joint decisions and to ensure discipline in the ranks of the negotiators. Many factors militated in favour of a positive outcome, not the least being the dynamics of glasnost, the bankruptcy of the apartheid approach, and the skill of the American facilitators led by Chester Crocker. But perhaps the most important aspect missing from previous attempts was the need to ensure a joint approach from the beginning.

An important part of the South African Department of Foreign Affairs' brief was to develop a good working relationship with their own military, not least to prevent them from undoing what had been achieved at the negotiating table, since the 'securocrat' mindset in those bad old days was largely ignorant or dismissive of international realities. Even though some strategic thinkers within the military had realised that their strategy was doomed to failure, questioning the axiomatic doctrine of 'Total Onslaught' and 'Total National Strategy' meant crossing swords with State President P W Botha – a dangerous exercise. For many in the military, negotiating with the enemy – internal or external – was not on, and, in fact, negotiations themselves were often viewed as the enemy, a strategy of cowards and defeatists. It was no small task to get officials in that frame of mind into the same room as Cubans, Angolans and Soviets – the very people who had until shortly before represented the 'Rooi Gevaar' (Red Danger, i.e. a communist take-over).

However, the Chief of the SADF, General Jannie Geldenhuys, was seen by all parties as a major force for realistic, honest bargaining, and an impressive strategic thinker. He was 'a pragmatist, an astute person who wanted to see a solution and who recognised that he was in command of a military which had finite resources.' South African foreign affairs officials had 'high regard for his perspicacity.' Or as Neil van Heerden said of his military counterpart: 'Luckily in Jannie Geldenhuys, I found a man who honestly believed the solution was 20% military and 80% political. He and I both decided that we needed, from the outset, to work and stick together, as we would not be able to achieve anything apart.'

Cubans interviewed have likewise expressed great respect for Geldenhuys as someone who was able to view the military events within the framework of the need for political negotiations. He also had to lead a group of generals, many of whom were not on board and who did not see the bigger picture – the effect of years of isolation from world thinking. The South African Foreign Affairs department was thus at pains to lead them gently towards a broader view of Pretoria's place in the world. One method of doing so was through simulation exercises. Early in the process, the South Africans participated in a role-playing scenario exercise for moving towards an independent Namibia. The contributions of the participants from Foreign Affairs, who were playing the roles of the UN or the US State Department or the Soviet Politburo, were reportedly frequently challenged by the military as not being realistic. 'Ag nee; hulle is darem nie so erg nie!' ('Oh, no; they [the UN, US or Soviets] are not as bad as that') apparently reverberated around the room a number of times.

All of this had other stresses and strains, and included officials having to 'sacrifice their liver for their country' in long drinking bouts intended to 'build respect' for the foreign affairs officials, derogatorily known in military parlance as 'die laventelbrigade' (the lavender brigade, or lounge lizards) – among their military counterparts. One of these sessions in Oshakati reputedly left one helicopter pilot asleep in a flower bed and the other sprawled on a concrete pathway leading to the barracks. They had apparently never heard Bismarck's comment that diplomats were superior to camels. 'Camels', he said, 'can only work for about 40 days without drinking. Diplomats can drink for far longer than that without working.' One foreign affairs official, however, admitted to defeat at five o'clock one morning aboard an SADF executive jet when a brigadier, who had worn his 32 Battalion T-shirt at every round of negotiations to taunt the Angolans, asked the flight attendant for a glass of brandy 'for the plaque on my teeth'.

The head of South Africa's intelligence department, Neil Barnard, made, in the opinion of his peers, some important tactical contributions to the discussion. As the 'eyes and ears of P W', or, as one foreign affairs member termed him, 'P W's extra-sensory perceptor', Barnard was viewed also as a good weather-vane of what concessions could be sold to the notoriously irascible State President.

Jonas Savimbi's Unita also had to be baby-sat, given that it had the capacity – with a little help from its friends – to wreck the process by actions on the ground. To keep him 'in the loop', he was informed before and after every negotiating round of what the South Africans intended doing and his input was considered. Initially that task was entrusted to the military, though to prevent a military bias to these briefings, foreign affairs officials subsequently traveled with the military to Jamba to carry out the briefings. Foreign Affairs also opened an office in Rundu in the north of Namibia to keep an ear on the ground.

Past efforts had failed because whenever agreement was close, either the military or intelligence services or the South African Police would derail the process. This time around, endless pre-meetings ensured that all departments signed off on a mandate before each round. And after each round, the heads of the South African delegation (Van Heerden, Barnard and Geldenhuys) immediately reported back directly to Pik Botha and Defence Minister Magnus Malan. This tactic limited opportunities for mischief-making and largely obviated the danger of distorted messages reaching the Cabinet. Moreover, given the multitude of egos involved, *how* things happened was all important and at times overshadowed the happenings themselves.

Personalities were important. Pik Botha was seen 'as abrasive but persuasive' in the process in 'getting through to people.' The Cairo summit 'nearly ended in disaster', recalls one former SA diplomat, 'when the Cuban foreign minister and Pik started to yell at each other. But then the Americans leant on us, and the Russians on the Cubans, and by the end of the evening, Pik and the Cuban were getting drunk together.' Even the much-maligned PW Botha played his part 'in ensuring that the SADF remained on board. They were so [on board] because he told them to be. They were all too good military in that respect. If P W said jump, they would say "how high?" For them, he was the Alpha and the Omega.' P W Botha had served as South Africa's Minister of Defence from 1966–78, and overseen the rise of the South African security establishment in policy as well as financial expenditure terms.

A fourth lesson illustrated the importance of monopolising the moral high ground. It became clear that the delegation that ended one meeting on the moral high ground started the next round at a distinct advantage.

Fifth, the choice of a professional facilitator with clout and extensive backroom backup was important. Chester Crocker was this person, and he cleverly used all manner of diplomatic techniques, including the 'single-text negotiating process'. When there was a deadlock, he would invite all sides to give him a written document of what they wanted. He then produced a third document which had important elements of what all sides wanted, but not all. When presented with this single text, there would be uproar but the negotiators would be berating the facilitator and not one another. He would then be asked to leave the room while the teams would sort it out amongst themselves. Crocker was seen as no favourite of either side, but both sides acknowledged that his role was crucial. In particular he orchestrated those countries with influence over the negotiating parties to pressurise and cajole their protégés into a reasonable course of action. Yet the Cubans and Angolans were surprised at the extent to which the South African team kept its distance from the Americans.

The venues were selected for various reasons, but were always a point of contention. The South Africans insisted on African destinations on the pretext that African problems should be resolved on African soil, a tactic that is familiar in post-apartheid South Africa. There was a more strategic political rationale, however, which related to white South Africa's isolation and search for political acceptance. Pretoria used the choice of venues to get into African states that would normally not have accepted them. This ploy was resisted by the Cubans and Angolans. Crocker eventually found a way around this by persuading the South Africans that Egypt was an African state, while selling Cairo to the others on the basis that Egypt was in the Middle East.

Sixth, small steps are important. The talks made better progress when easy targets and deadlines were set for each side. This built confidence and reassured the politicians, whereas attempting giant steps made them nervous. But it was also essential to maintain momentum and not to let too much time elapse between steps.

Seventh, expect wider ramifications. The Nationalist Party caucus signed off on negotiations in Namibia on the understanding that it was an offshore exercise to see whether one could negotiate with 'terrorists' without the sky falling on one's head. Many of them believed that if the results were not to their liking, the process could be reversed. Yet such a limited understanding of the dynamics of transition that made Namibian independence inevitable and similar ignorance of the tactics of negotiation were evident once more in the South African negotiations that followed in 1991–1994. Perhaps the National Party would not have been so frequently out-maneuvered by the ANC in the subsequent CODESA (Convention for a Democratic South Africa – the initial internal South African negotiating forum for majority rule) process and beyond if they had employed the technical and tactical expertise they had built up in the Namibia initiative.

Eighth, and perhaps most important, related to the above: the negotiations showed that not only were military solutions not workable in a southern African context, but that it was possible to achieve peaceful solutions through negotiations. These were not a 'zero-sum' game; indeed, if all sides wanted victory, one task of the negotiators was to ensure that both sides could be allowed to extract themselves with their honour intact. As Van Heerden put it:

'We knew all along that the Cubans had to have their honour intact. Rubbing their noses in it meant that they could have brought in another 15,000 troops and thrown themselves lemming-like against the Namibian border.'

The ninth lesson highlights the importance of allowing all sides to portray the negotiations – and the outcome – in their own terms. Honour demanded that Castro, in spite of (and perhaps because of) his military losses, be allowed to claim a huge military victory. Such propaganda permitted the process to move ahead.

The tenth and final lesson brought home the importance of recognising and valuing the qualities of excellence, expertise, method and determination that made the negotiations a success – qualities which, Neil van Heerden reflects, 'we should invoke in securing our today and our tomorrow.'

Assessing the Impact of Cuito Cuanavale

Castro argued that the South Africans, by exploiting their big victory over the Angolans in October 1987, 'created a crisis and forced me to act' and that his intervention had significantly changed 'the correlation of forces'. Medals were struck for the heroes of Cuito Cuanavale as the Cubans trumpeted a great victory and the town entered into Cuban – and Angolan and liberation movement – legend.

Crocker, the purveyor of the Reagan administration's policy of 'constructive engagement' says in his book *High Noon in Southern Africa: Making Peace in a Rough Neighbourhood*[8] that 'whatever Castro's rhetorical bombast, he could not dictate South Africa's choice, and his behaviour during 1988 suggests that he realised his own limits'. It was, he notes, 'beyond Cuba's capacity to dominate the Southern African military balance'. Castro's 'risky adventure in grand strategy was dependent, in practice', he argues, 'on American diplomacy and South African common sense and steady nerves'.

Likewise, with access to official SADF sources, Helmoed Römer-Heitman's early account of the *War in Angola: The Final South African Phase*[9] argues that it was never the intention to take Cuito, given the political damage 'of holding on to a town in Angola, or the propaganda damage of their withdrawal being turned into a great Fapla victory'.

And Fred Bridgland's *The War for Africa: 12 Months that Transformed a Continent*[10] agrees that the Cuban assertion that an over-extended SADF force became surrounded at Cuito and therefore entered negotiations to enable a retreat, is 'nonsense' as 'No-one can surround anyone in south-eastern Angola. The vastness, wilderness, tangled vegetation and sparse population of the terrain make that impossible'. This, he argues, is reinforced by the limited number of troops that were deployed by all sides over a vast area. Although the author had earlier claimed that the South Africans had 'smashed themselves against the Angolan-Cuban resistance', Bridgland cites a later speech of Castro's in support of the author's view in which the Cuban refers only to the 'thwarting' of the South Africans at Cuito Cuanavale.

SADF soldiers who fought at Cuito concur. There was no attempt, they say, to take the town, as it was not a strategic or tactical target, and they could never have held onto it nor had any reason to want to do so. The only tactical reasoning for taking Cuito Cuanavale was to cut the Angolan brigades off that had retreated there and to then 'destroy them at leisure'. But this objective was passed up in favour of attempting to destroy the Fapla force east of Cuito, forcing the Angolans, as Heitman puts it, 'to accept battle on their terms' and to prevent them from being able to relaunch an offensive against Unita in 1988. The limited size of the SADF force there (always less than brigade strength of 4,000 men) and their relatively modest equipment and personnel losses suggest their intentions on Cuito Cuanavale were more opportunistic than militarily deliberate. And the costs of taking a town they could never have held meant that the South Africans could not, as the American scholar Jeffrey Herbst aptly put it at the time, 'afford a victory, much less a defeat.'[11]

But, in the opinion of one South African diplomat, by the time Cuito happened, 'was die koeël reeds deur die kerk' ('the bullet had already gone through the church' – the matter was settled or had reached a point of no return). According to this viewpoint, the South Africans had, even before Cuito, realised they had to get out of Angola and Namibia, and that the political cards were stacked against Pretoria remaining there. The worsening military situation (from a South African point of view) and rapidly changing global geo-strategic landscape had persuaded the powers-that-be in Pretoria that the time was ripe for withdrawal.

Winners and Losers?

So, who won at Cuito Cuanavale?

The answer is that the tactical stalemate at the end of a long run of victories for the SADF/Unita coalition, represented, in fact, a psychological victory for the MPLA/Swapo/Cuban/ANC alliance. It proved to Pretoria that there were strict limits on how much they could achieve in Angola; and that they had to consider what losses the white public back home was prepared to accept for distant, indistinct and undeclared objectives. Add a dose of machismo on the part of Castro by his raising of the military stakes, coupled with the SADF's until-then near-invincibility, and you have a 'victory' – which was how anything other than a major defeat must have looked at the time to the Angolans and Cubans. As Crocker observes, 'While Castro was waging a political contest, the SADF leadership concentrated on battlefield logic'. The legend of Cuito thus owes much to Castro's personality, since 'the South Africans were no match for Castro in the battle of perceptions'. As Risquet puts it, 'Cuito was a symbol, more than just its importance on the battlefield' and was a 'trump' complementing the Cuban advance on the Namibian border. Jannie Geldenhuys and Neil van Heerden concur in recognising that, unlike Cuba, South African propaganda would

not be ratcheted up, as it was part of the (white) South African mythology that this was a Unita war. As a result, 'it only made the headlines in South Africa when the SADF lost soldiers, so it seemed as if all that was happening to South Africa in Angola was that it was having its soldiers killed.'

In a sense, it was a victory, in that it was not a defeat for the Cuban and Angolan government forces. Or, as a former South African foreign affairs official summed it up:

'Cuito Cuanavale was a stand-off with an inconclusive military result but with a realisation that a military victory was not possible or only at a price that neither side was prepared to pay. Thus it led to a renewed sense of urgency to find a political solution and to establish linkage between what was happening in Angola to events in Namibia.'

Cuban officials today maintain that they had great respect for South African military prowess, particularly the G5 and G6 guns. These were accurate and 'kept them underground', with the result that Cuban artillery was out-ranged 'and did not hit its objectives'. Yet when Pretoria 'emerged from its long night of diplomatic hibernation . . . to find that these artful military tactics were not good enough', the South Africans converted the SADF's position at Cuito into a 'bargaining chip' according to Crocker. Cuban 'bravado' kept the South Africans engaged at Cuito, while the SADF would not withdraw until 'concrete, reciprocal agreements' were reached.

Although South African diplomats had little respect for Risquet's diplomatic skills (given that at the Cairo meeting he reportedly nearly brought the entire diplomatic exercise to a halt with his confrontational and doctrinaire approach), they did regard the veteran Cuban revolutionary as being dead right about the

SADF's obsession with detail at the expense of the bigger picture. While the South African Department of Foreign Affairs regarded the SADF as undoubtedly more organised and disciplined and with much bigger budgets and resources than themselves, they argued that many of the South African soldiers suffered from 'tunnel vision'.

Cuba's chief negotiator, Carlos Aldana, was, however, widely respected by the South Africans, being seen as a warm and forthcoming man who had the knack of looking past the positions that various delegations took and working out what his interlocutors really wanted or feared. The chemistry between him and Neil van Heerden was viewed as contributing significantly to the success of negotiations. 'Carlos Aldana and I had a particularly warm personal relationship,' recalls Van Heerden. 'Without him I am not sure we could have had the outcome we reached – certainly not in the timeframe in which it happened. He was a man who made you feel he was genuinely pursuing a path of peace. In the midst of the negotiations he said to me: "Why don't we go somewhere to meet offshore – somewhere in the Cape Verde Islands?" So just the two of us went there with an interpreter. It was a very interesting experience as we were outside the atmosphere of the formal negotiations. We enjoyed long walks together and spoke about the melting pot aspect of Cuba. He thought that it was something Cuba could help South Africa with in the inevitable future melting pot we faced.'

The South African military had a number of face-to-face meetings with their Cuban counterparts, mostly on Sol Island in the Atlantic. They were usually cordial and productive affairs, since the 'military people understood each other.' At one meeting, the Cuban delegation called for a short break as they wanted to introduce someone to the South African delegates, one of whom recalled: 'The doors burst open, and an imposing fellow walked in. It was the Cuban Commander-in-Chief in Angola, General Arnaldo Ochoa Sánchez. With General Geldenhuys leading our delegation, this was the first time we had the two commanders of the opposing sides in the same room at the same time.' General Ochoa was later arrested and executed by Havana on charges of drug trafficking and other 'economic crimes', though it is widely suspected he was executed more for his potential as a coup plotter since he had challenged Castro's military policies in Angola.[12]

Whatever the personal fate of the negotiators, for the Angolan government, the Cubans and the South Africans it was a strategic victory in terms of adding to the impetus – hastened by the disintegration of the Soviet empire – to conclude the Angolan-Namibian peace accords, an event which, critically, added impetus to democratic change within South Africa itself.

Ironically, the Namibia-Angola agreement linked, too, the end of SADF support for Unita (which nonetheless continued for some time beyond this period and into the early 1990s) with the closure of the ANC's Angolan bases. But this fact is relegated to a footnote of history by the liberation movements in their appraisal of the events in and around Cuito in 1987–88, which has become the stuff of legend. After all, all sides need at least one military victory to cement their credentials. This explains why Nelson Mandela said, when he visited Havana in July 1991: 'We come here with a sense of the great debt that is owed to the people of Cuba. What other country can point to a record of greater selflessness than Cuba has displayed in its relations with Africa?'[13]

Visiting Angola

It was not possible to visit Cuito Cuanavale for the writing of this chapter. Not only are internal (Angolan) airflights infrequent and subject to constant changes, but the terrain around Cuito Cuanavale is still saturated with landmines.

However, for further information on visiting Angola, see www.embangola-can.org/tourism11.html

For details on business opportunities in Angola (which may help in understanding the political environment) go to www.us-angola.org/aboutchamber.htm

REFERENCES AND FURTHER READING

Chester Crocker, *High Noon in Southern Africa; Making Peace in a Rough Neighbourhood*. Johannesburg: Jonathan Ball, 1992.

Piero Glenijeses, *Conflicting Missions: Havana, Washington and Africa, 1959–1976*. Chapel Hill: The University of North Carolina Press, 2002.

Helmoed Römer-Heitman, *War in Angola: The Final South African Phase*. Gibraltar: Ashanti, 1990.

Fred Bridgland, *The War for Africa: 12 Months that Transformed a Continent*. Gibraltar: Ashanti, 1990.

NOTES

1   For details on this historical background, see Greg Mills and Simon Baynham, 'South African Foreign Policy, 1945–90', in Greg Mills (ed.), *From Pariah to Participant: South Africa's Evolving Foreign Relations, 1990–1994*. Johannesburg: South African Institute of International Affairs, 1994, pp.10–36. The interviews portrayed in this chapter were conducted by Greg Mills in Cuba and South Africa in 2004 and 2005. Anonymity was respected where requested.

2   The Angolans supplied food on an intermittent basis, and partly paid for the demobilisation of Cuban forces. One chartered Soviet aircraft traveled weekly from Angola to Cuba. But the Angolan supply chains were unreliable. On one occasion Cuban troops went without boots, which the Angolans were supposed to furnish.

3   Fred Bridgland, *Jonas Savimbi: A Key to Africa*. London: Hodder and Stoughton, 1988, p.201.

4   Piero Glenijeses, *Conflicting Missions: Havana, Washington and Africa, 1959–1976*. Chapel Hill: The University of North Carolina Press, 2002, p.375.

5   Cited in *Ibid*, p.391. For the Cuban account of what happened at Cuito Cuanavale, see *The Peace of Cuito Cuanavale: Documents of a Process*. La Habana: Editora Politica, 1990.

6   *Ibid*, p.377.

7   Cited in *The Independent*, 12 November 1987.

8   Chester Crocker, *High Noon in Southern Africa; Making Peace in a Rough Neighbourhood*. Johannesburg: Jonathan Ball, 1992.

9   Helmoed Römer-Heitman, *War in Angola: The Final South African Phase*. Gibraltar: Ashanti, 1990.

10 Fred Bridgland, *The War for Africa: 12 Months that Transformed a Continent*. Gibraltar: Ashanti, 1990.

11 See his paper 'Showdown at Cuito Cuanavale: Understanding the Politics of the Cuban Escalation in Angola', presented at the 31st Annual Meeting of the American African Studies Association, Chicago, 28–31 October 1988.

12 Javier Corrales, 'Gatekeeper State: Limited Economic Reform and Regime Survival in Cuba, 1989–2002.' September 2002. At *http://www.amherst.edu/~jcorrale/The%20Gatekeeper%20State%203.pdf*.

13 Cited in Glenijeses, *op cit*, p.394.

About the Authors

DR GREG MILLS holds a BA Honours degree from the University of Cape Town, and a Masters and PhD from the University of Lancaster. Having taught at the Universities of Western Cape and Cape Town, he joined the South African Institute of International Affairs (SAIIA) in January 1994, first as Director of Studies and, from July 1996– March 2005, as National Director. During his tenure at SAIIA he published more than 20 books, including most recently *Poverty to Prosperity: Globalisation, Good Governance and African Recovery* (Tafelberg, 2002); with Jeffrey Herbst of Princeton University, *The Future of Africa: New Order in Sight?* (Oxford University Press, 2003); and *The Security Intersection: The Paradox of Power in an Age of Terror* (Wits University Press, 2005). He is also widely published in international journals and the local and international press. Dr Mills has, since April 2005, been the director of The Brenthurst Foundation, which is dedi-  cated to strengthening Africa's economic performance. *www.thebrenthurstfoundation.org*

Dr Mills is married to the acclaimed artist Janet Wilson. They have two daughters, Amelia and Beatrix, and a son William.

DAVID WILLIAMS, an Associate Deputy Editor of the *Financial Mail* and an SAIIA Research Associate, is acknowledged as an expert on the El Alamein battles and the desert campaigns, and has regularly given talks in South Africa on military subjects. His initial national service was with 1 Signal Regiment at Voortrekkerhoogte; later he qualified as a Citizen Force infantry section leader. An experienced radio and TV broadcaster, he has covered military affairs for the *Financial Mail*, notably during the transition years 1990–1995, and has also specialised in coverage of investment, education, railways and politics. He has published two books on sport: *Great Games* (Penguin, 1998) and *Toughest of Them All* with Grant Harding (Penguin, 2001). He was educated at King Edward VII School and at Wits University.

David Williams lives in Johannesburg and is married to Patricia; they have two sons, Robbie and Morgan.

Index

Page references in italics indicate illustrations.